Unholy Kinship

ISBN-10: 1-56163-482-4
ISBN-13: 978-1-56163-482-8
© 2006 Naomi Nowak
Printed in China

5   4   3   2   1

Unholy Kinship

Naomi Nowak

nbm
ComicsLit

Naomi Nowak is a child of the mid-eighties. She was born in Stockholm, Sweden and grew up loving comics. Starting out as a painter and an illustrator, she has gradually expanded her working area into graphic novels, where she combines her artistic and story-telling skills. Her inspirations are a mix of the European and Asian comic traditions, but she also strives to learn from how stories are told in cinema. In her spare time she likes to play the accordion, dance and read books and comics.

We have over 200 graphic novels in print,
write for our color catalog:
NBM, 40 Exchange Pl., Ste. 1308
New York, NY 10005
www.nbmpublishing.com

ComicsLit is an imprint
and trademark of

NANTIER • BEALL • MINOUSTCHINE
Publishing inc.
new york

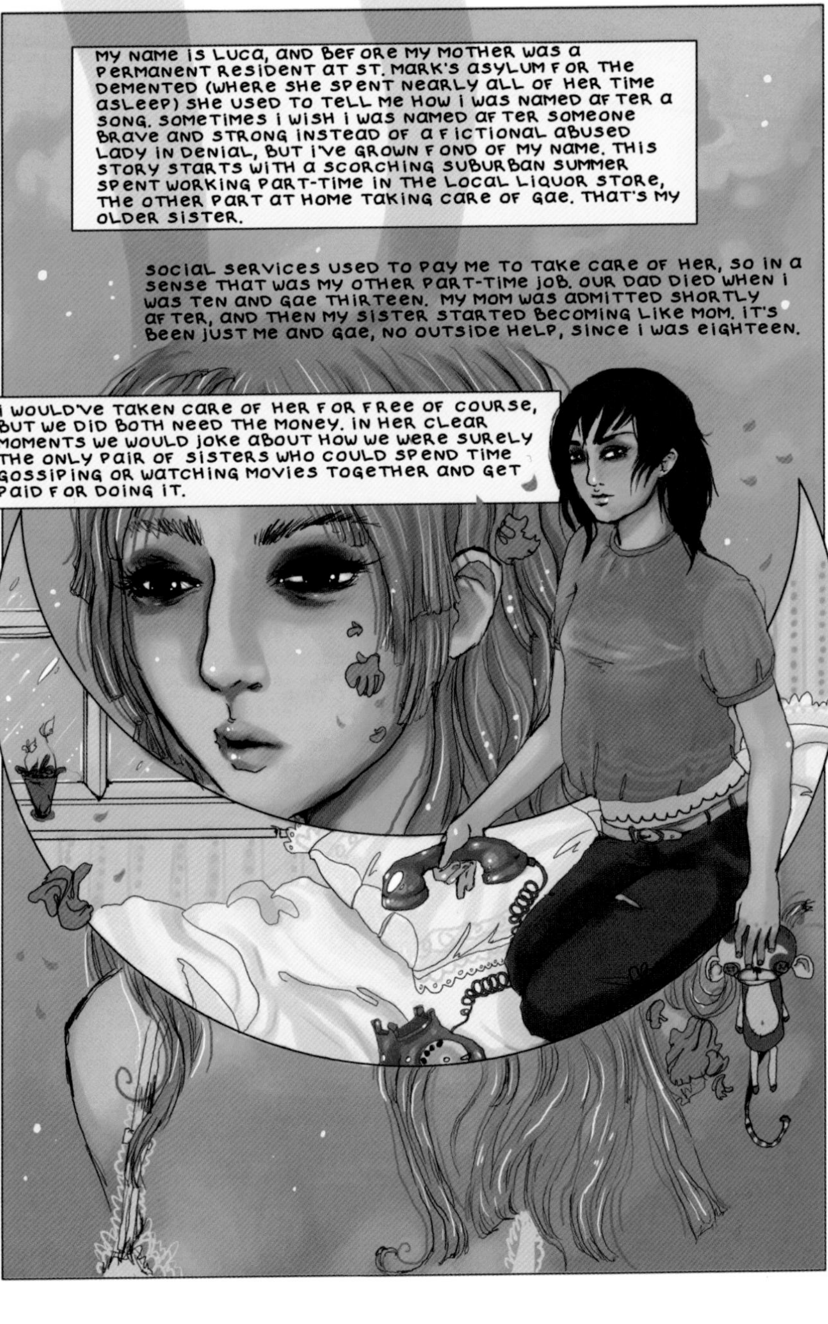
MY NAME IS LUCA, AND BEFORE MY MOTHER WAS A PERMANENT RESIDENT AT ST. MARK'S ASYLUM FOR THE DEMENTED (WHERE SHE SPENT NEARLY ALL OF HER TIME ASLEEP) SHE USED TO TELL ME HOW I WAS NAMED AFTER A SONG. SOMETIMES I WISH I WAS NAMED AFTER SOMEONE BRAVE AND STRONG INSTEAD OF A FICTIONAL ABUSED LADY IN DENIAL, BUT I'VE GROWN FOND OF MY NAME. THIS STORY STARTS WITH A SCORCHING SUBURBAN SUMMER SPENT WORKING PART-TIME IN THE LOCAL LIQUOR STORE, THE OTHER PART AT HOME TAKING CARE OF GAE. THAT'S MY OLDER SISTER.
SOCIAL SERVICES USED TO PAY ME TO TAKE CARE OF HER, SO IN A SENSE THAT WAS MY OTHER PART-TIME JOB. OUR DAD DIED WHEN I WAS TEN AND GAE THIRTEEN. MY MOM WAS ADMITTED SHORTLY AFTER, AND THEN MY SISTER STARTED BECOMING LIKE MOM. IT'S BEEN JUST ME AND GAE, NO OUTSIDE HELP, SINCE I WAS EIGHTEEN.
I WOULD'VE TAKEN CARE OF HER FOR FREE OF COURSE, BUT WE DID BOTH NEED THE MONEY. IN HER CLEAR MOMENTS WE WOULD JOKE ABOUT HOW WE WERE SURELY THE ONLY PAIR OF SISTERS WHO COULD SPEND TIME GOSSIPING OR WATCHING MOVIES TOGETHER AND GET PAID FOR DOING IT.

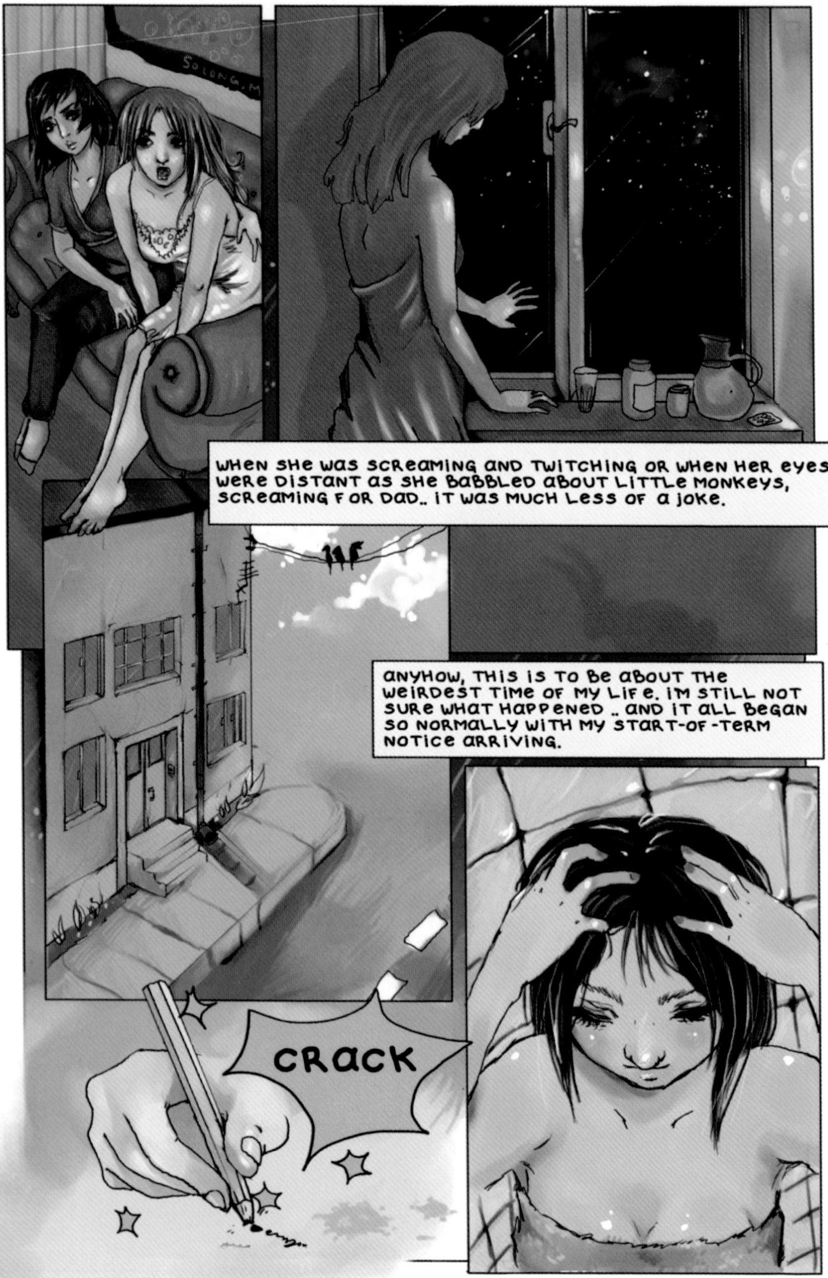
SO LONG M
WHEN SHE WAS SCREAMING AND TWITCHING OR WHEN HER EYES WERE DISTANT AS SHE BABBLED ABOUT LITTLE MONKEYS, SCREAMING FOR DAD.. IT WAS MUCH LESS OF A JOKE.
ANYHOW, THIS IS TO BE ABOUT THE WEIRDEST TIME OF MY LIFE. IM STILL NOT SURE WHAT HAPPENED .. AND IT ALL BEGAN SO NORMALLY WITH MY START-OF-TERM NOTICE ARRIVING.
CRACK

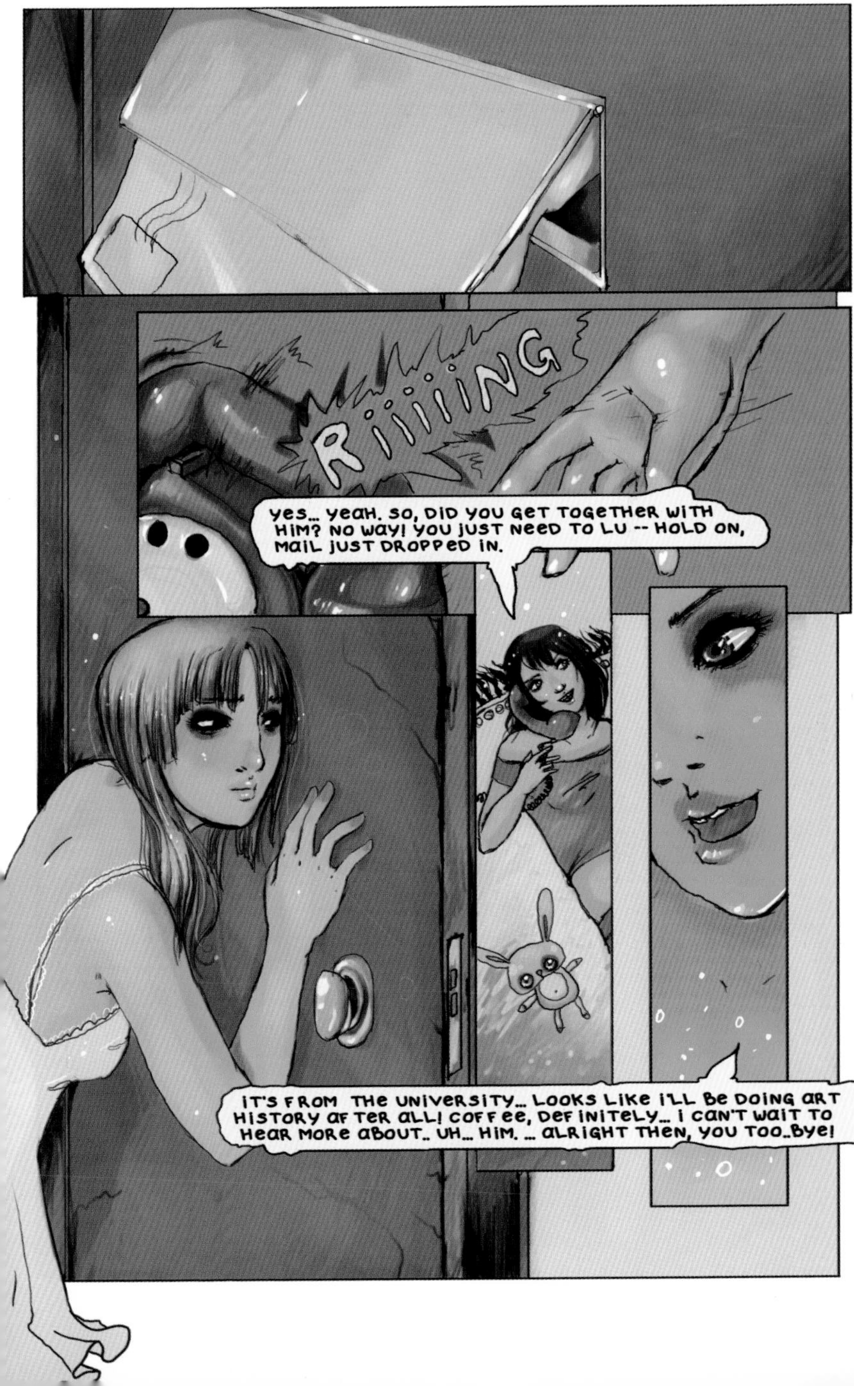
RiiiiNG
yes... yeah. so, did you get together with him? no way! you just need to lu -- hold on, mail just dropped in.
it's from the university... looks like i'll be doing art history after all! coffee, definitely... i can't wait to hear more about.. uh... him. ... alright then, you too..bye!

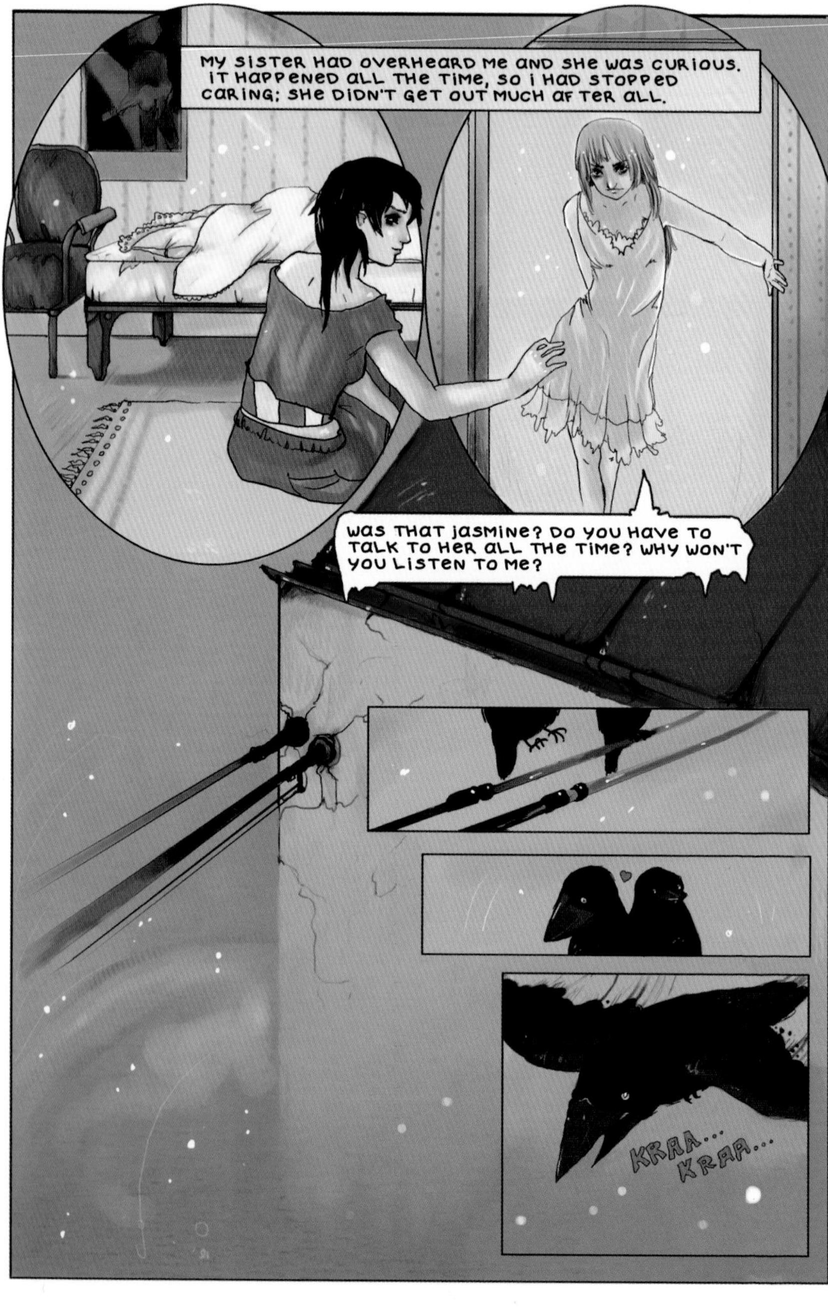
MY SISTER HAD OVERHEARD ME AND SHE WAS CURIOUS. IT HAPPENED ALL THE TIME, SO I HAD STOPPED CARING; SHE DIDN'T GET OUT MUCH AFTER ALL.
WAS THAT JASMINE? DO YOU HAVE TO TALK TO HER ALL THE TIME? WHY WON'T YOU LISTEN TO ME?
KRAA... KRAA...

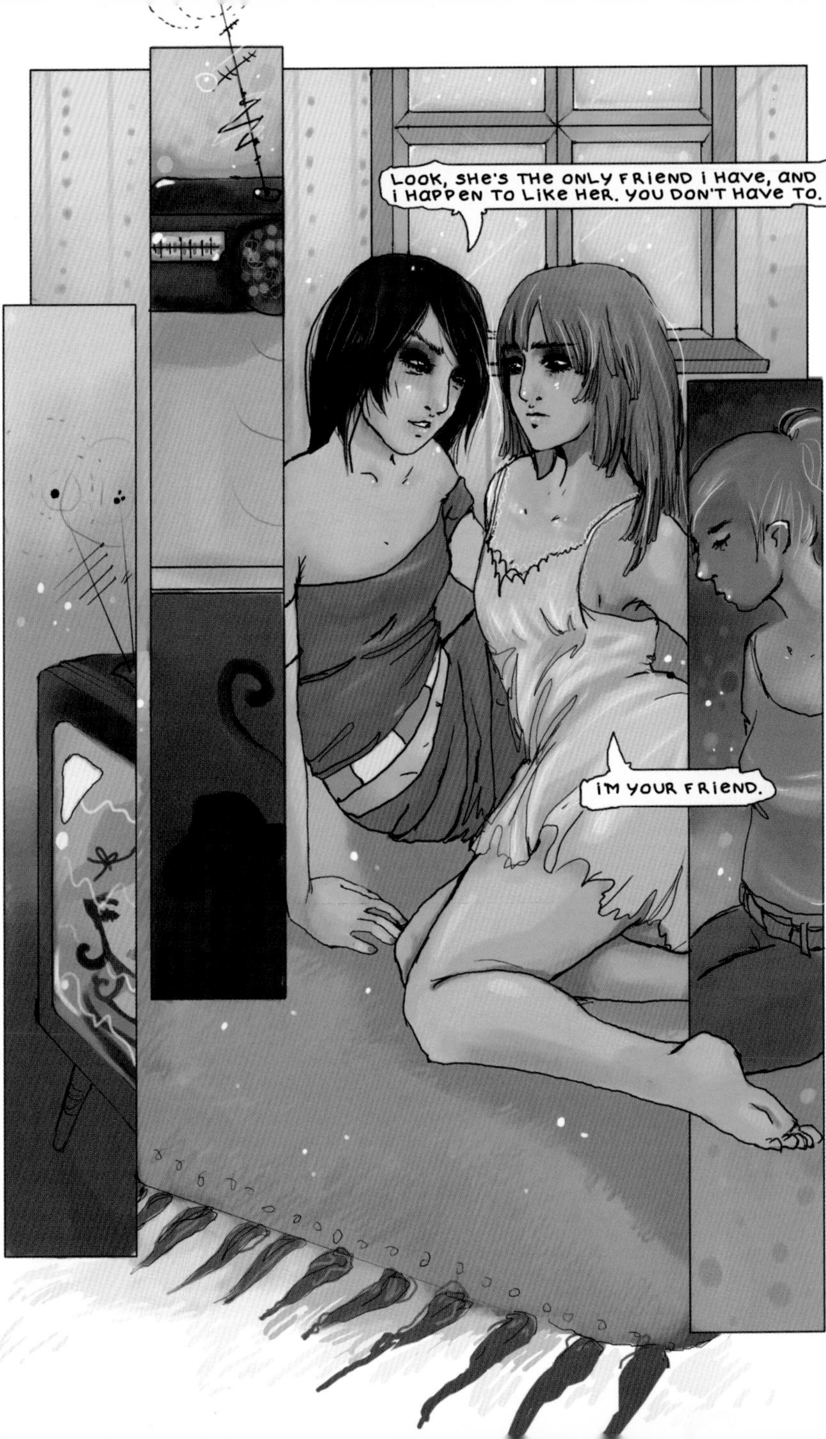
LOOK, SHE'S THE ONLY FRIEND I HAVE, AND I HAPPEN TO LIKE HER. YOU DON'T HAVE TO.
I'M YOUR FRIEND.

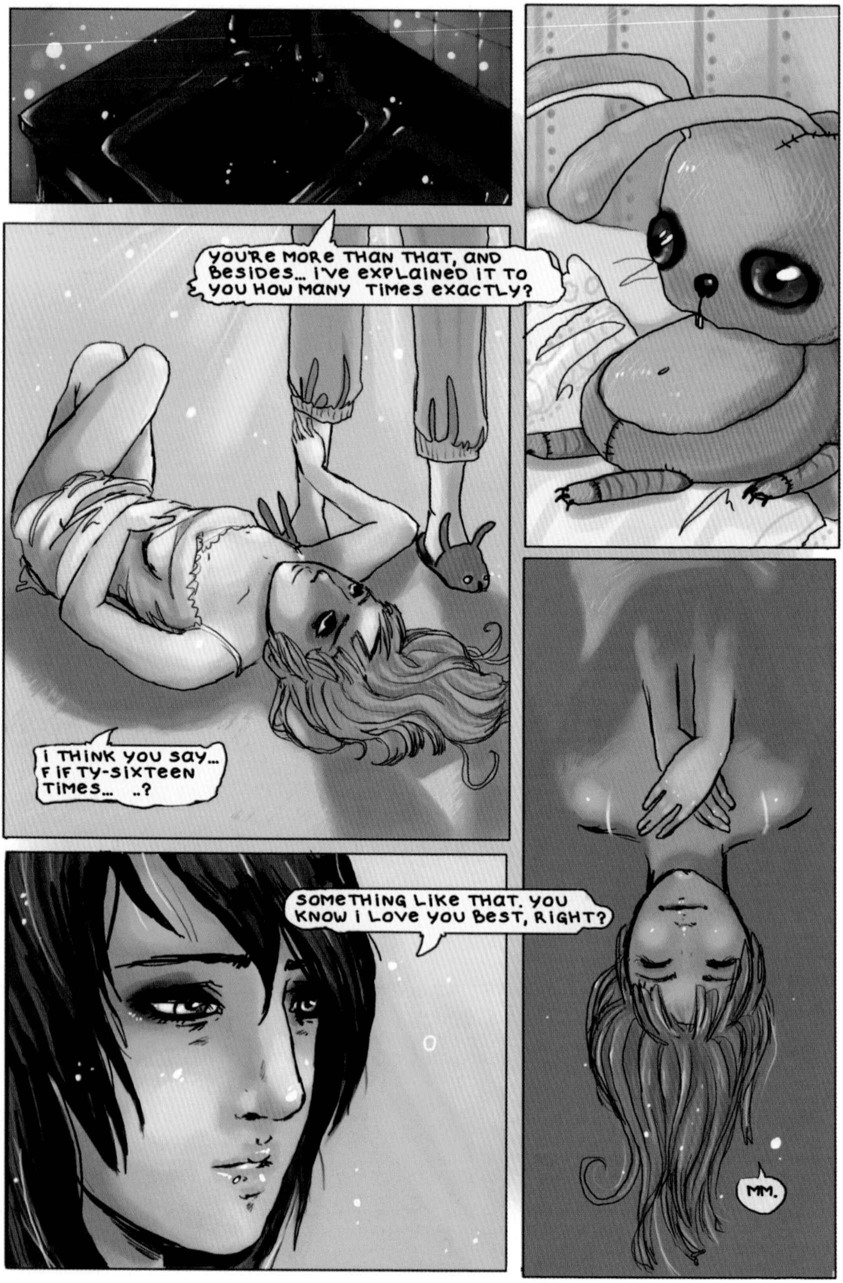
YOU'RE MORE THAN THAT, AND BESIDES... I'VE EXPLAINED IT TO YOU HOW MANY TIMES EXACTLY?
I THINK YOU SAY... FIFTY-SIXTEEN TIMES... ..?
SOMETHING LIKE THAT. YOU KNOW I LOVE YOU BEST, RIGHT?
MM.

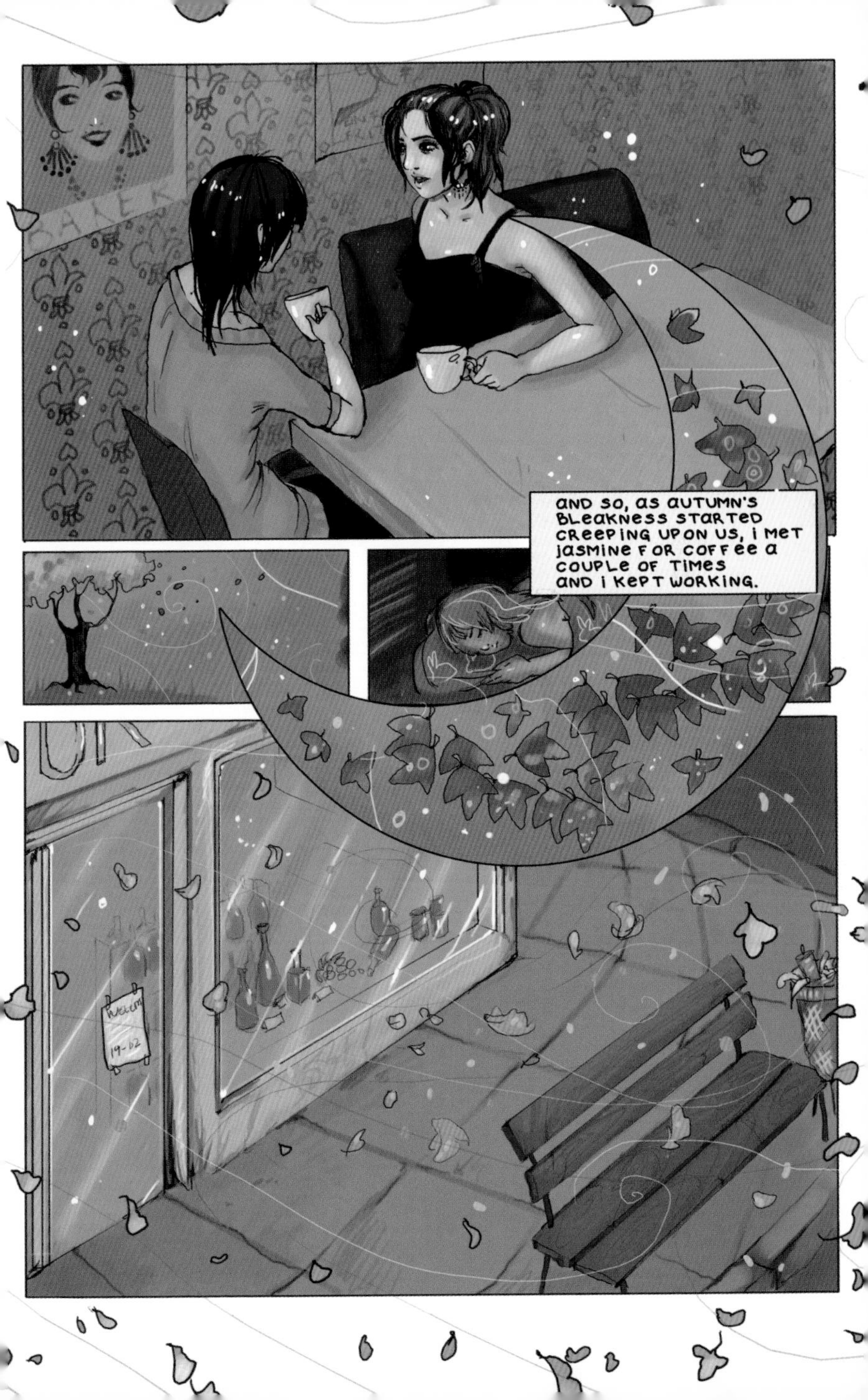
and so, as autumn's bleakness started creeping upon us, i met jasmine for coffee a couple of times and i kept working.

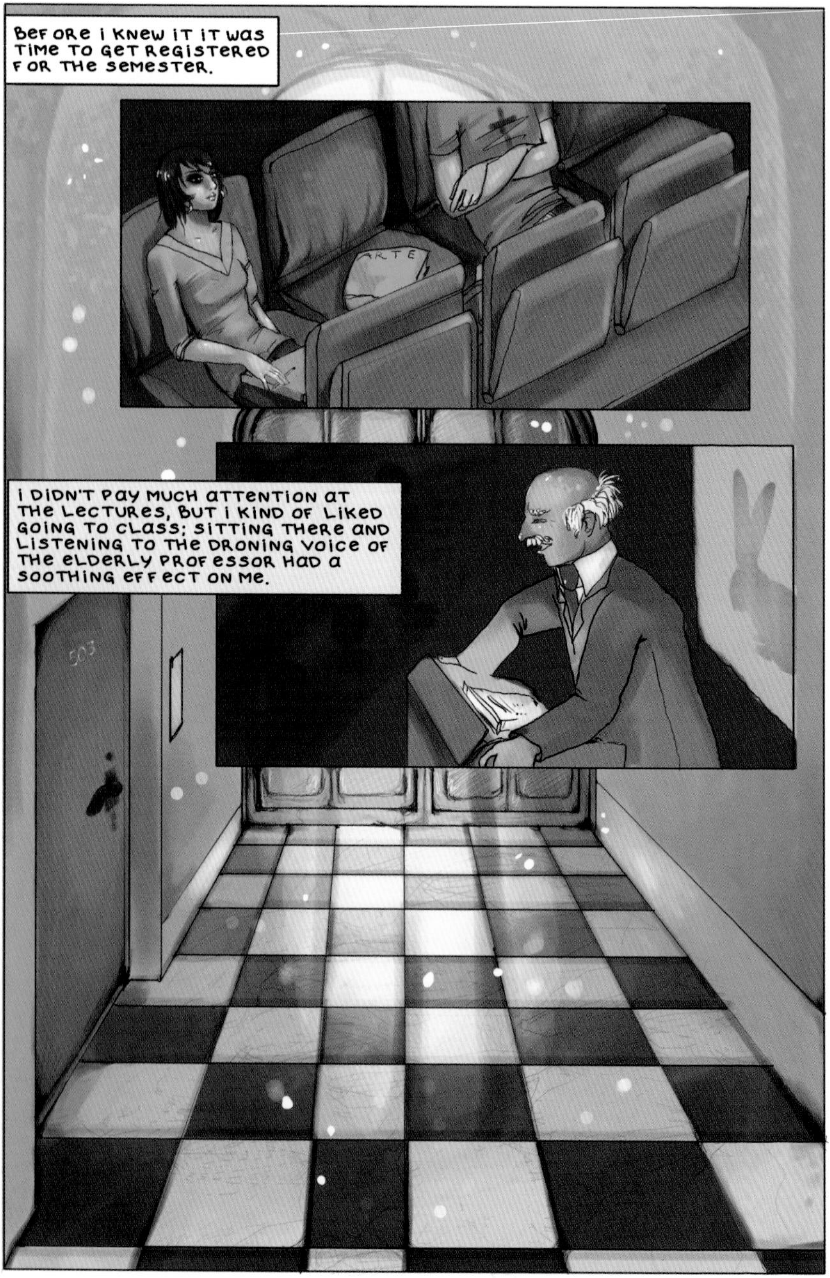
BEFORE I KNEW IT IT WAS TIME TO GET REGISTERED FOR THE SEMESTER.
ARTE
I DIDN'T PAY MUCH ATTENTION AT THE LECTURES, BUT I KIND OF LIKED GOING TO CLASS; SITTING THERE AND LISTENING TO THE DRONING VOICE OF THE ELDERLY PROFESSOR HAD A SOOTHING EFFECT ON ME.
503

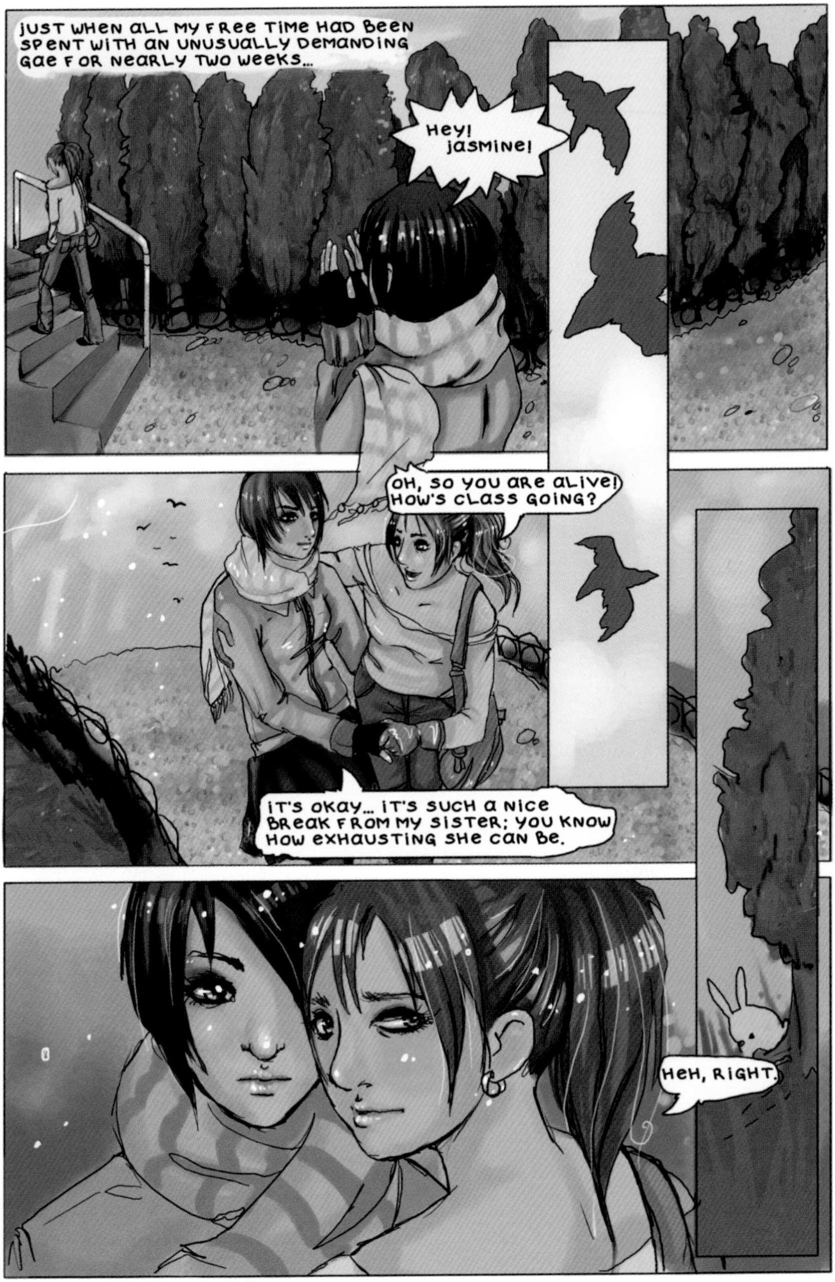
JUST WHEN ALL MY FREE TIME HAD BEEN SPENT WITH AN UNUSUALLY DEMANDING GAE FOR NEARLY TWO WEEKS...
HEY! JASMINE!
OH, SO YOU ARE ALIVE! HOW'S CLASS GOING?
IT'S OKAY... IT'S SUCH A NICE BREAK FROM MY SISTER; YOU KNOW HOW EXHAUSTING SHE CAN BE.
HEH, RIGHT.

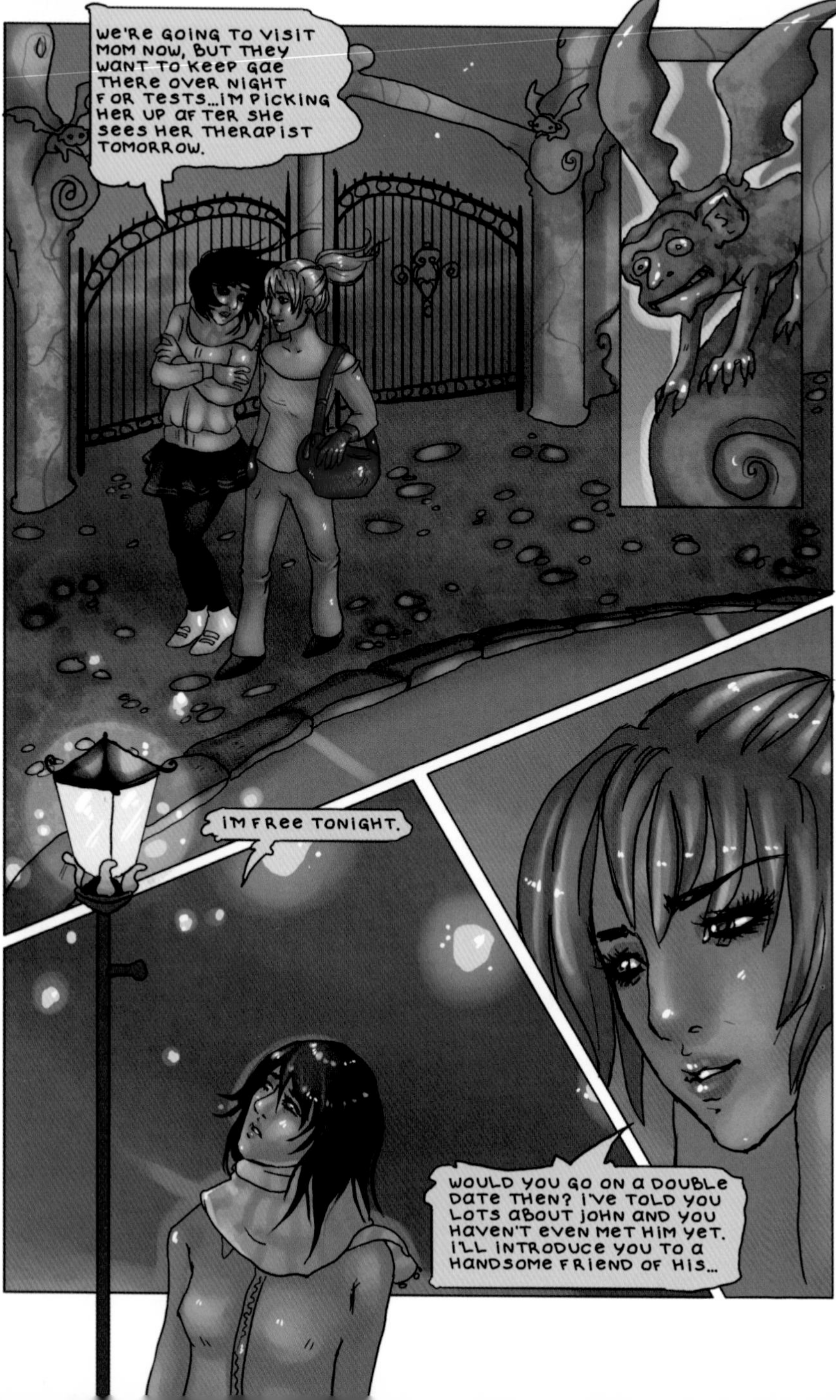
WE'RE GOING TO VISIT MOM NOW, BUT THEY WANT TO KEEP GAE THERE OVER NIGHT FOR TESTS...IM PICKING HER UP AFTER SHE SEES HER THERAPIST TOMORROW.
IM FREE TONIGHT.
WOULD YOU GO ON A DOUBLE DATE THEN? I'VE TOLD YOU LOTS ABOUT JOHN AND YOU HAVEN'T EVEN MET HIM YET. I'LL INTRODUCE YOU TO A HANDSOME FRIEND OF HIS...

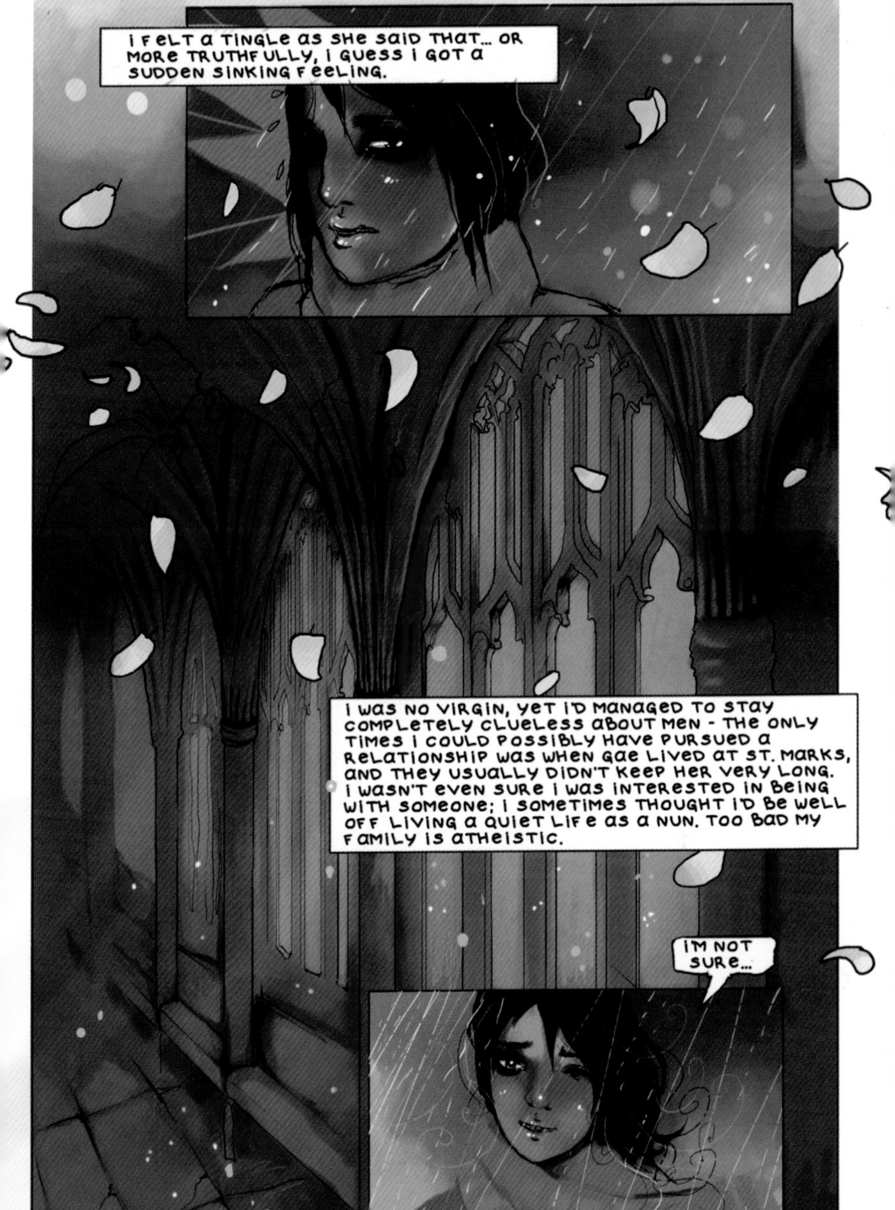
I FELT A TINGLE AS SHE SAID THAT... OR MORE TRUTHFULLY, I GUESS I GOT A SUDDEN SINKING FEELING.
I WAS NO VIRGIN, YET I'D MANAGED TO STAY COMPLETELY CLUELESS ABOUT MEN - THE ONLY TIMES I COULD POSSIBLY HAVE PURSUED A RELATIONSHIP WAS WHEN GAE LIVED AT ST. MARKS, AND THEY USUALLY DIDN'T KEEP HER VERY LONG. I WASN'T EVEN SURE I WAS INTERESTED IN BEING WITH SOMEONE; I SOMETIMES THOUGHT I'D BE WELL OFF LIVING A QUIET LIFE AS A NUN. TOO BAD MY FAMILY IS ATHEISTIC.
I'M NOT SURE...

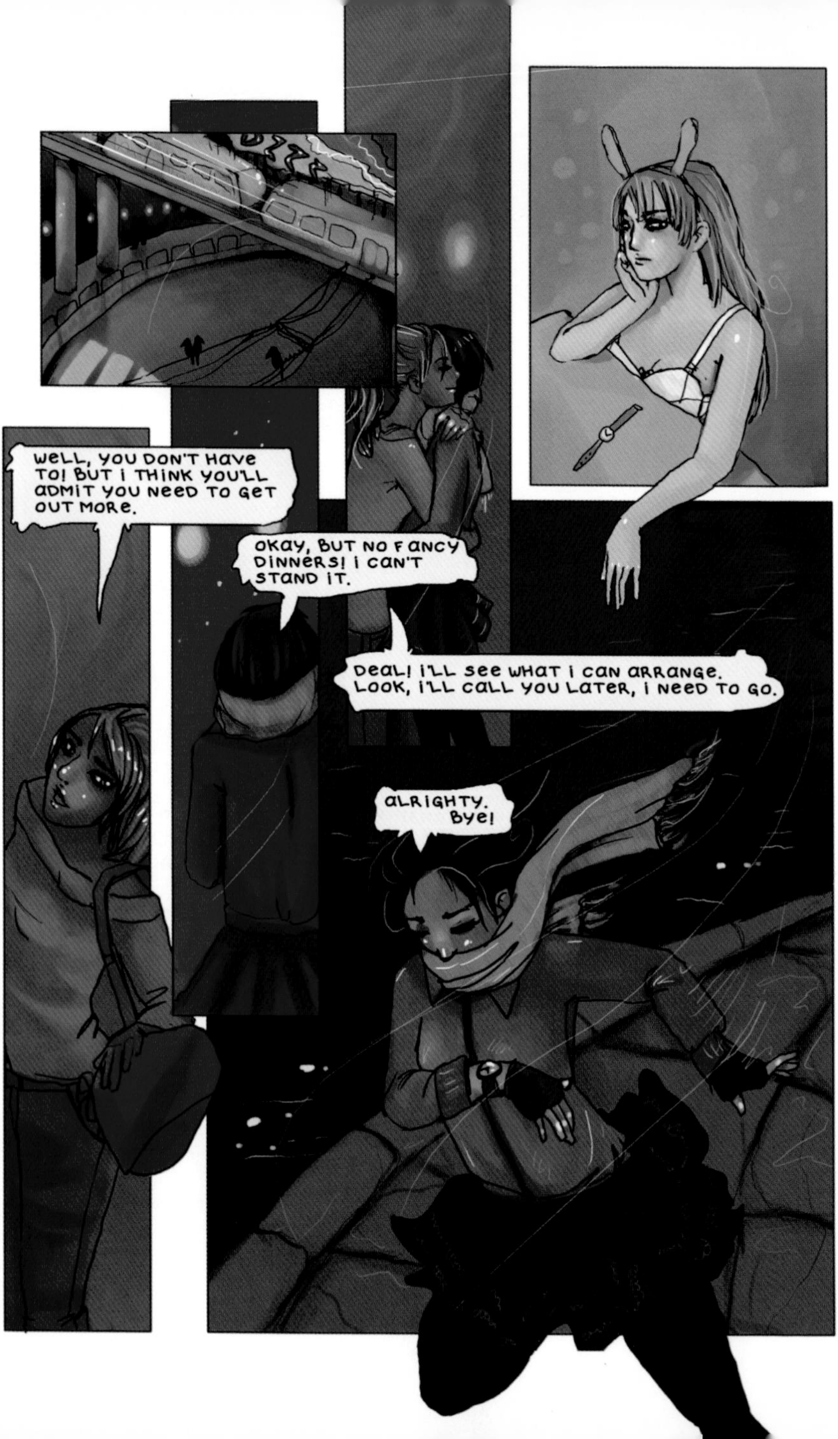
WELL, YOU DON'T HAVE TO! BUT I THINK YOU'LL ADMIT YOU NEED TO GET OUT MORE.
OKAY, BUT NO FANCY DINNERS! I CAN'T STAND IT.
DEAL! I'LL SEE WHAT I CAN ARRANGE. LOOK, I'LL CALL YOU LATER, I NEED TO GO.
ALRIGHTY. BYE!

as i sat on the bus on the way home i thought about jasmine. she'd never been any good with her choice of men; throughout our friendship i'd seen her hurt, abandoned, even bitter. but at least she was out there. me...

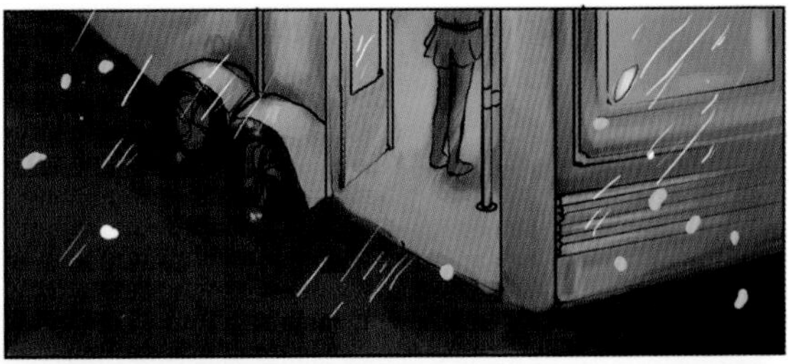

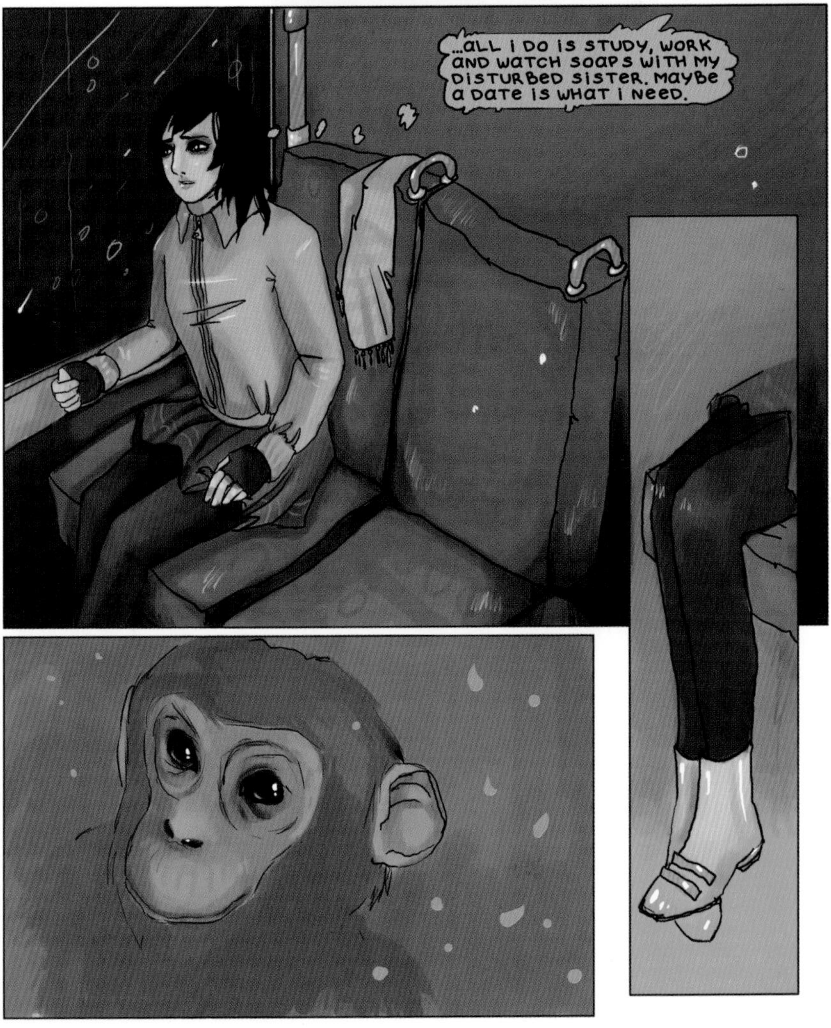
...all i do is study, work and watch soaps with my disturbed sister. maybe a date is what i need.

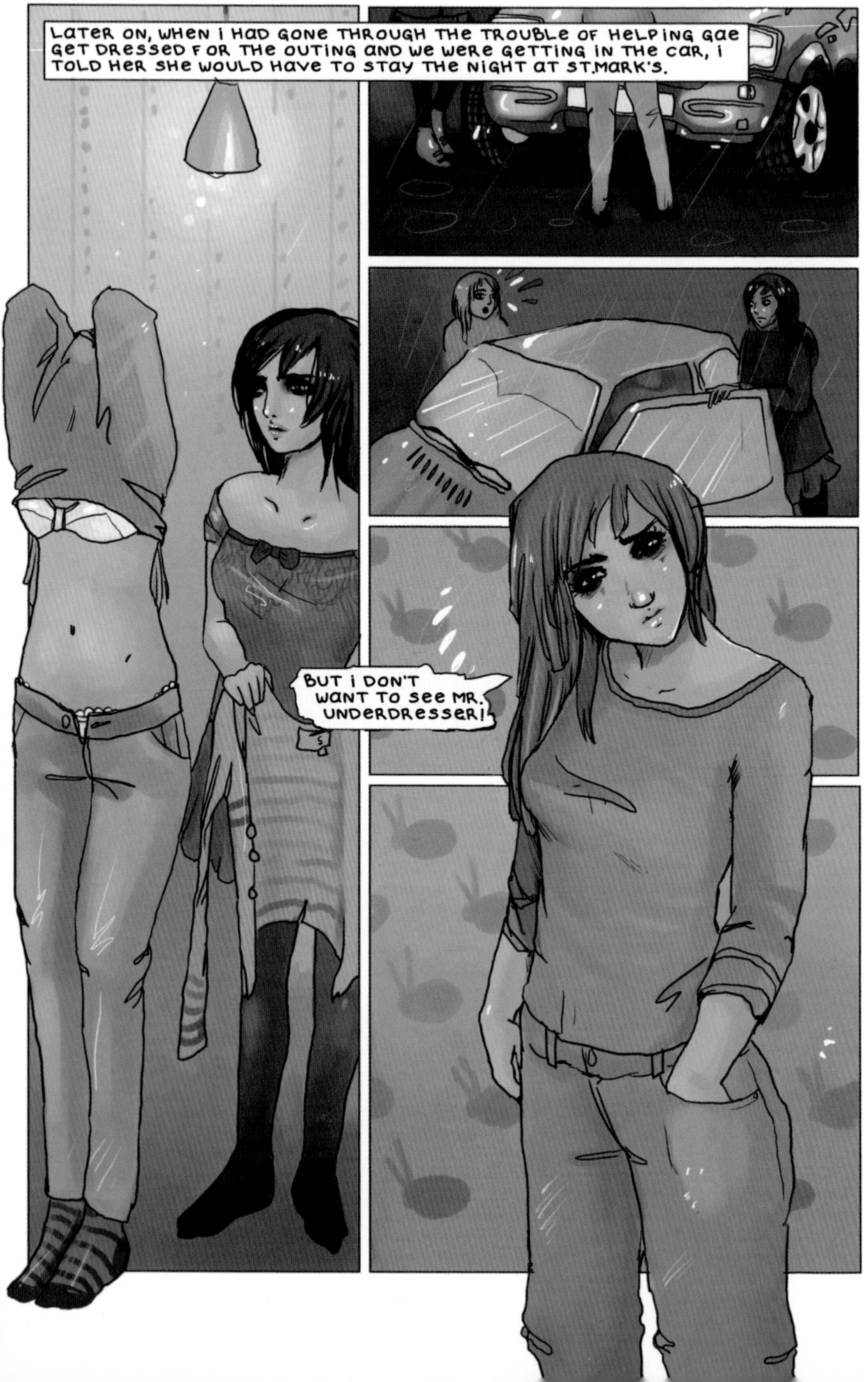
LATER ON, WHEN I HAD GONE THROUGH THE TROUBLE OF HELPING GAE GET DRESSED FOR THE OUTING AND WE WERE GETTING IN THE CAR, I TOLD HER SHE WOULD HAVE TO STAY THE NIGHT AT ST.MARK'S.
BUT I DON'T WANT TO SEE MR. UNDERDRESSER!

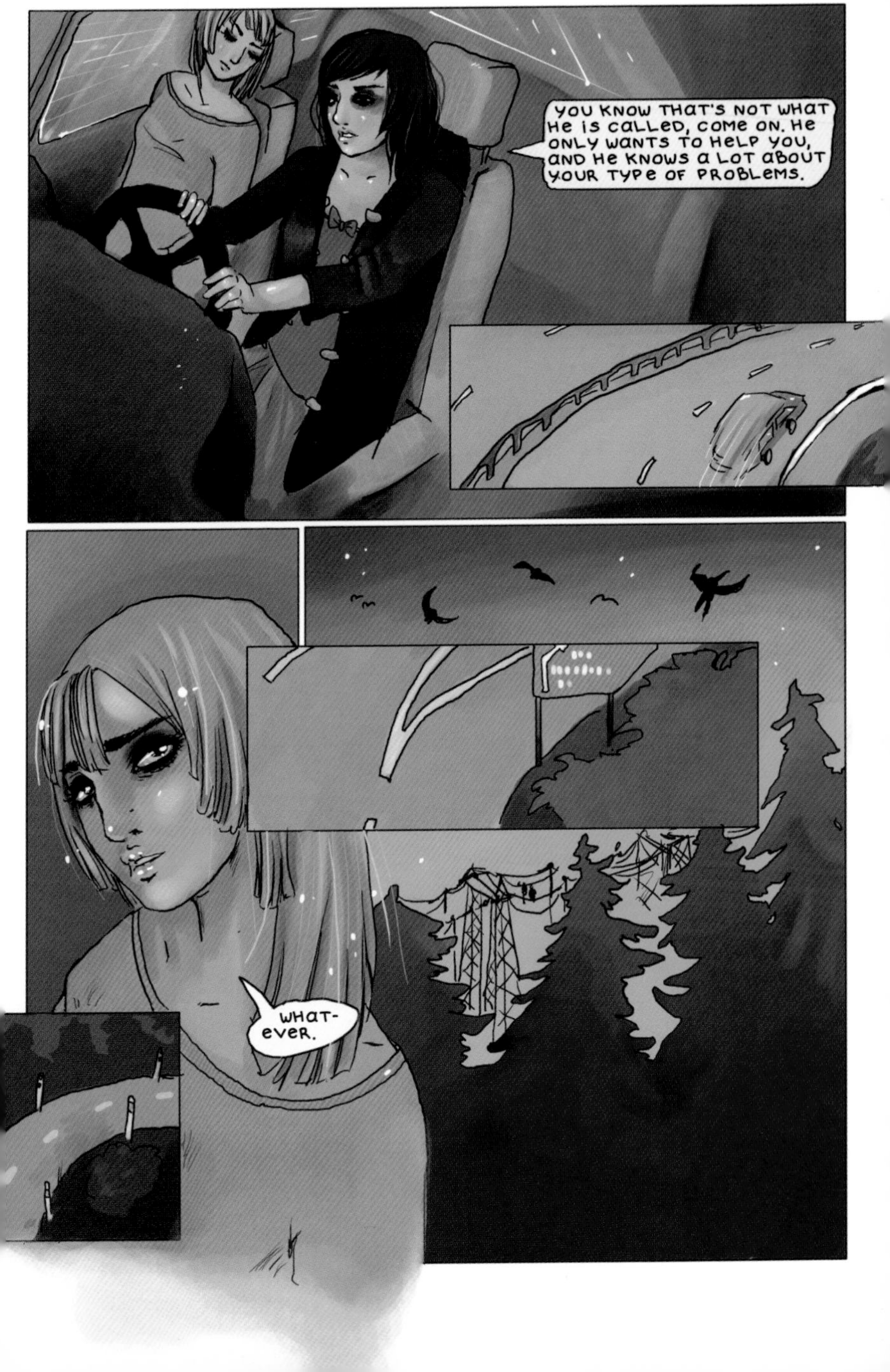
YOU KNOW THAT'S NOT WHAT HE IS CALLED, COME ON. HE ONLY WANTS TO HELP YOU, AND HE KNOWS A LOT ABOUT YOUR TYPE OF PROBLEMS.
WHAT-EVER.

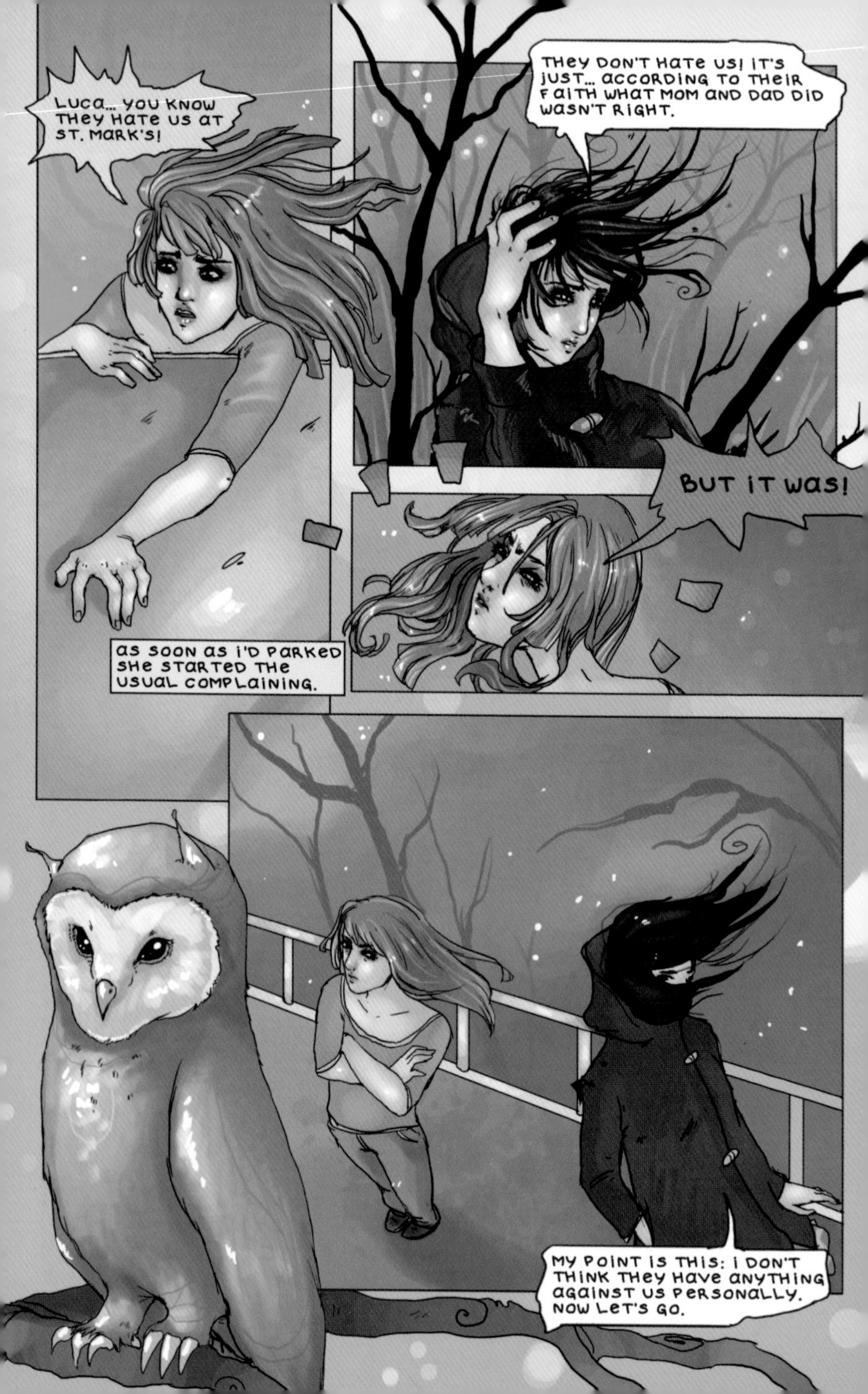
LUCA... YOU KNOW THEY HATE US AT ST. MARK'S!
THEY DON'T HATE US! IT'S JUST... ACCORDING TO THEIR FAITH WHAT MOM AND DAD DID WASN'T RIGHT.
AS SOON AS I'D PARKED SHE STARTED THE USUAL COMPLAINING.
BUT IT WAS!
MY POINT IS THIS: I DON'T THINK THEY HAVE ANYTHING AGAINST US PERSONALLY. NOW LET'S GO.

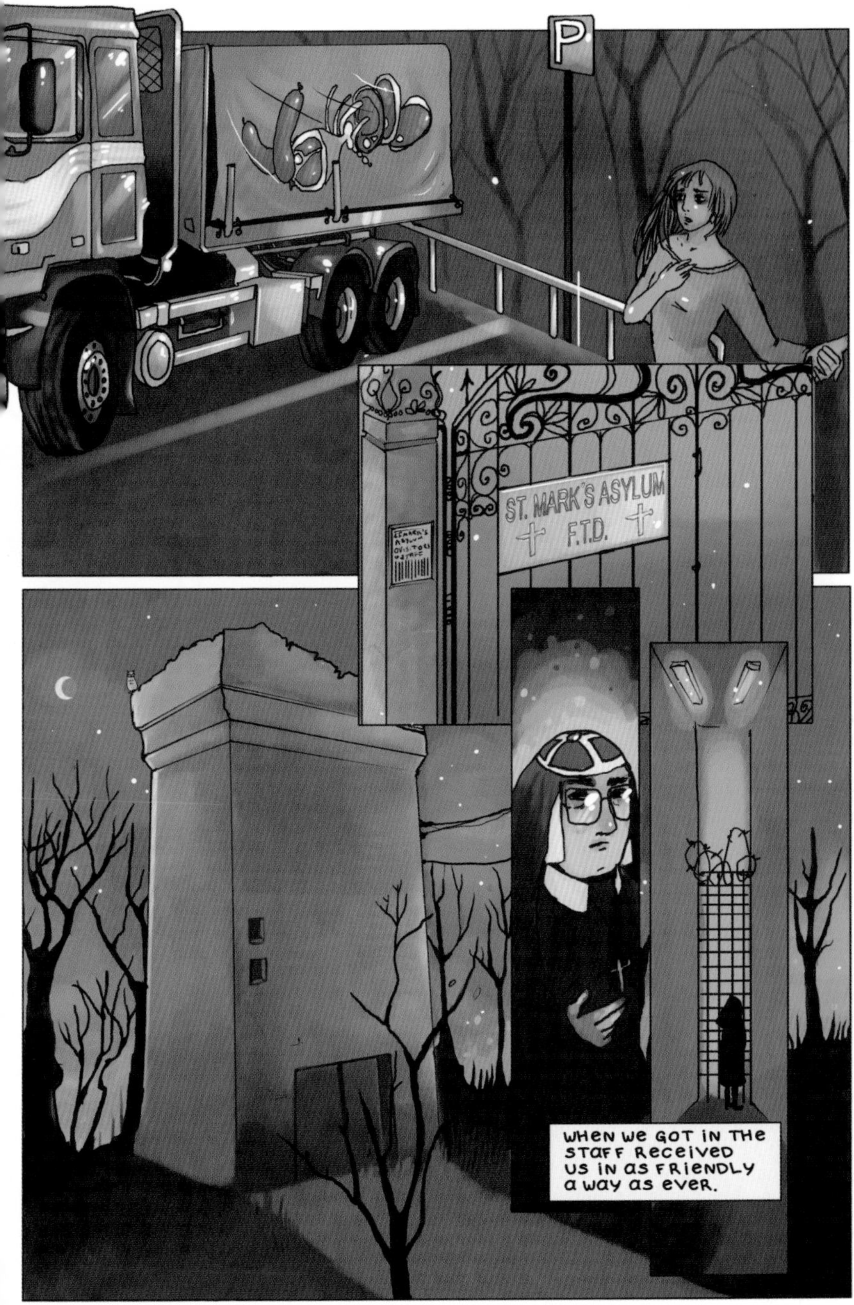
P
ST. MARK'S ASYLUM
F.T.D.
WHEN WE GOT IN THE STAFF RECEIVED US IN AS FRIENDLY A WAY AS EVER.

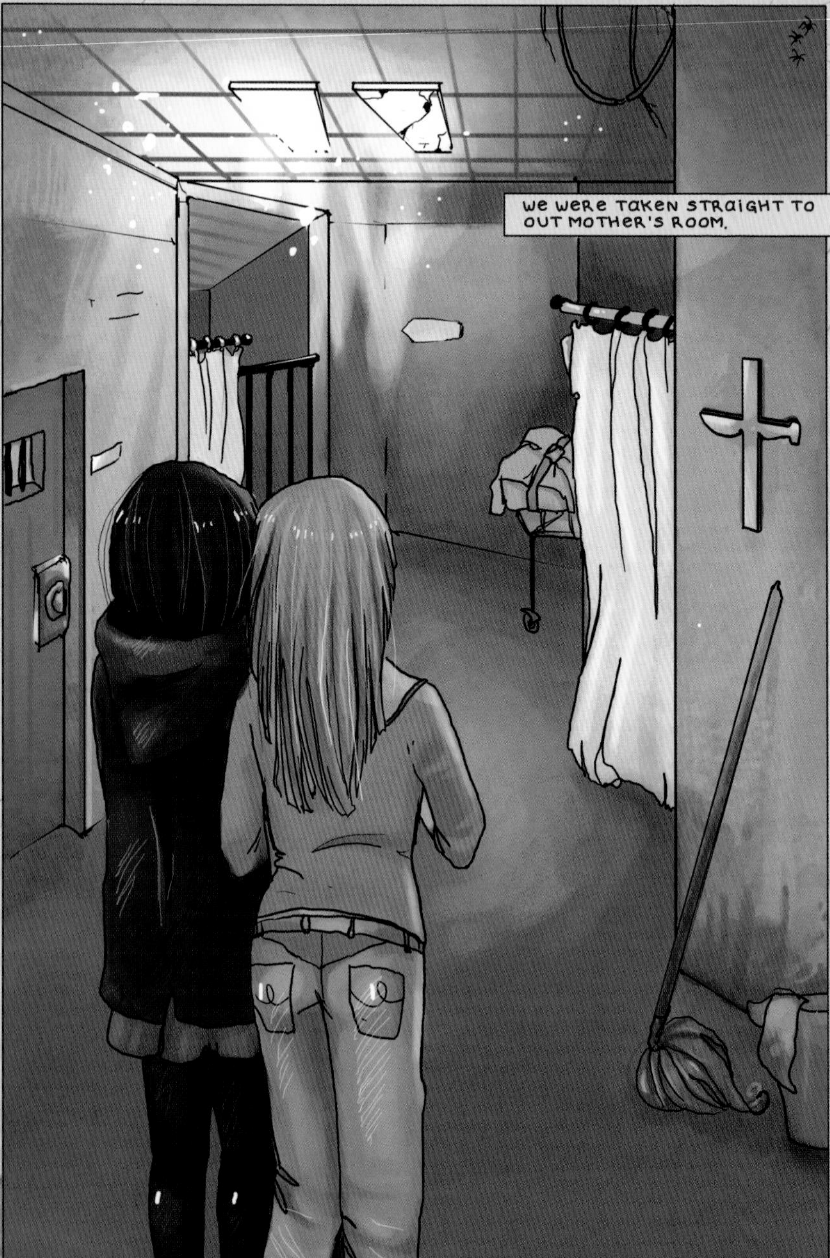
WE WERE TAKEN STRAIGHT TO OUT MOTHER'S ROOM.

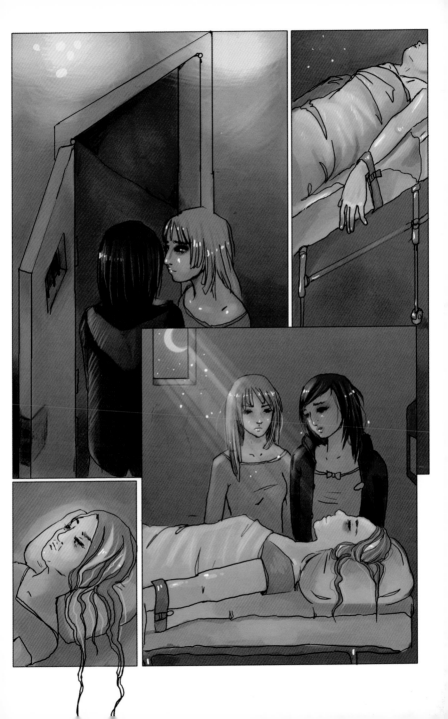

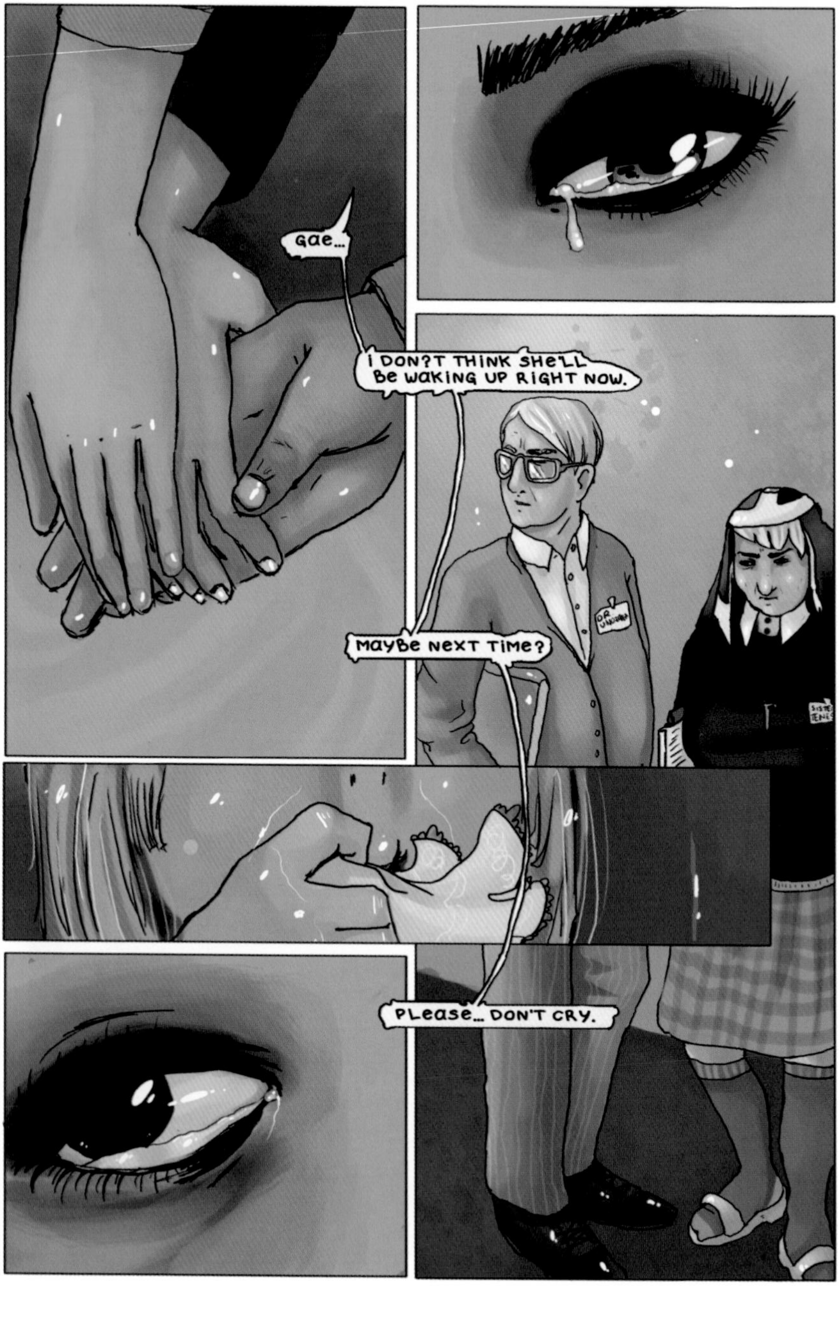
Gae...
I DON?T THINK SHE'LL Be WAKING UP RIGHT NOW.
MayBe NEXT TIME?
PLease... DON'T CRY.

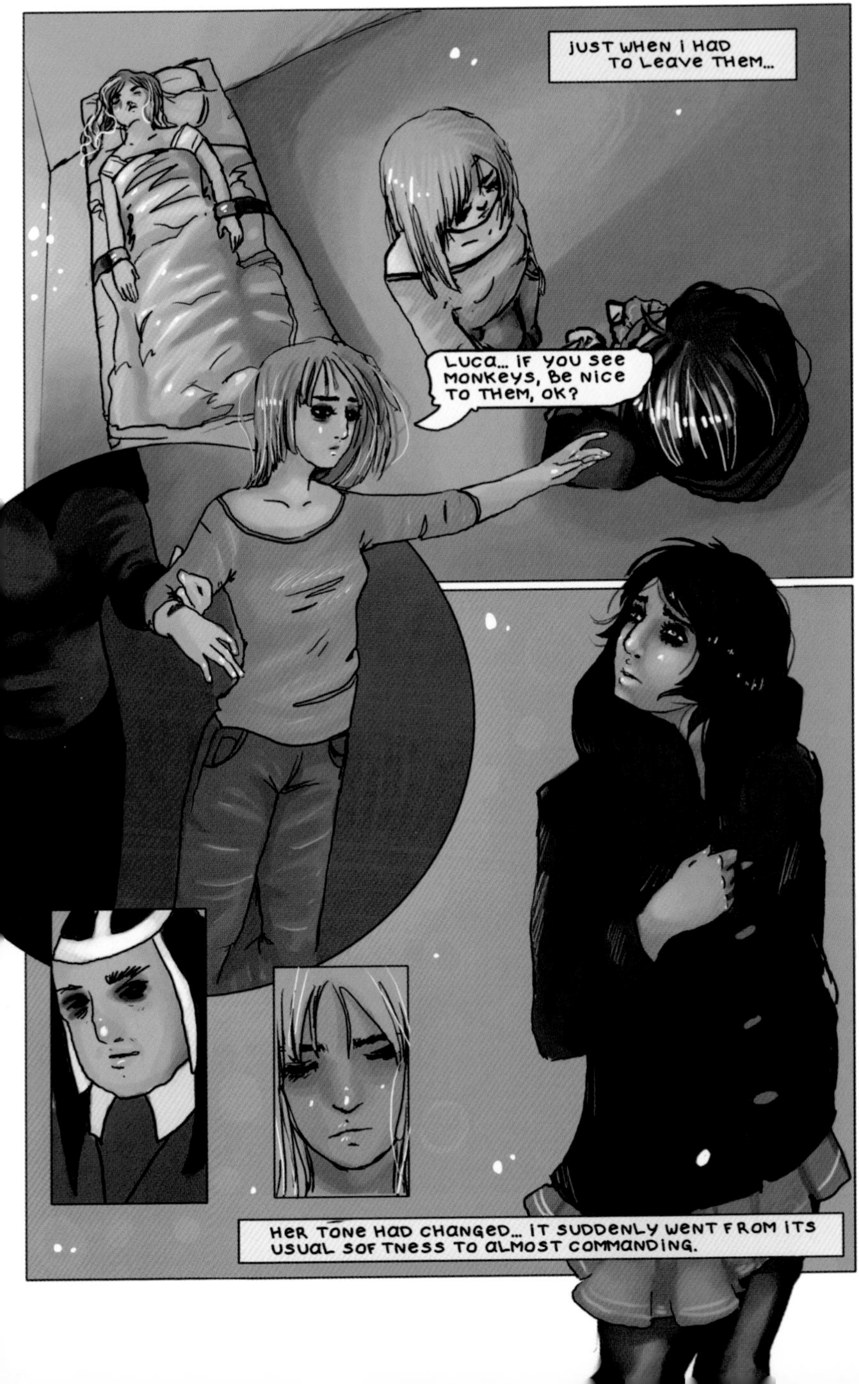
JUST WHEN I HAD TO LEAVE THEM...
LUCA... IF YOU SEE MONKEYS, BE NICE TO THEM, OK?
HER TONE HAD CHANGED... IT SUDDENLY WENT FROM ITS USUAL SOFTNESS TO ALMOST COMMANDING.

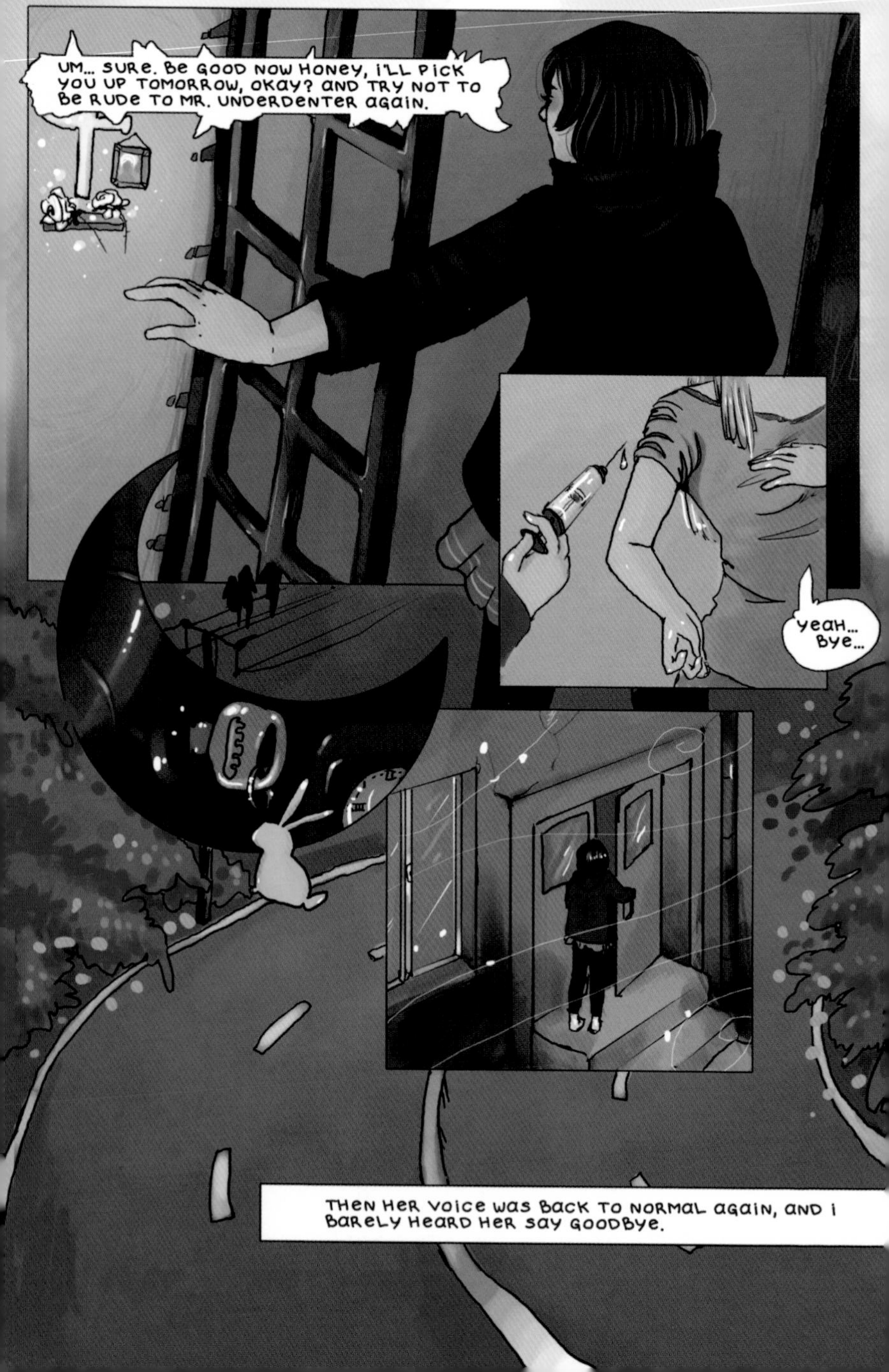
UM... SURE. BE GOOD NOW HONEY, I'LL PICK YOU UP TOMORROW, OKAY? AND TRY NOT TO BE RUDE TO MR. UNDERDENTER AGAIN.
YEAH... BYE...
THEN HER VOICE WAS BACK TO NORMAL AGAIN, AND I BARELY HEARD HER SAY GOODBYE.

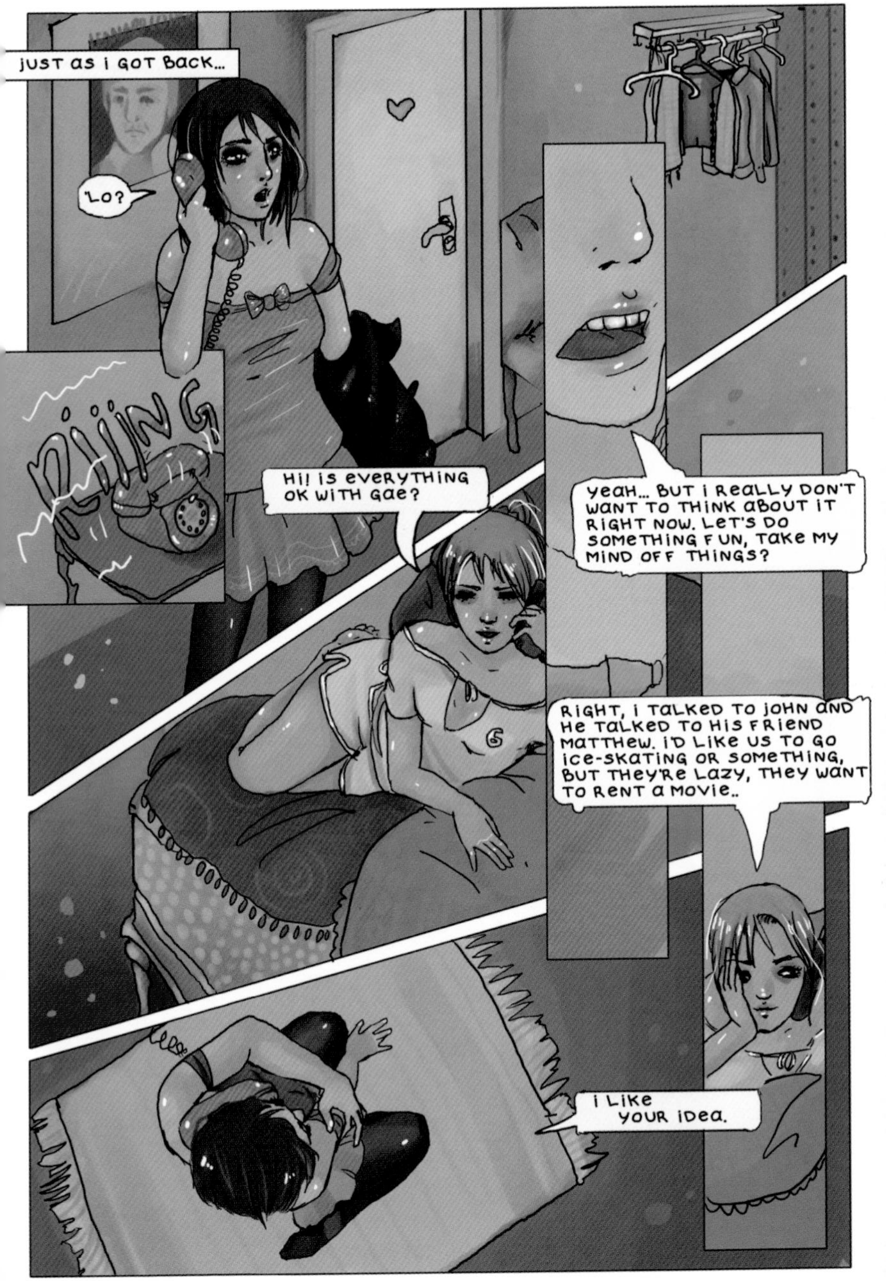
JUST AS I GOT BACK...
'LO?
RIIING
HI! IS EVERYTHING OK WITH GAE?
YEAH... BUT I REALLY DON'T WANT TO THINK ABOUT IT RIGHT NOW. LET'S DO SOMETHING FUN, TAKE MY MIND OFF THINGS?
RIGHT, I TALKED TO JOHN AND HE TALKED TO HIS FRIEND MATTHEW. I'D LIKE US TO GO ICE-SKATING OR SOMETHING, BUT THEY'RE LAZY, THEY WANT TO RENT A MOVIE..
I LIKE YOUR IDEA.

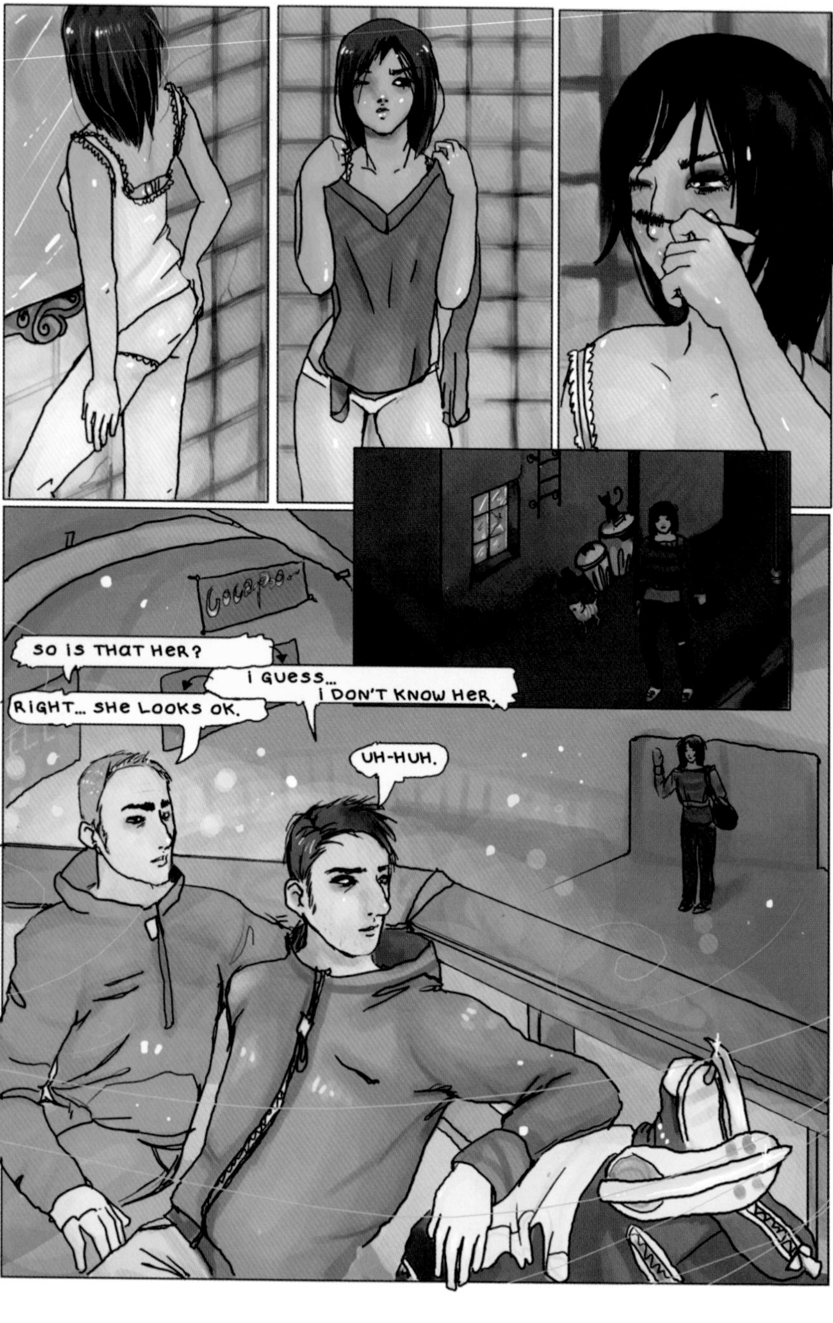
SO IS THAT HER?
I GUESS... I DON'T KNOW HER.
RIGHT... SHE LOOKS OK.
UH-HUH.

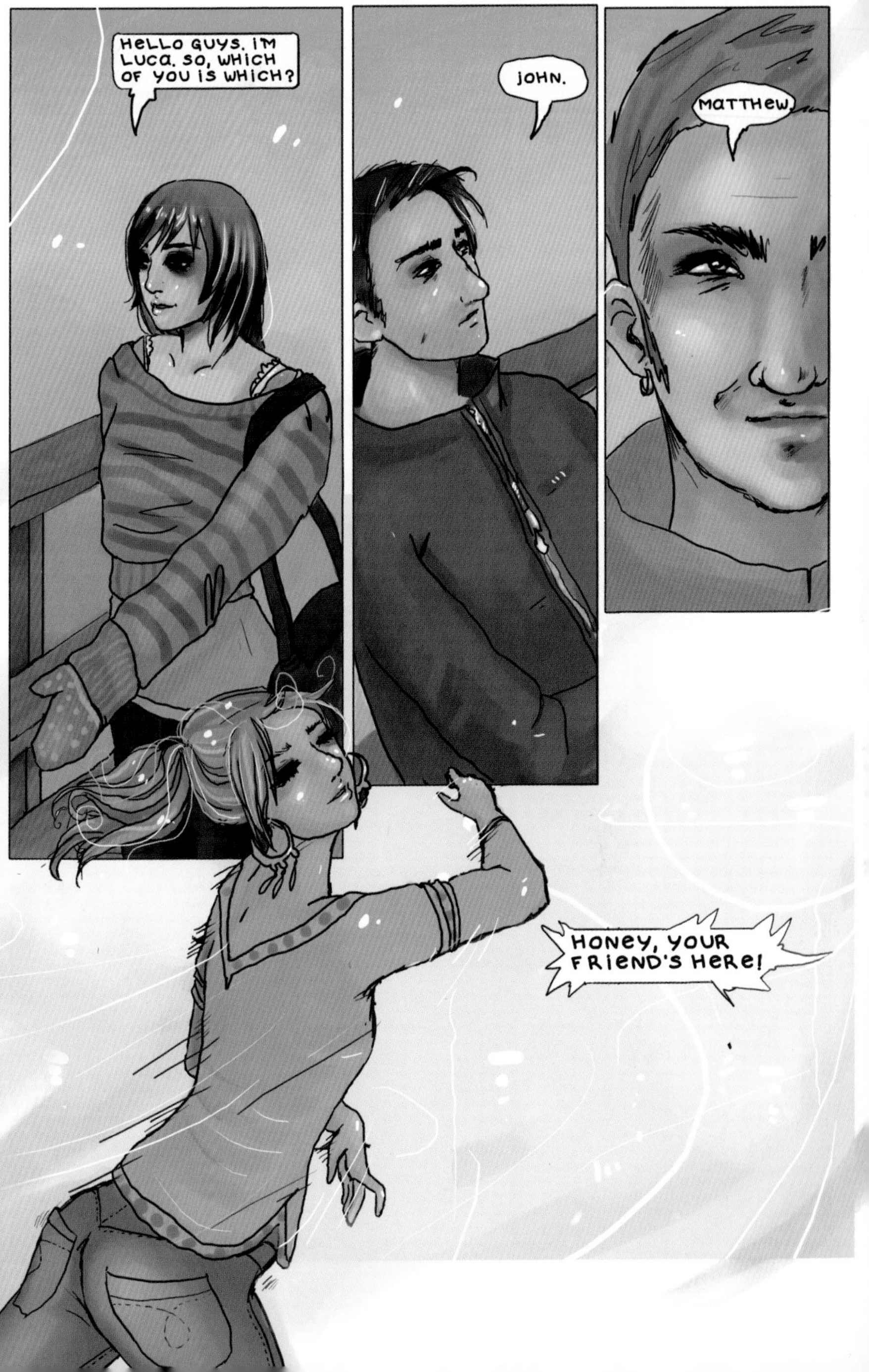
HELLO GUYS. I'M LUCA. SO, WHICH OF YOU IS WHICH?
JOHN.
MATTHEW.
HONEY, YOUR FRIEND'S HERE!

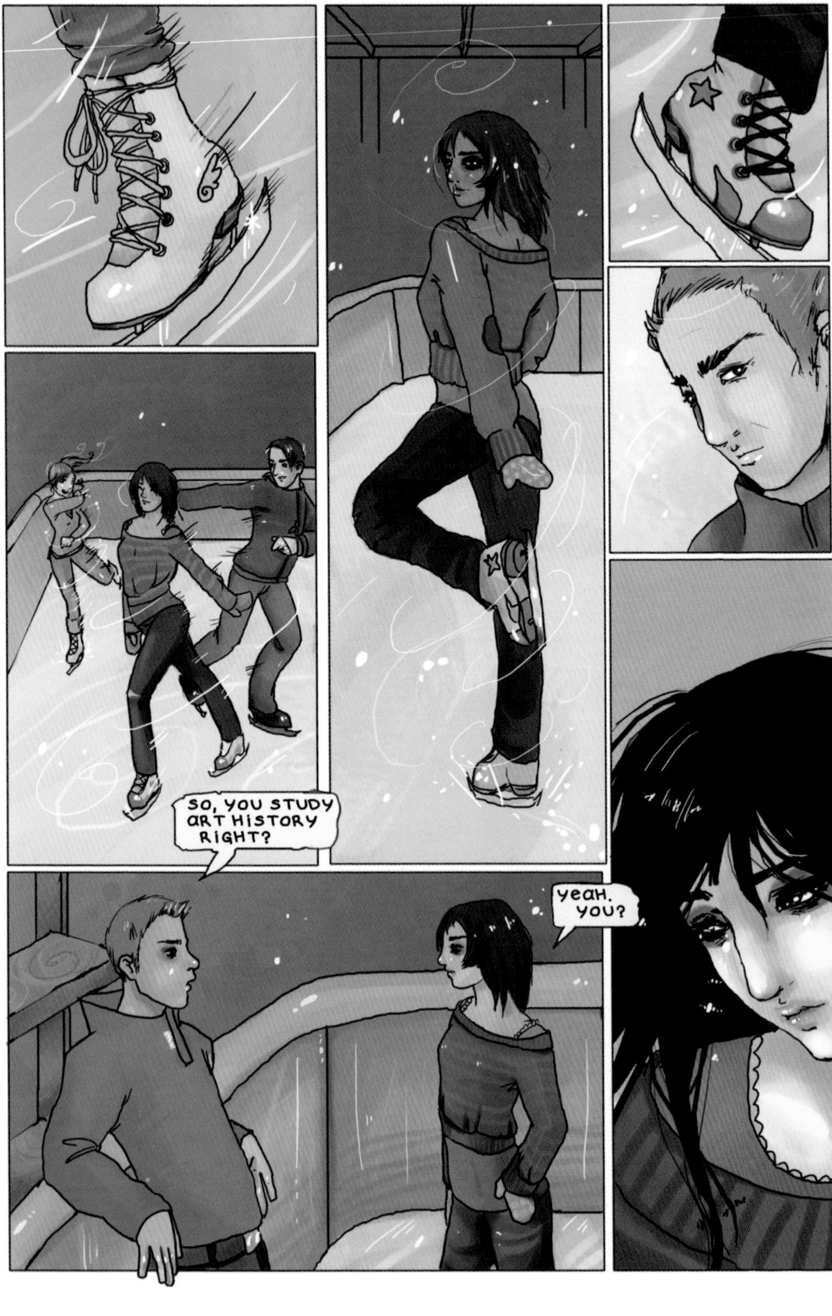
SO, YOU STUDY ART HISTORY RIGHT?
yeah. you?

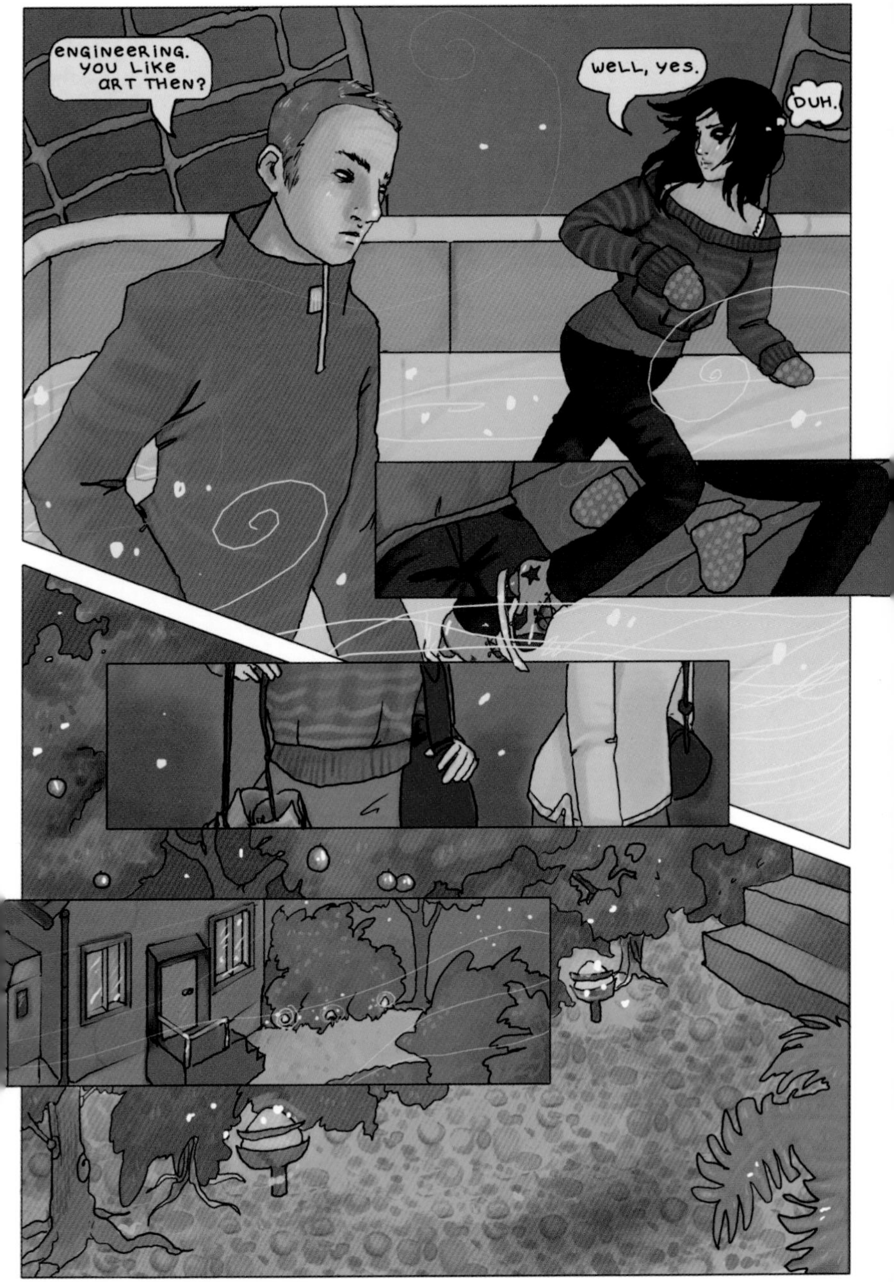
ENGINEERING. YOU LIKE ART THEN?
WELL, YES.
DUH.

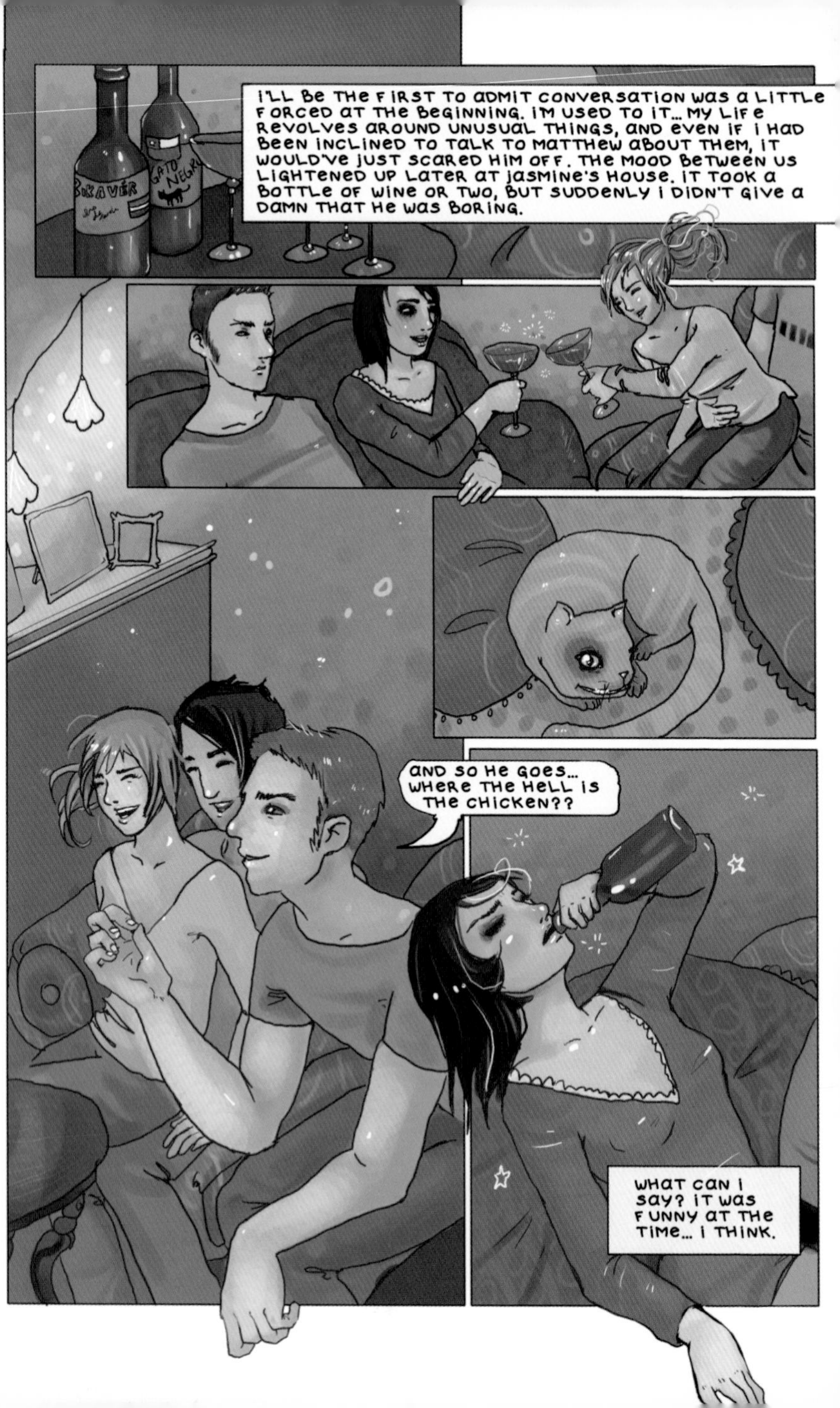
I'LL BE THE FIRST TO ADMIT CONVERSATION WAS A LITTLE FORCED AT THE BEGINNING. I'M USED TO IT... MY LIFE REVOLVES AROUND UNUSUAL THINGS, AND EVEN IF I HAD BEEN INCLINED TO TALK TO MATTHEW ABOUT THEM, IT WOULD'VE JUST SCARED HIM OFF. THE MOOD BETWEEN US LIGHTENED UP LATER AT JASMINE'S HOUSE. IT TOOK A BOTTLE OF WINE OR TWO, BUT SUDDENLY I DIDN'T GIVE A DAMN THAT HE WAS BORING.
AND SO HE GOES... WHERE THE HELL IS THE CHICKEN??
WHAT CAN I SAY? IT WAS FUNNY AT THE TIME... I THINK.

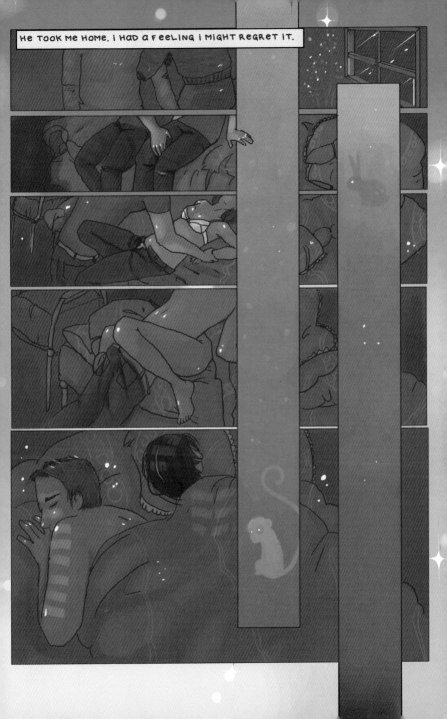

HE TOOK ME HOME. I HAD A FEELING I MIGHT REGRET IT.

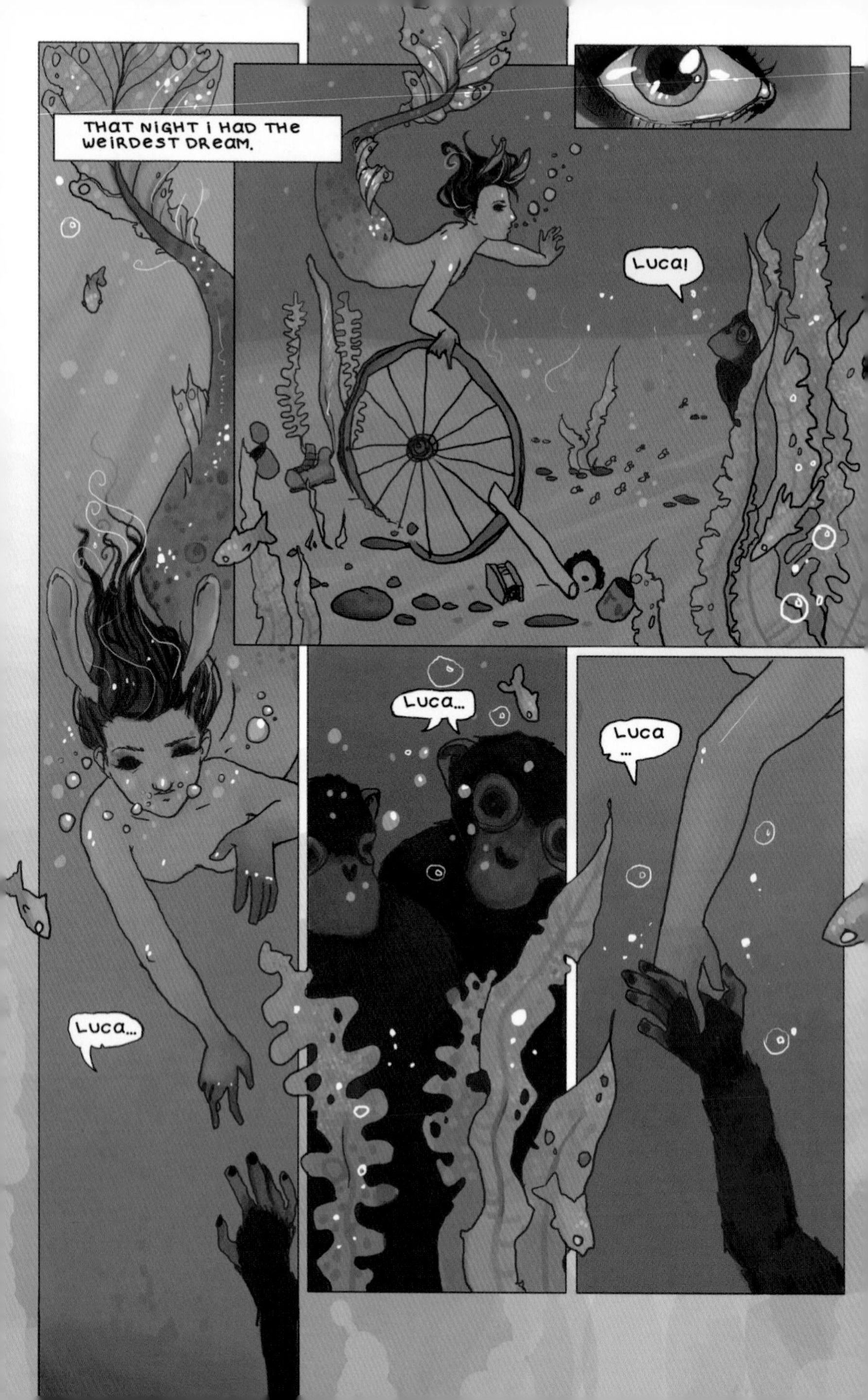
THAT NIGHT I HAD THE WEIRDEST DREAM.
Luca!
Luca...
Luca...
Luca
...

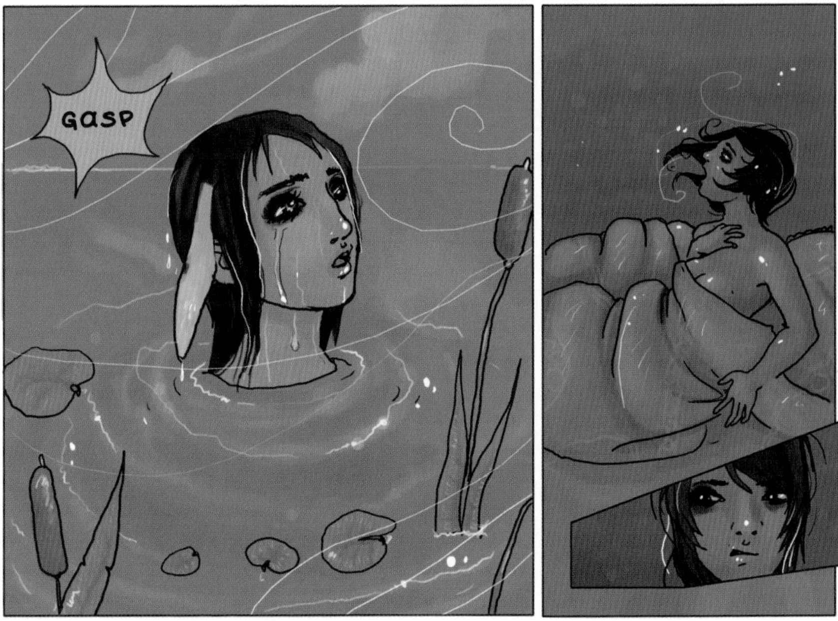
GASP

a couple of days later.

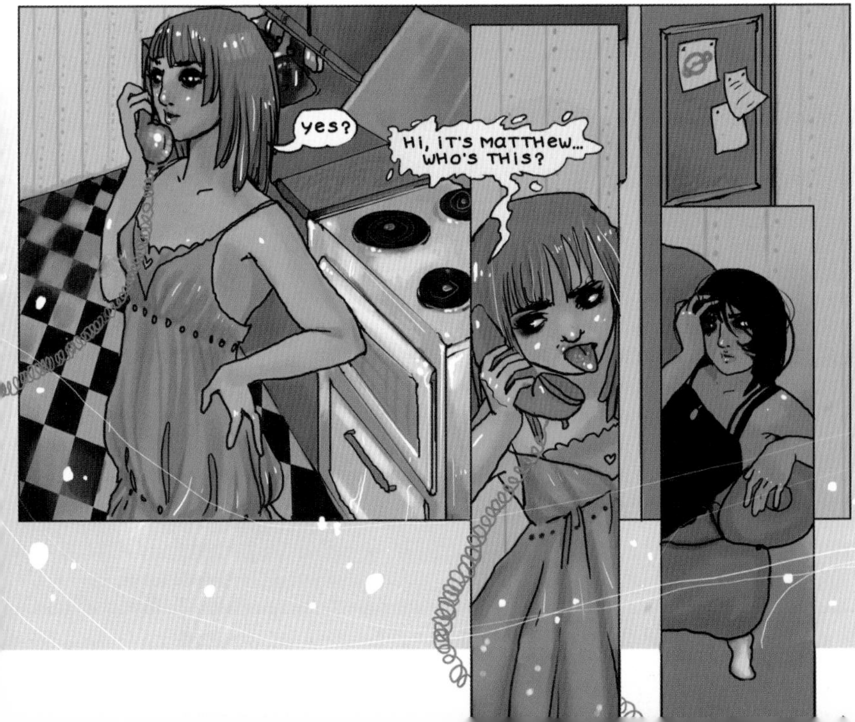
yes?
Hi, it's Matthew...
who's this?

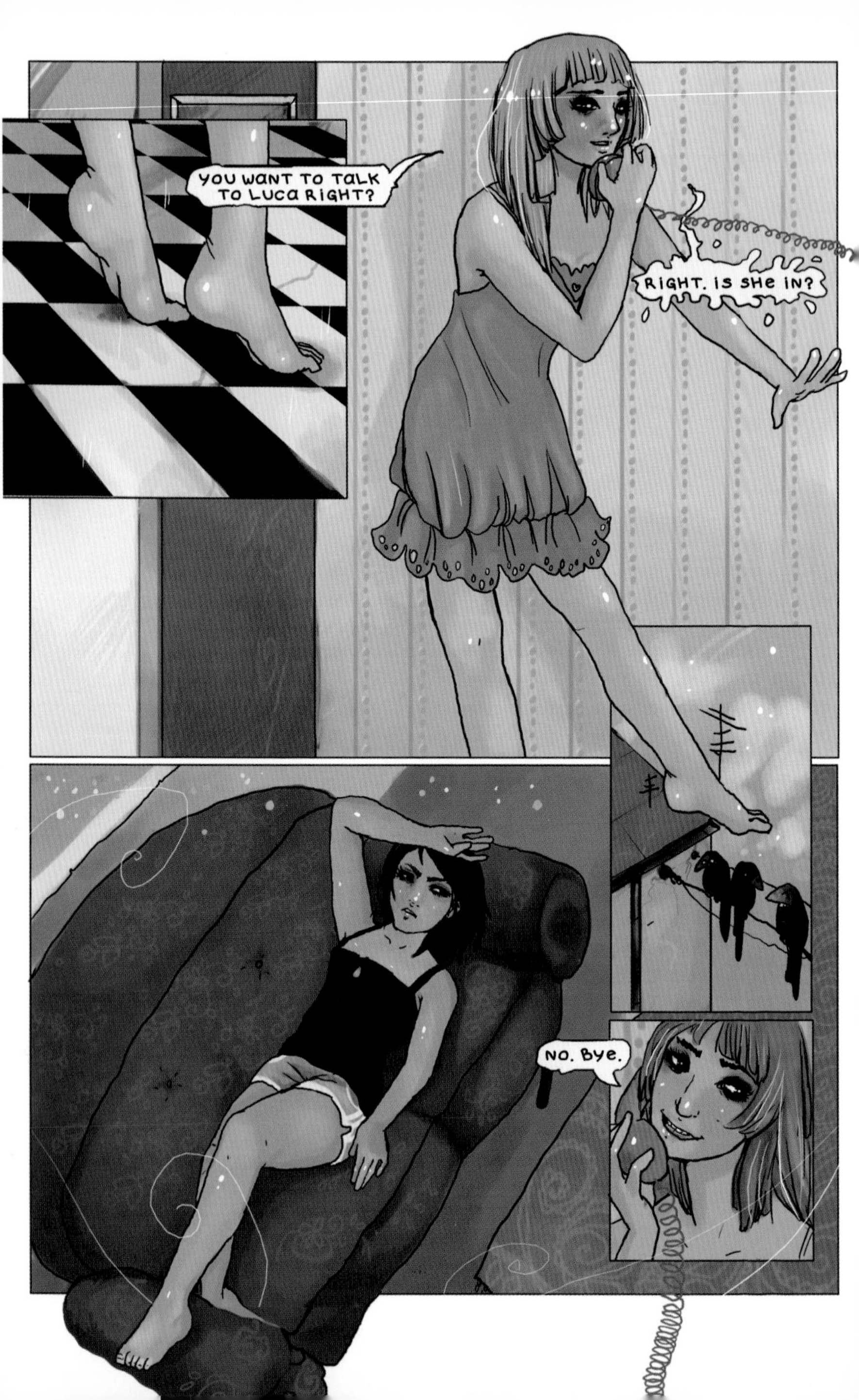
YOU WANT TO TALK TO LUCA RIGHT?
RIGHT. IS SHE IN?
NO. BYE.

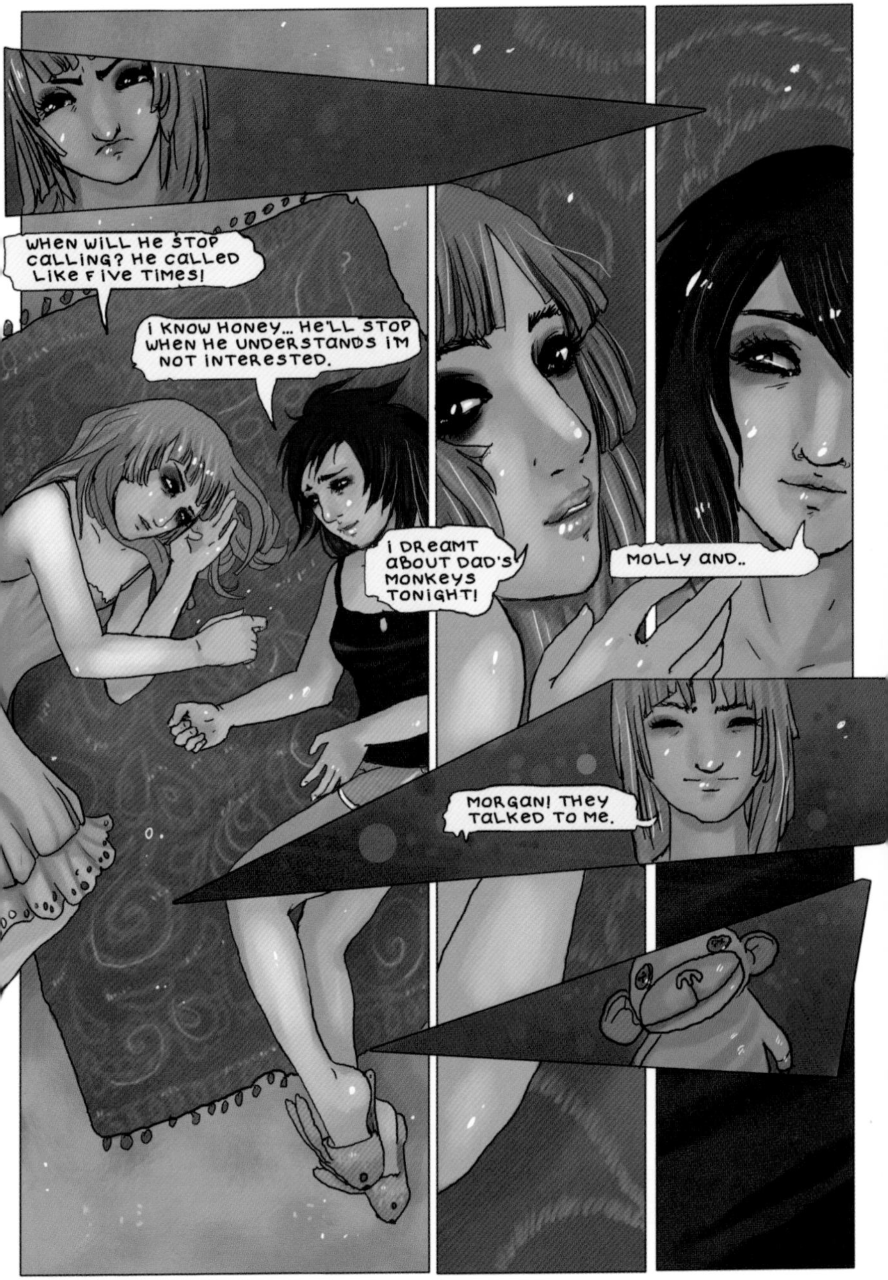
WHEN WILL HE STOP CALLING? HE CALLED LIKE FIVE TIMES!
I KNOW HONEY... HE'LL STOP WHEN HE UNDERSTANDS I'M NOT INTERESTED.
I DREAMT ABOUT DAD'S MONKEYS TONIGHT!
MOLLY AND..
MORGAN! THEY TALKED TO ME.

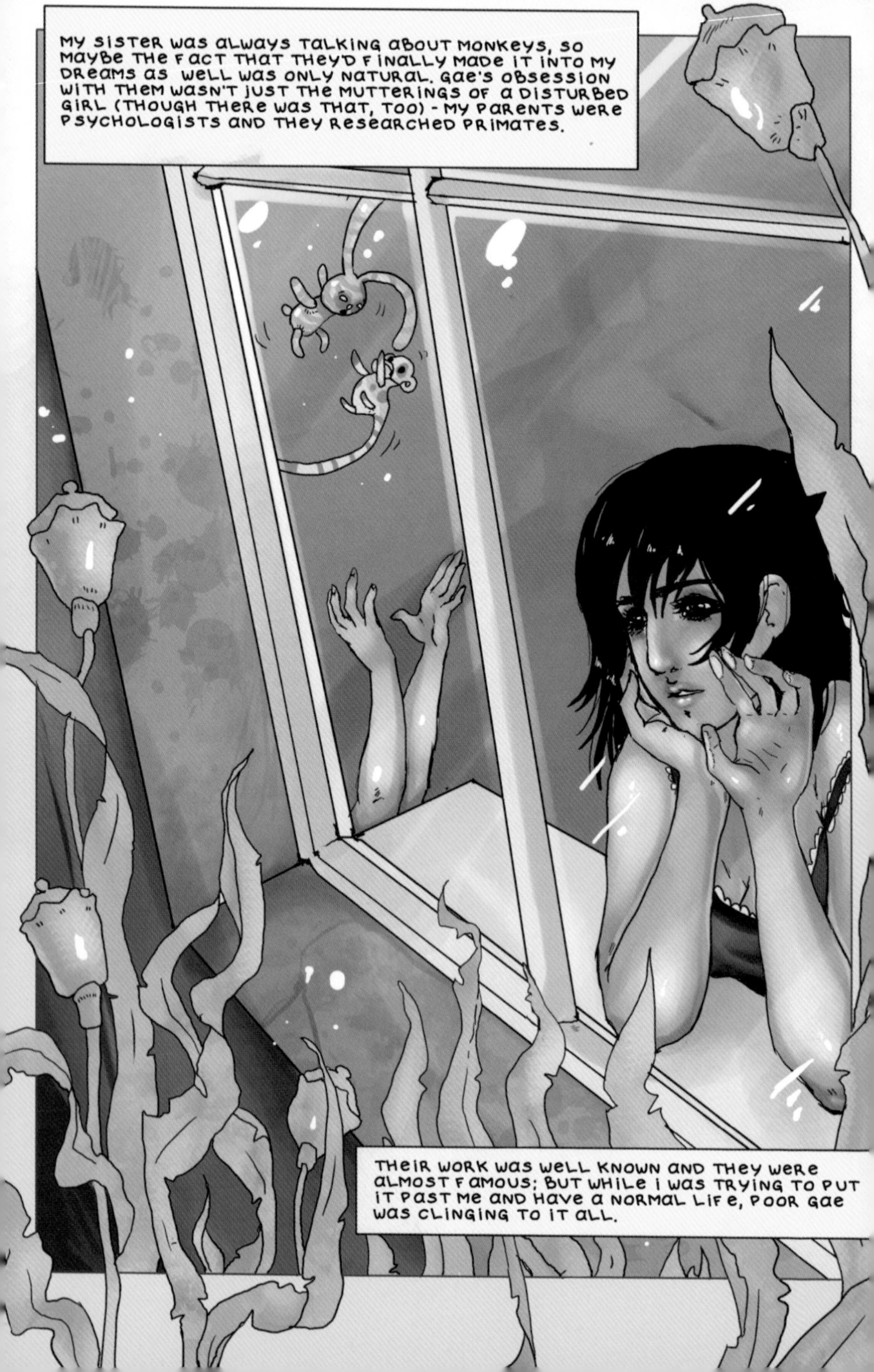
MY SISTER WAS ALWAYS TALKING ABOUT MONKEYS, SO MAYBE THE FACT THAT THEY'D FINALLY MADE IT INTO MY DREAMS AS WELL WAS ONLY NATURAL. GAE'S OBSESSION WITH THEM WASN'T JUST THE MUTTERINGS OF A DISTURBED GIRL (THOUGH THERE WAS THAT, TOO) - MY PARENTS WERE PSYCHOLOGISTS AND THEY RESEARCHED PRIMATES.
THEIR WORK WAS WELL KNOWN AND THEY WERE ALMOST FAMOUS; BUT WHILE I WAS TRYING TO PUT IT PAST ME AND HAVE A NORMAL LIFE, POOR GAE WAS CLINGING TO IT ALL.

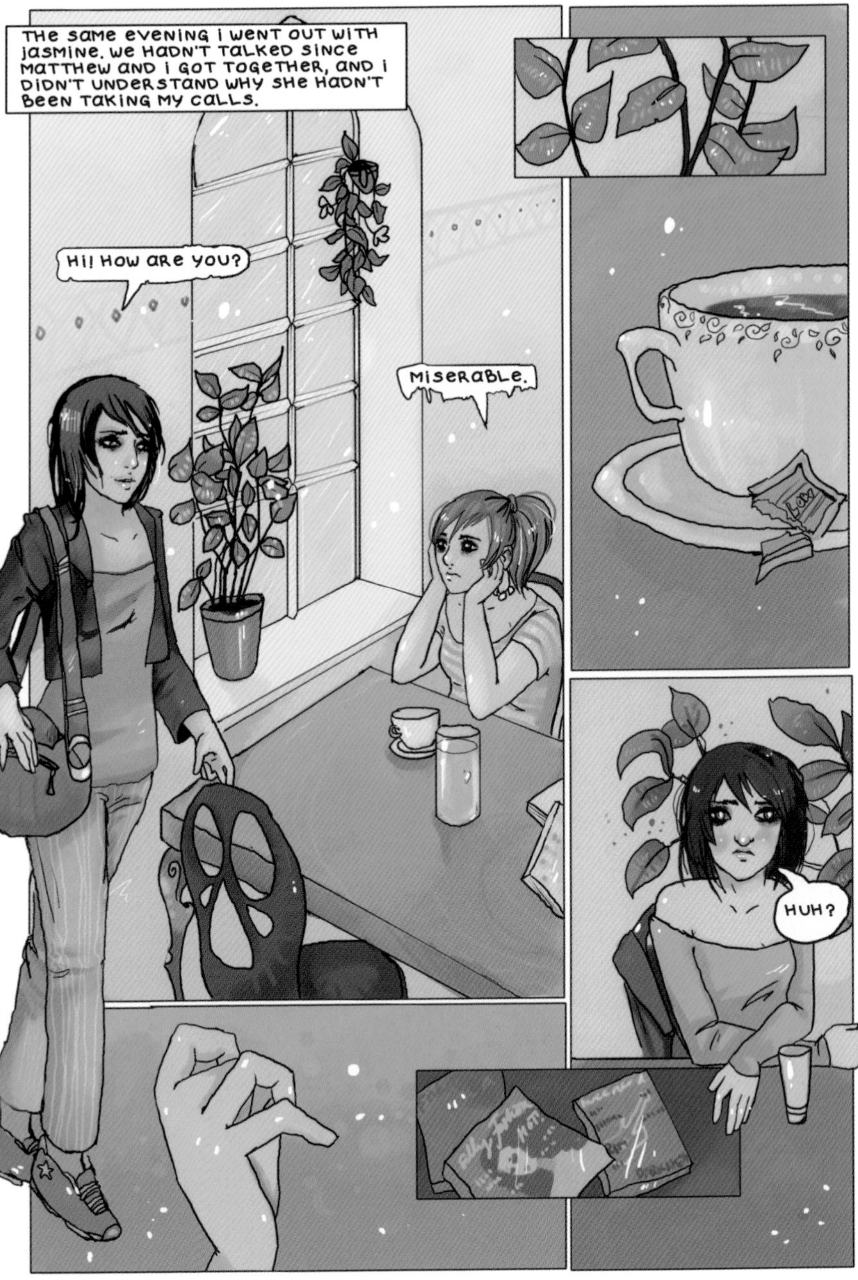
The same evening i went out with jasmine. We hadn't talked since Matthew and i got together, and i didn't understand why she hadn't been taking my calls.
Hi! How are you?
Miserable.
Huh?

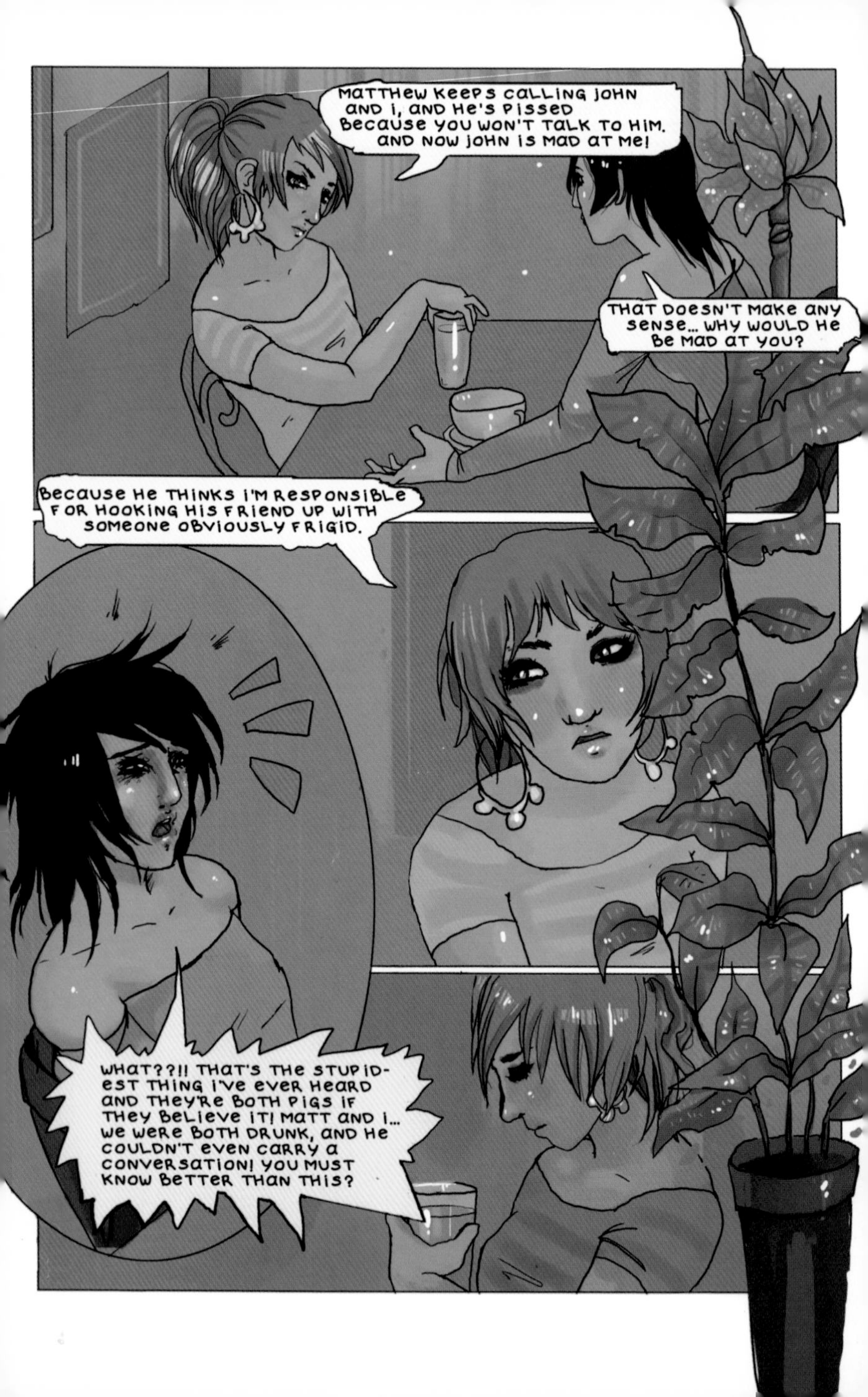
MATTHEW KEEPS CALLING JOHN AND I, AND HE'S PISSED BECAUSE YOU WON'T TALK TO HIM. AND NOW JOHN IS MAD AT ME!
THAT DOESN'T MAKE ANY SENSE... WHY WOULD HE BE MAD AT YOU?
BECAUSE HE THINKS I'M RESPONSIBLE FOR HOOKING HIS FRIEND UP WITH SOMEONE OBVIOUSLY FRIGID.
WHAT??!! THAT'S THE STUPID-EST THING I'VE EVER HEARD AND THEY'RE BOTH PIGS IF THEY BELIEVE IT! MATT AND I... WE WERE BOTH DRUNK, AND HE COULDN'T EVEN CARRY A CONVERSATION! YOU MUST KNOW BETTER THAN THIS?

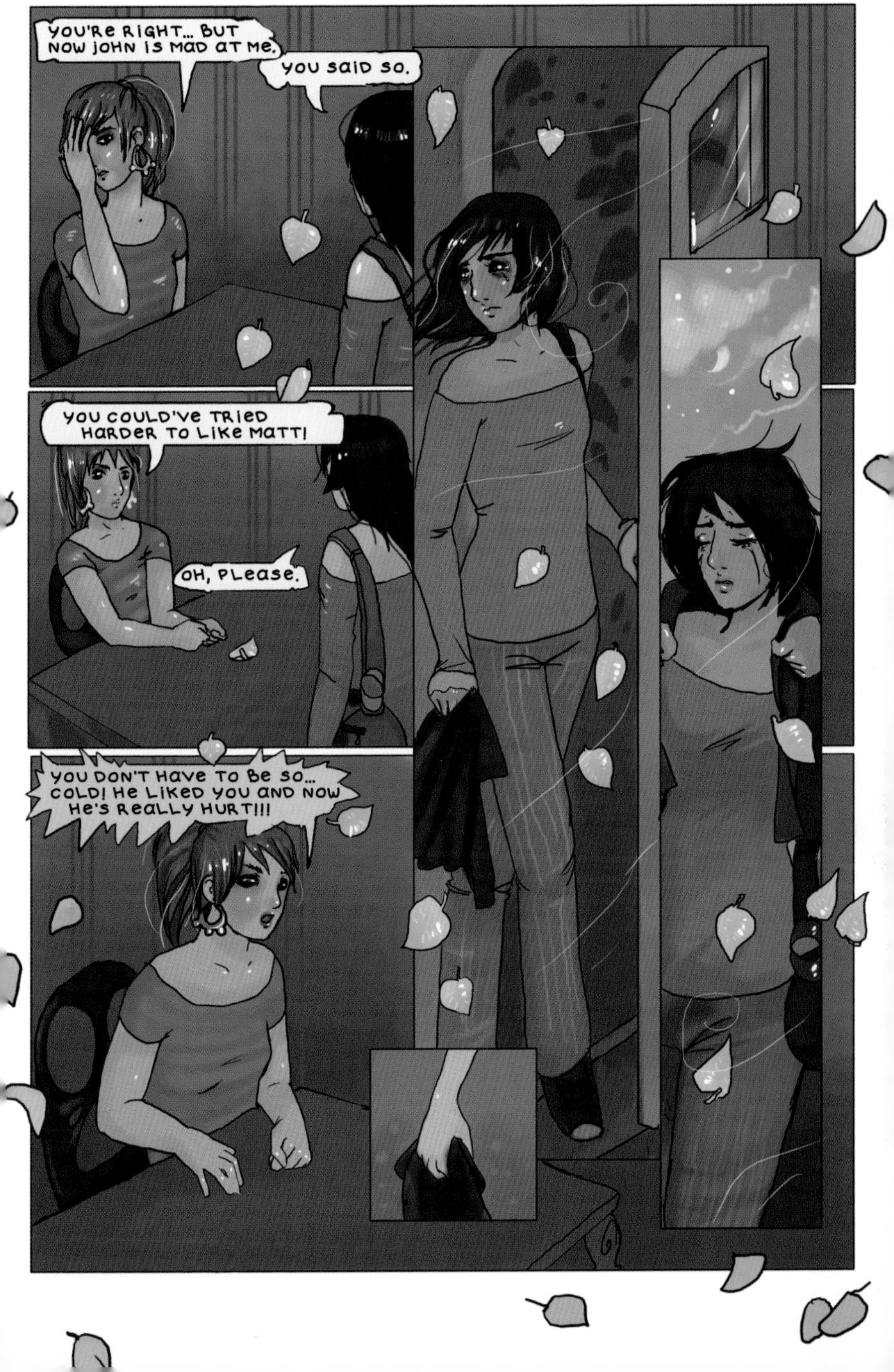
YOU'RE RIGHT... BUT NOW JOHN IS MAD AT ME.
YOU SAID SO.
YOU COULD'VE TRIED HARDER TO LIKE MATT!
OH, PLEASE.
YOU DON'T HAVE TO BE SO... COLD! HE LIKED YOU AND NOW HE'S REALLY HURT!!!

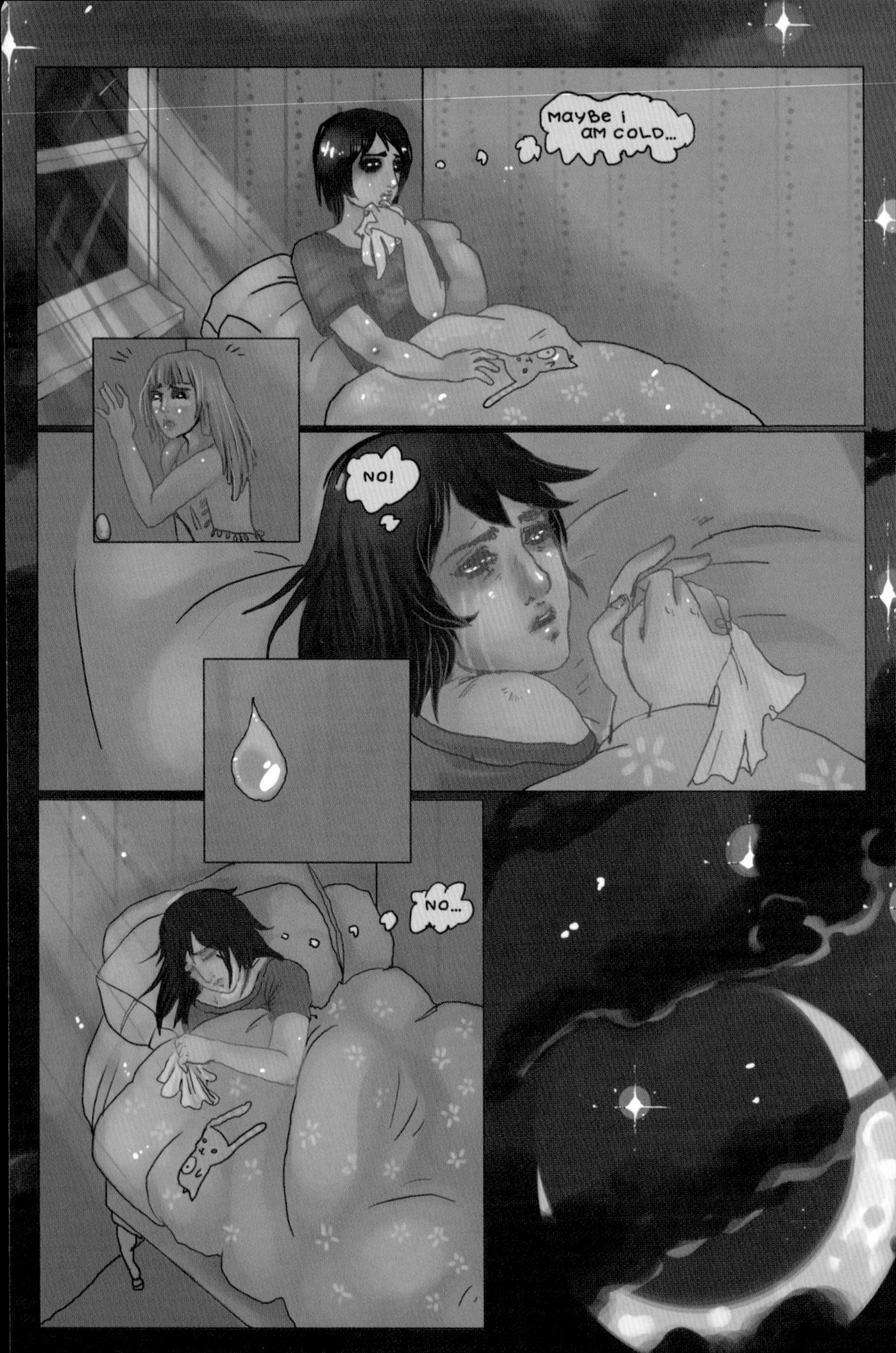
MayBe i am COLD...
NO!
NO...

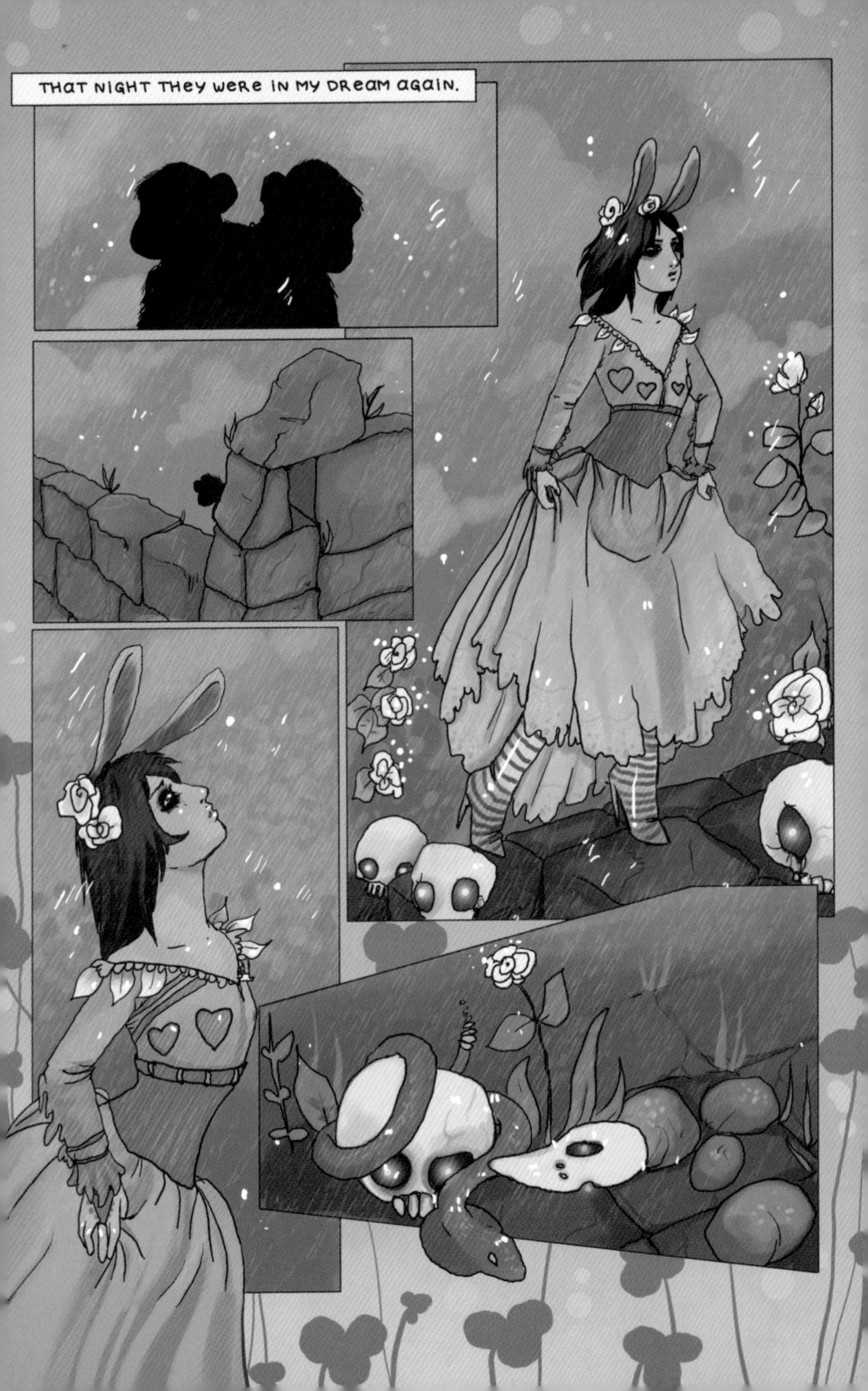
THAT NIGHT THEY WERE IN MY DREAM AGAIN.

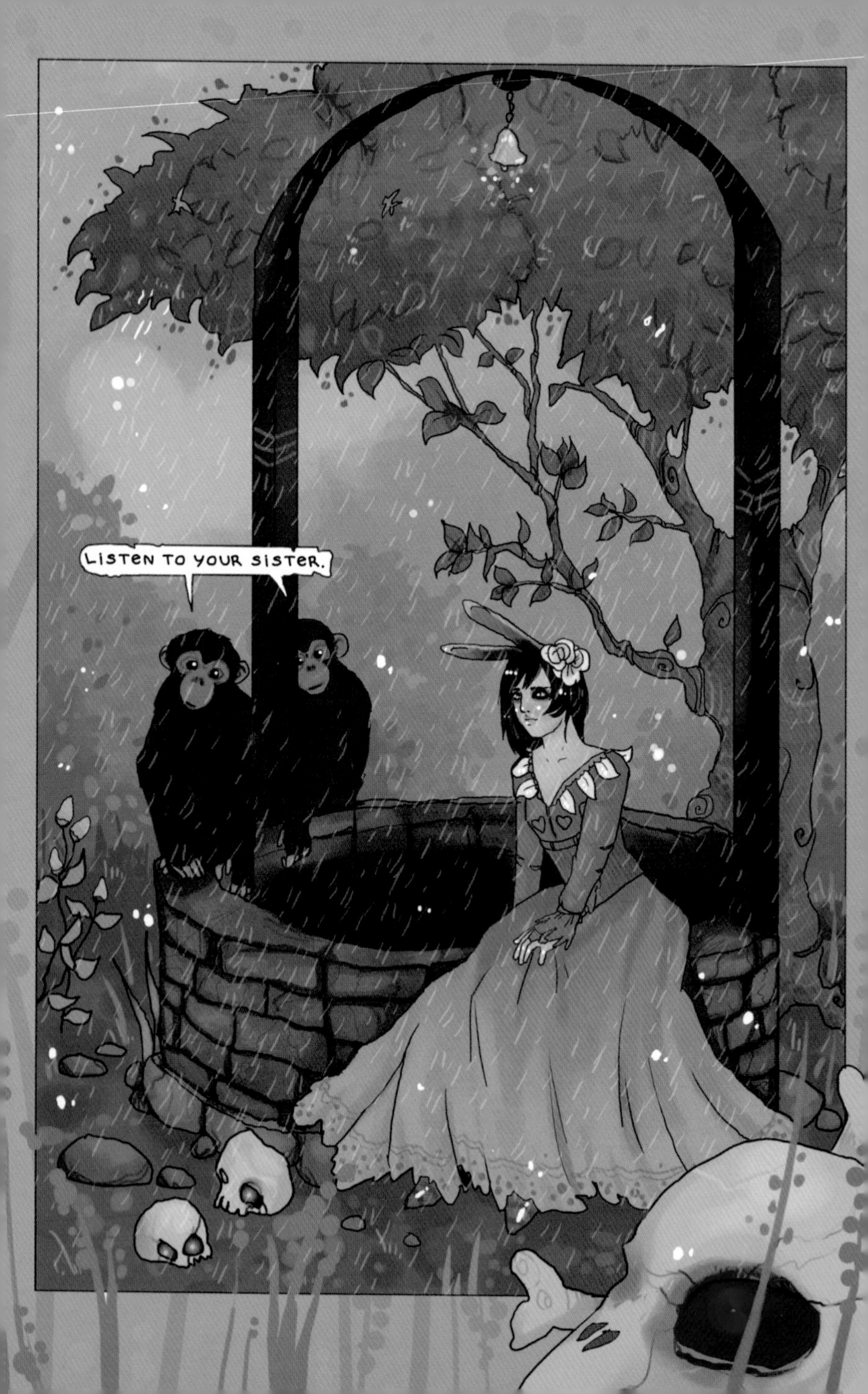
LISTEN TO YOUR SISTER.

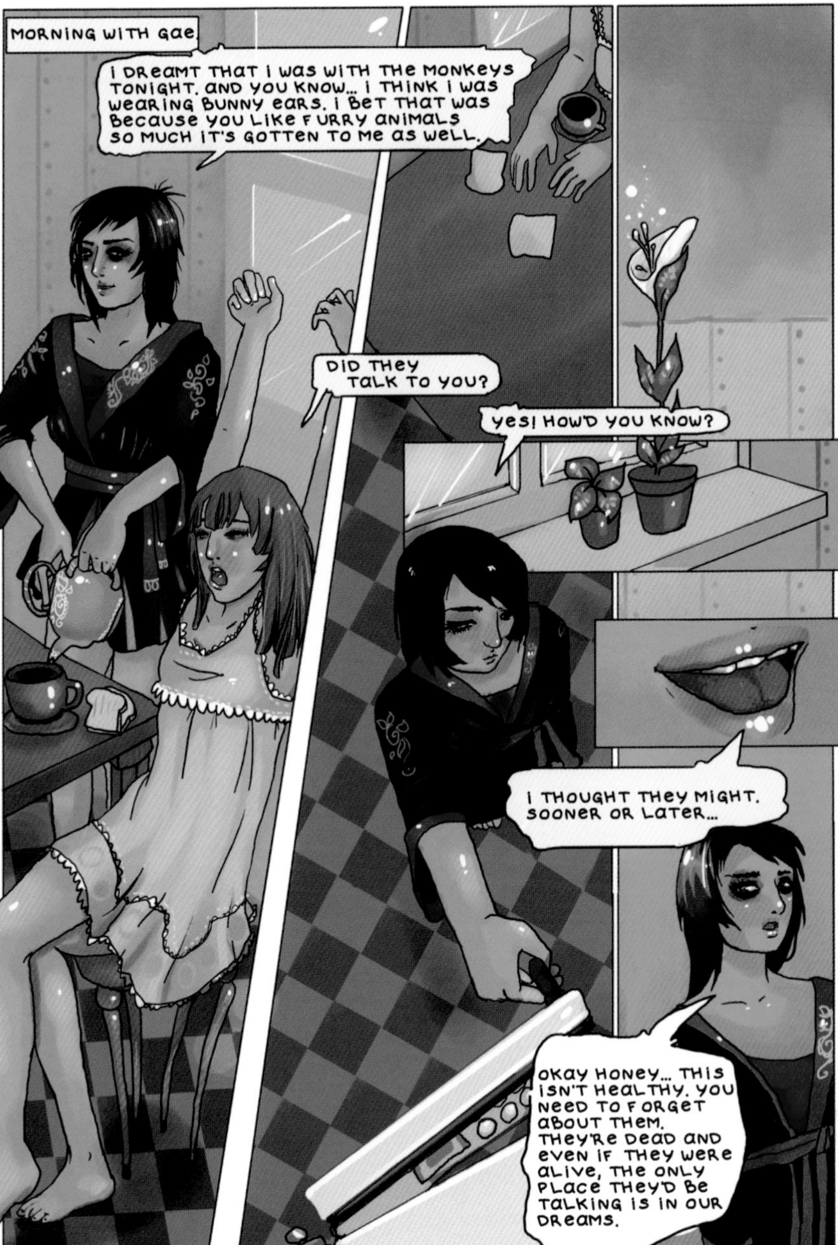
MORNING WITH GAE
I DREAMT THAT I WAS WITH THE MONKEYS TONIGHT. AND YOU KNOW... I THINK I WAS WEARING BUNNY EARS. I BET THAT WAS BECAUSE YOU LIKE FURRY ANIMALS SO MUCH IT'S GOTTEN TO ME AS WELL.
DID THEY TALK TO YOU?
YES! HOW'D YOU KNOW?
I THOUGHT THEY MIGHT. SOONER OR LATER...
OKAY HONEY... THIS ISN'T HEALTHY. YOU NEED TO FORGET ABOUT THEM. THEY'RE DEAD AND EVEN IF THEY WERE ALIVE, THE ONLY PLACE THEY'D BE TALKING IS IN OUR DREAMS.

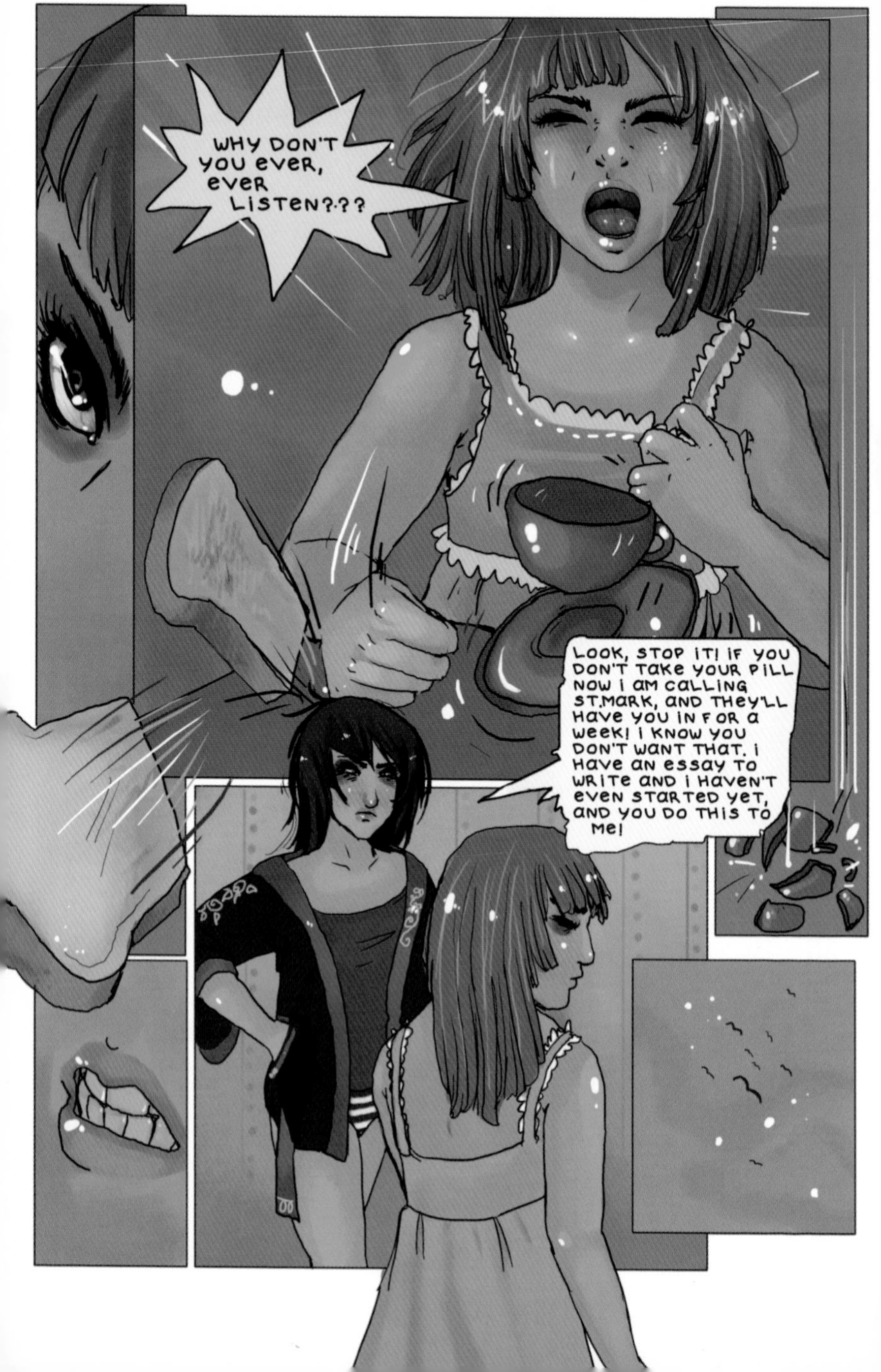
WHY DON'T YOU ever, ever LISTEN???
LOOK, STOP IT! IF YOU DON'T TAKE YOUR PILL NOW I AM CALLING ST.MARK, AND THEY'LL HAVE YOU IN FOR A WEEK! I KNOW YOU DON'T WANT THAT. I HAVE AN ESSAY TO WRITE AND I HAVEN'T EVEN STARTED YET, AND YOU DO THIS TO ME!

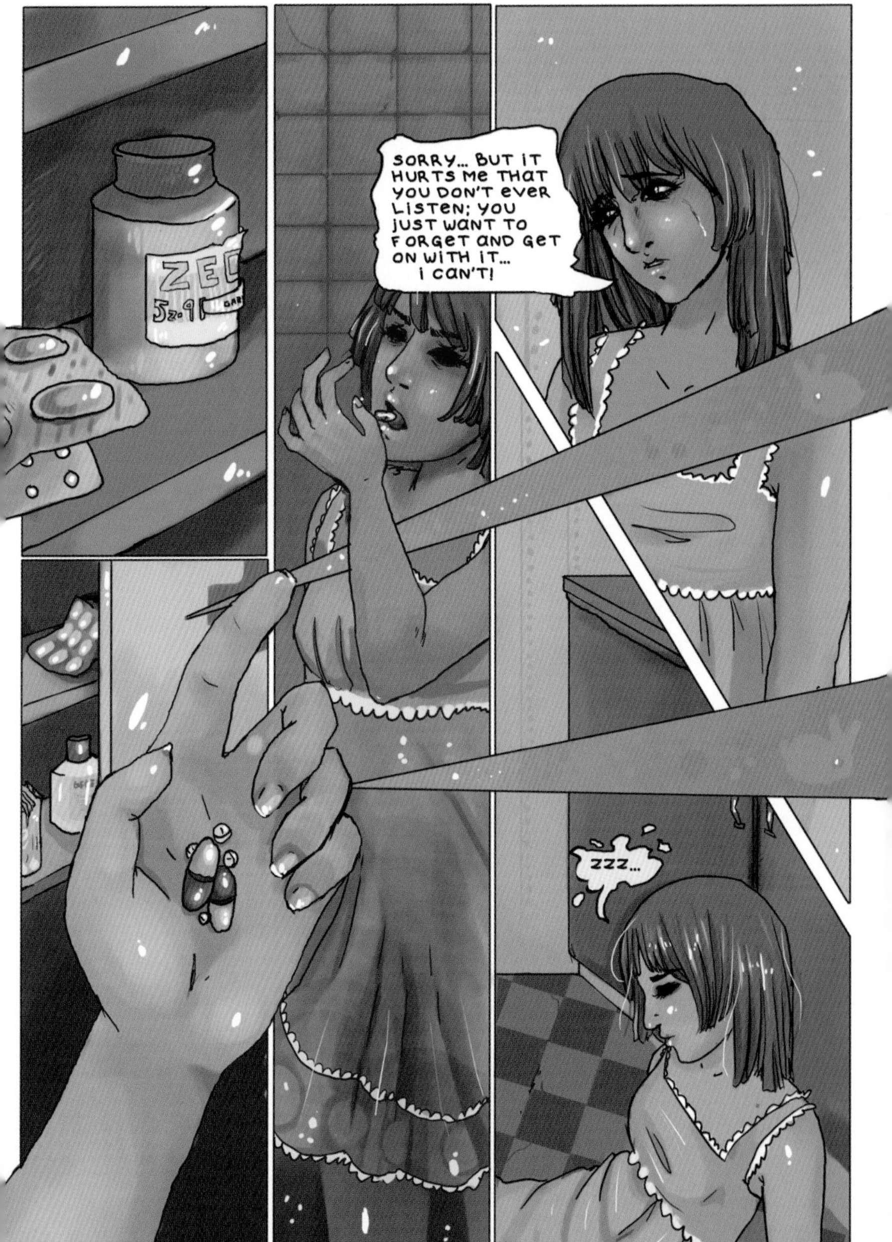
SORRY... BUT IT HURTS ME THAT YOU DON'T EVER LISTEN; YOU JUST WANT TO FORGET AND GET ON WITH IT... I CAN'T!
ZZZ...

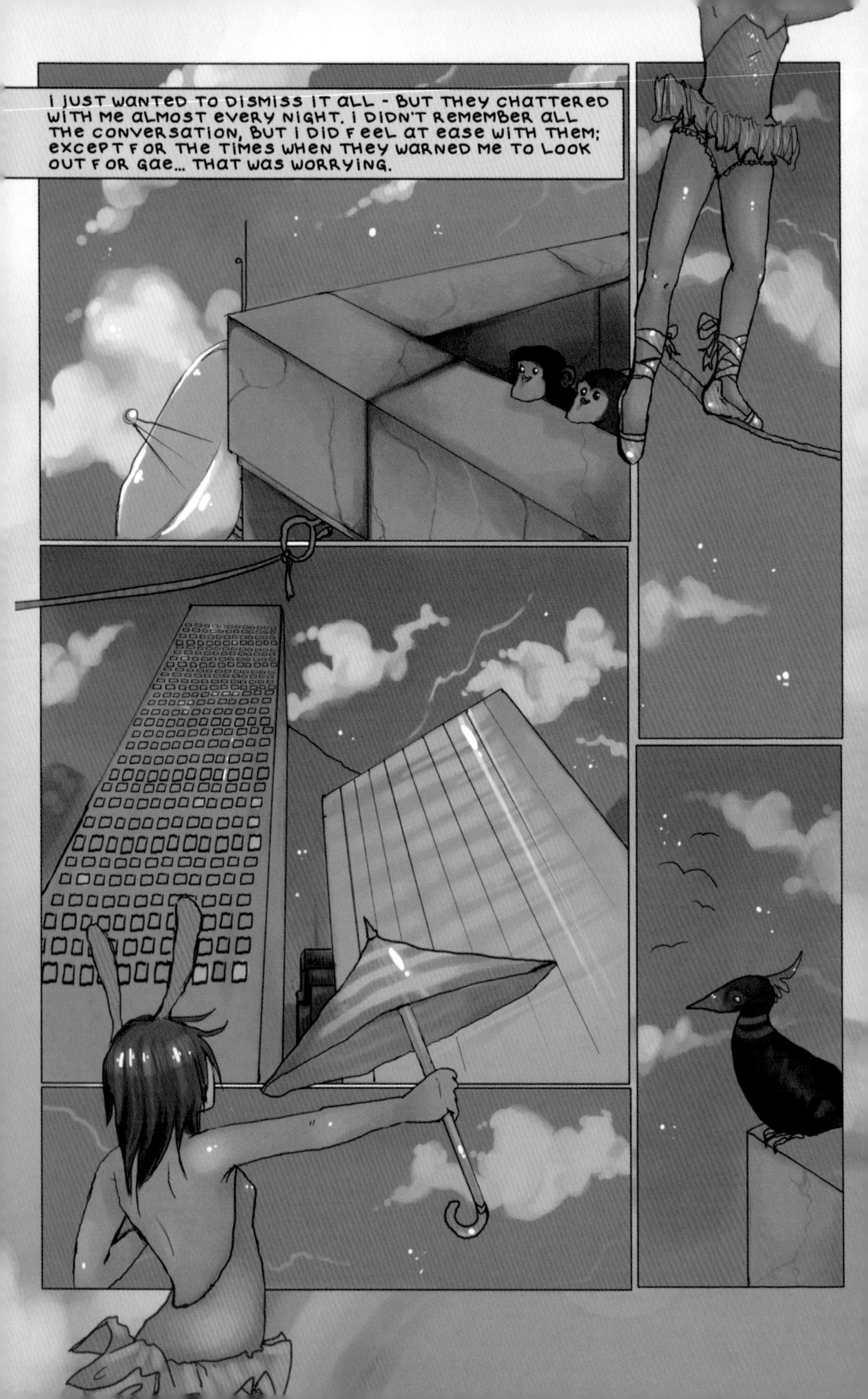
I JUST WANTED TO DISMISS IT ALL - BUT THEY CHATTERED WITH ME ALMOST EVERY NIGHT. I DIDN'T REMEMBER ALL THE CONVERSATION, BUT I DID FEEL AT EASE WITH THEM; EXCEPT FOR THE TIMES WHEN THEY WARNED ME TO LOOK OUT FOR GAE... THAT WAS WORRYING.

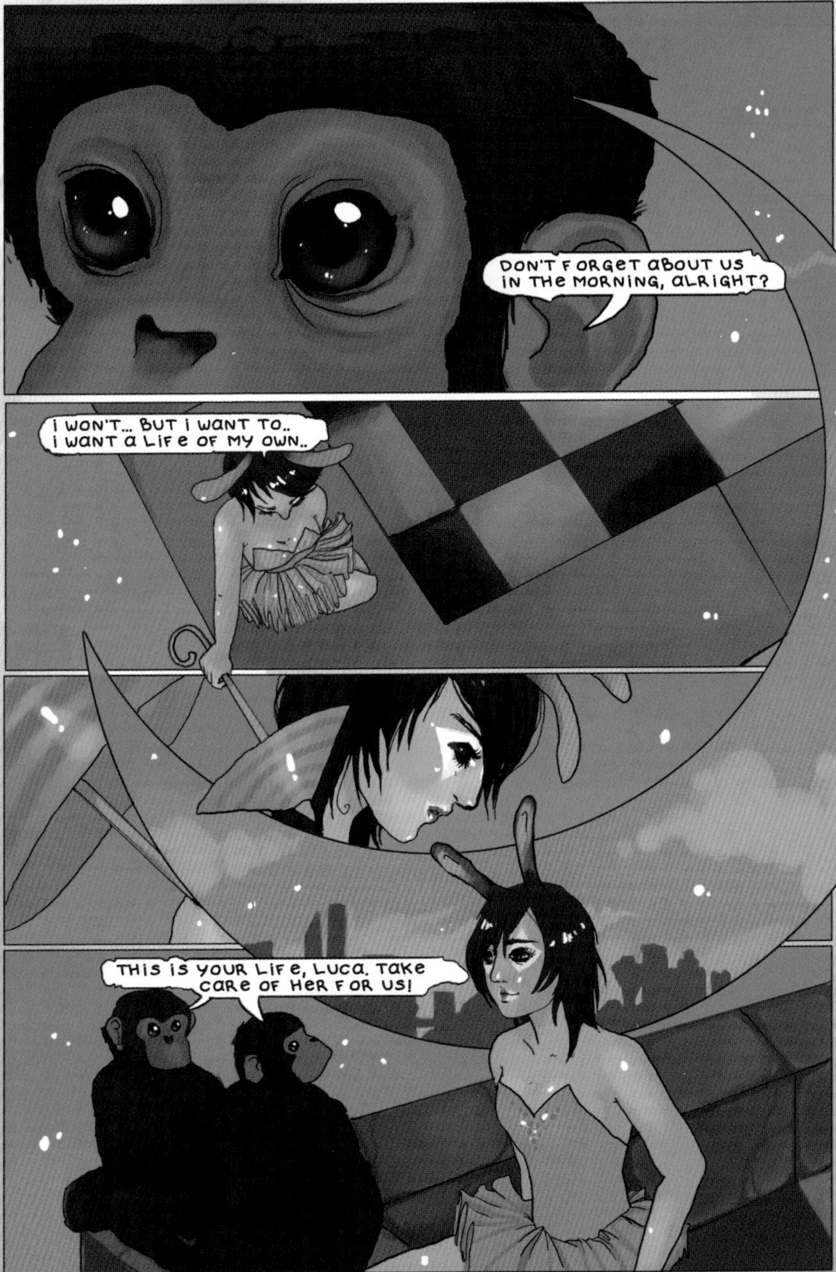
DON'T FORGET ABOUT US IN THE MORNING, ALRIGHT?
I WON'T... BUT I WANT TO.. I WANT A LIFE OF MY OWN..
THIS IS YOUR LIFE, LUCA. TAKE CARE OF HER FOR US!

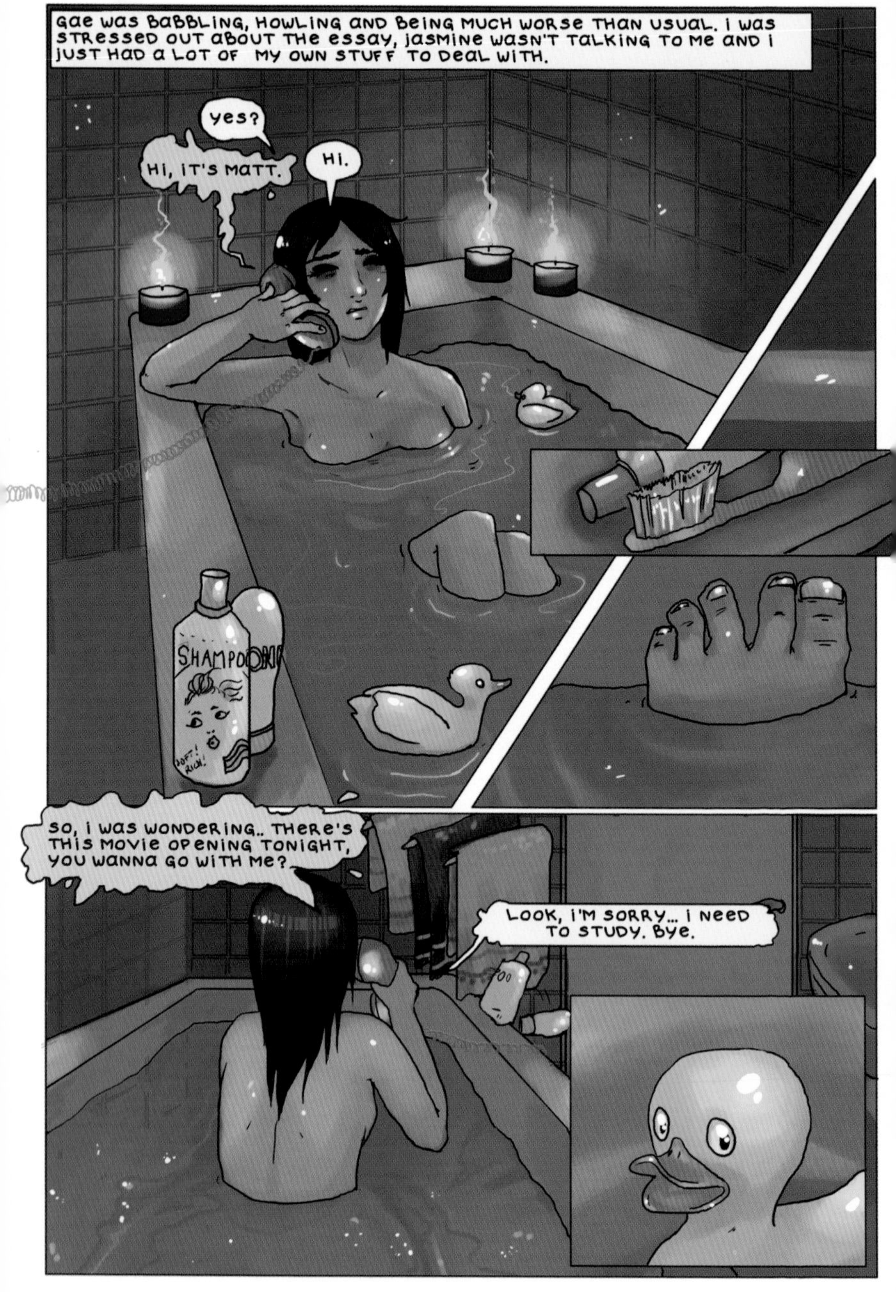
gae was babbling, howling and being much worse than usual. i was stressed out about the essay, jasmine wasn't talking to me and i just had a lot of my own stuff to deal with.
yes?
Hi, it's matt.
Hi.
SHAMPO
So, i was wondering.. there's this movie opening tonight, you wanna go with me?
Look, i'm sorry... i need to study. Bye.

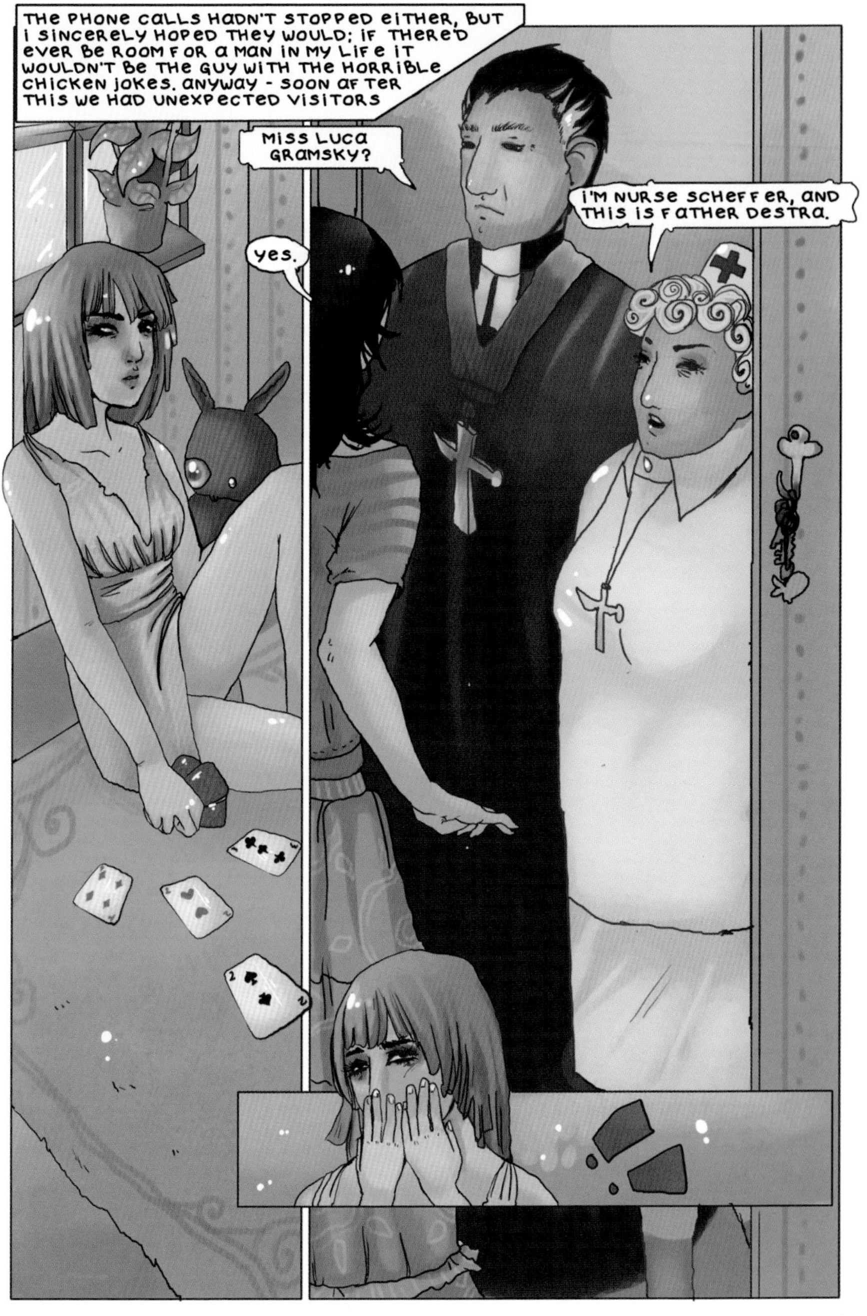
THE PHONE CALLS HADN'T STOPPED EITHER, BUT I SINCERELY HOPED THEY WOULD; IF THERE'D EVER BE ROOM FOR A MAN IN MY LIFE IT WOULDN'T BE THE GUY WITH THE HORRIBLE CHICKEN JOKES. ANYWAY - SOON AFTER THIS WE HAD UNEXPECTED VISITORS
MISS LUCA GRAMSKY?
YES.
I'M NURSE SCHEFFER, AND THIS IS FATHER DESTRA.

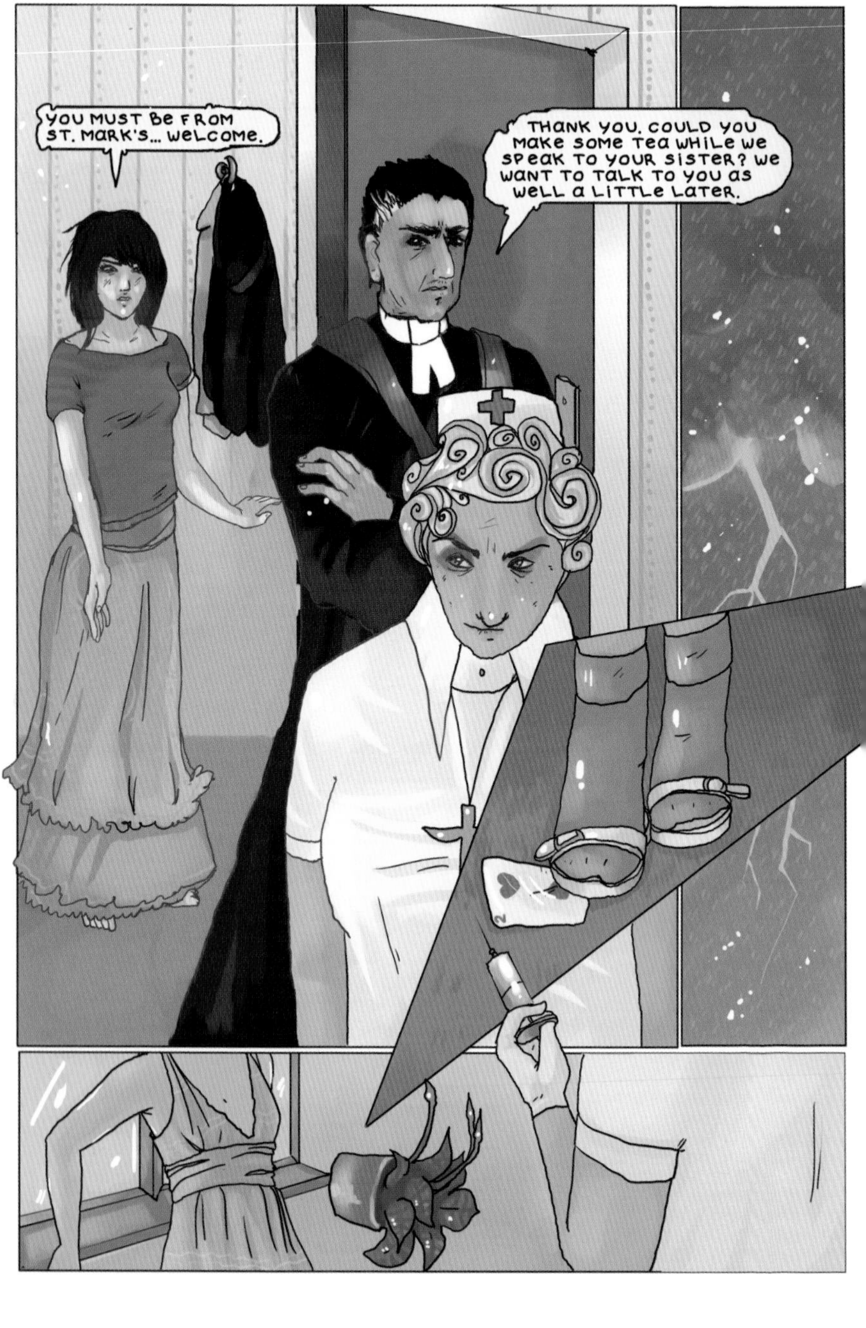
YOU MUST BE FROM ST. MARK'S... WELCOME.
THANK YOU. COULD YOU MAKE SOME TEA WHILE WE SPEAK TO YOUR SISTER? WE WANT TO TALK TO YOU AS WELL A LITTLE LATER.

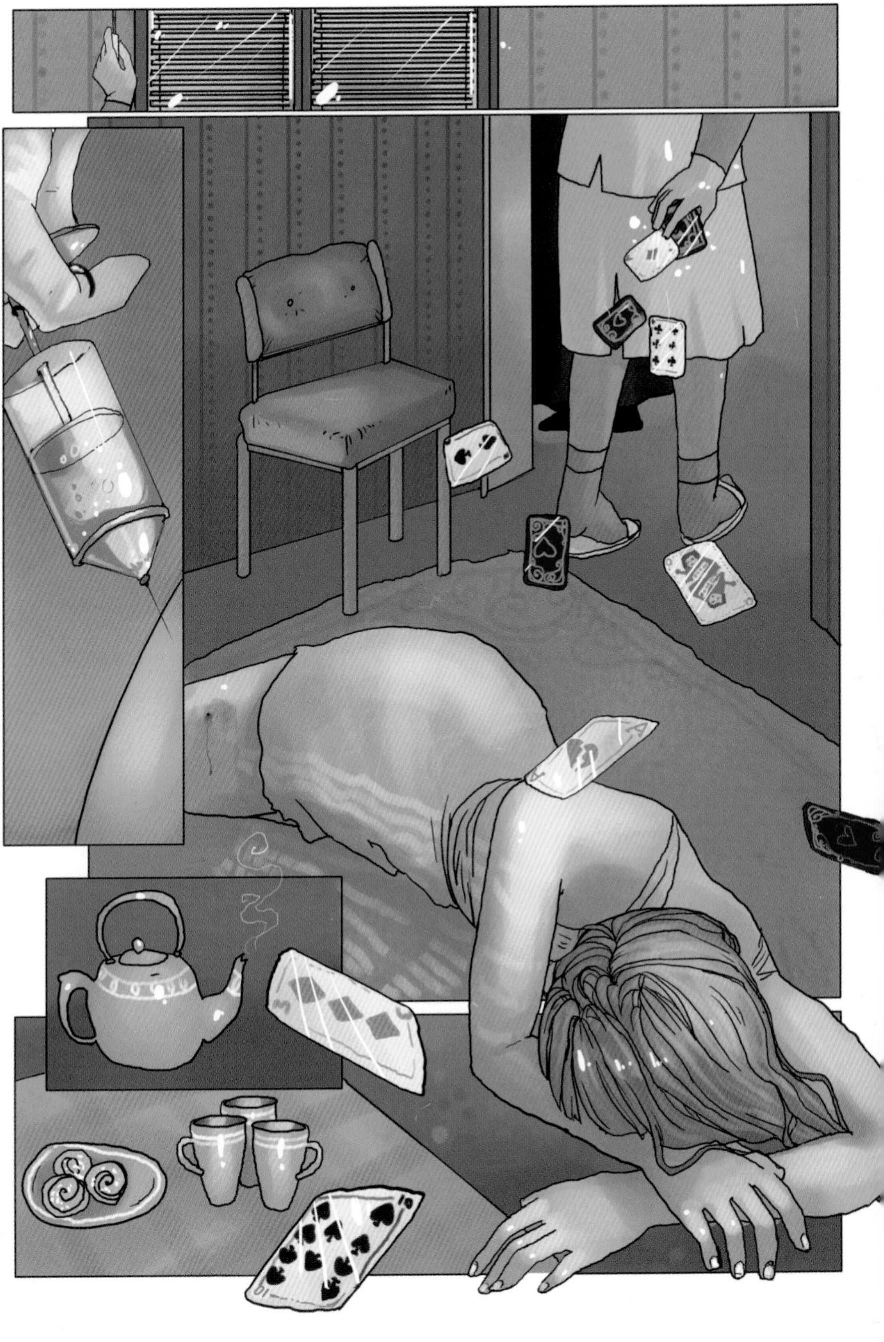

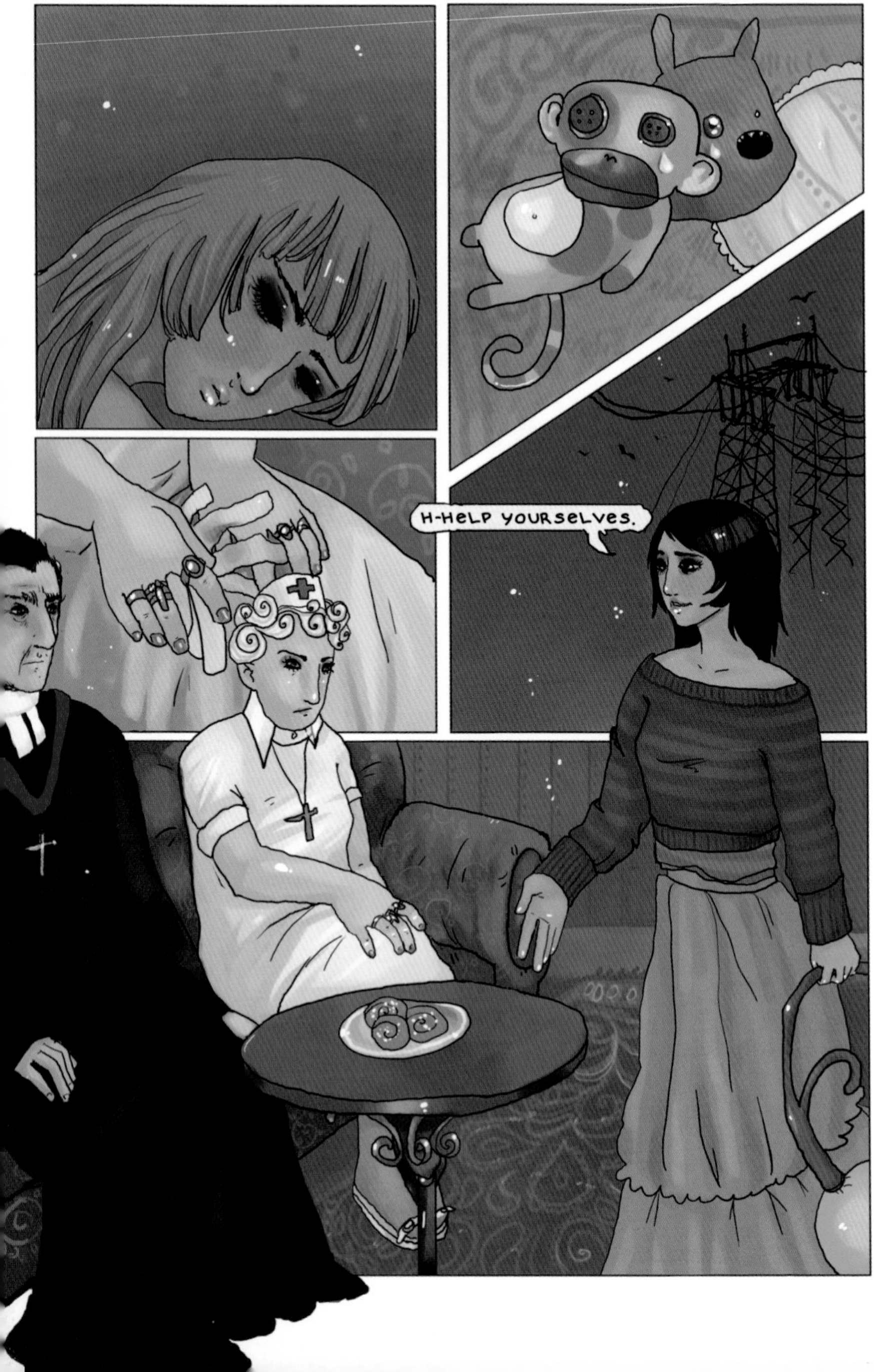
H-HELP YOURSELVES.

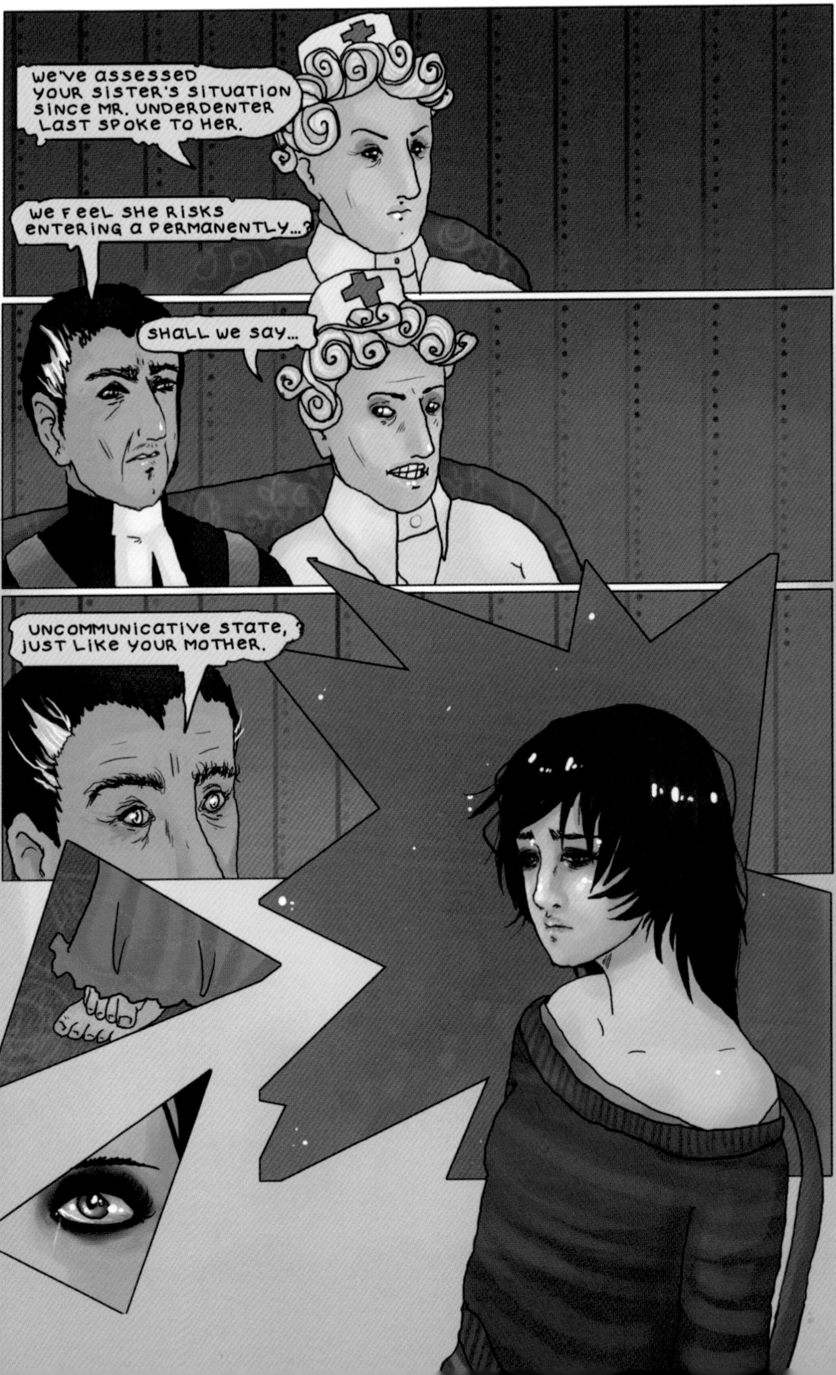
we've assessed your sister's situation since Mr. Underdenter last spoke to her.
we feel she risks entering a permanently...?
shall we say...
uncommunicative state, just like your mother.

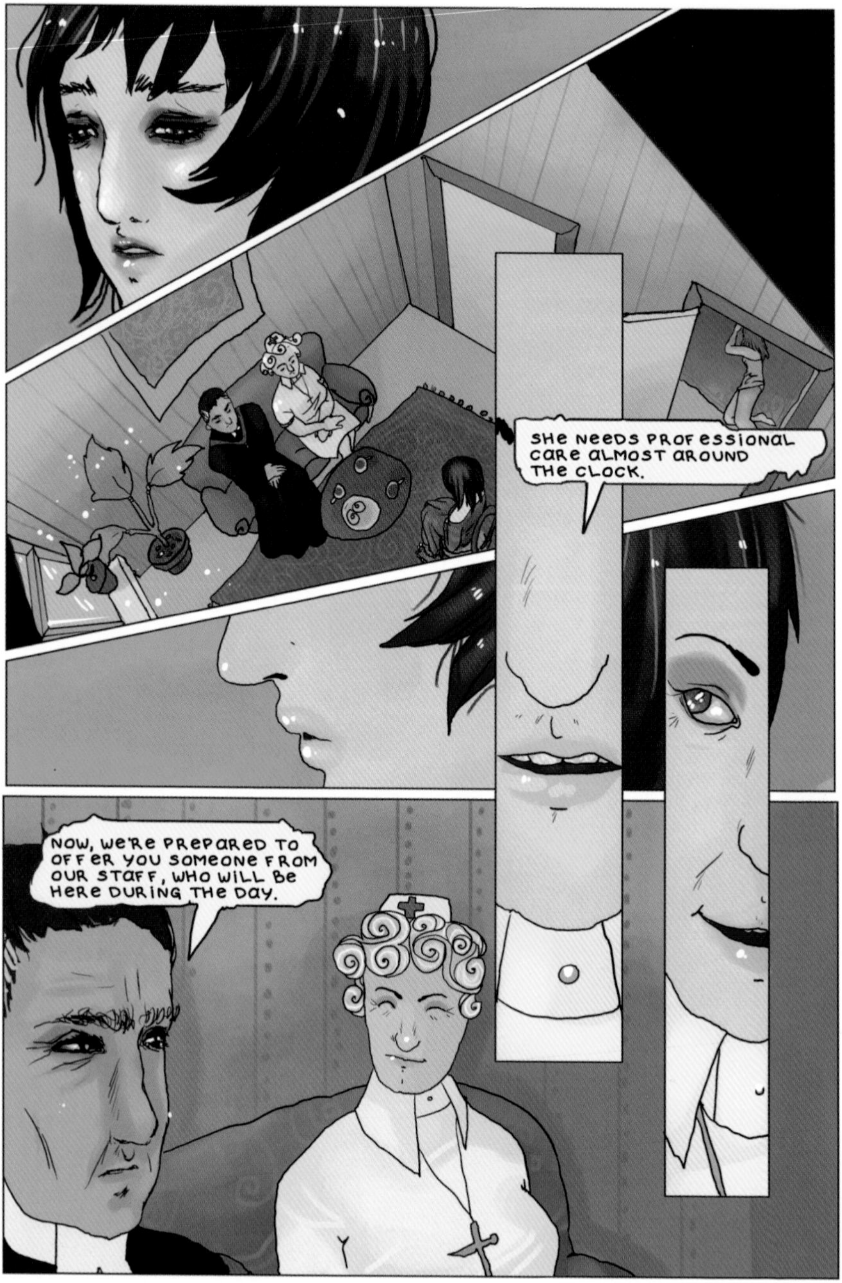
SHE NEEDS PROFESSIONAL CARE ALMOST AROUND THE CLOCK.
NOW, WE'RE PREPARED TO OFFER YOU SOMEONE FROM OUR STAFF, WHO WILL BE HERE DURING THE DAY.

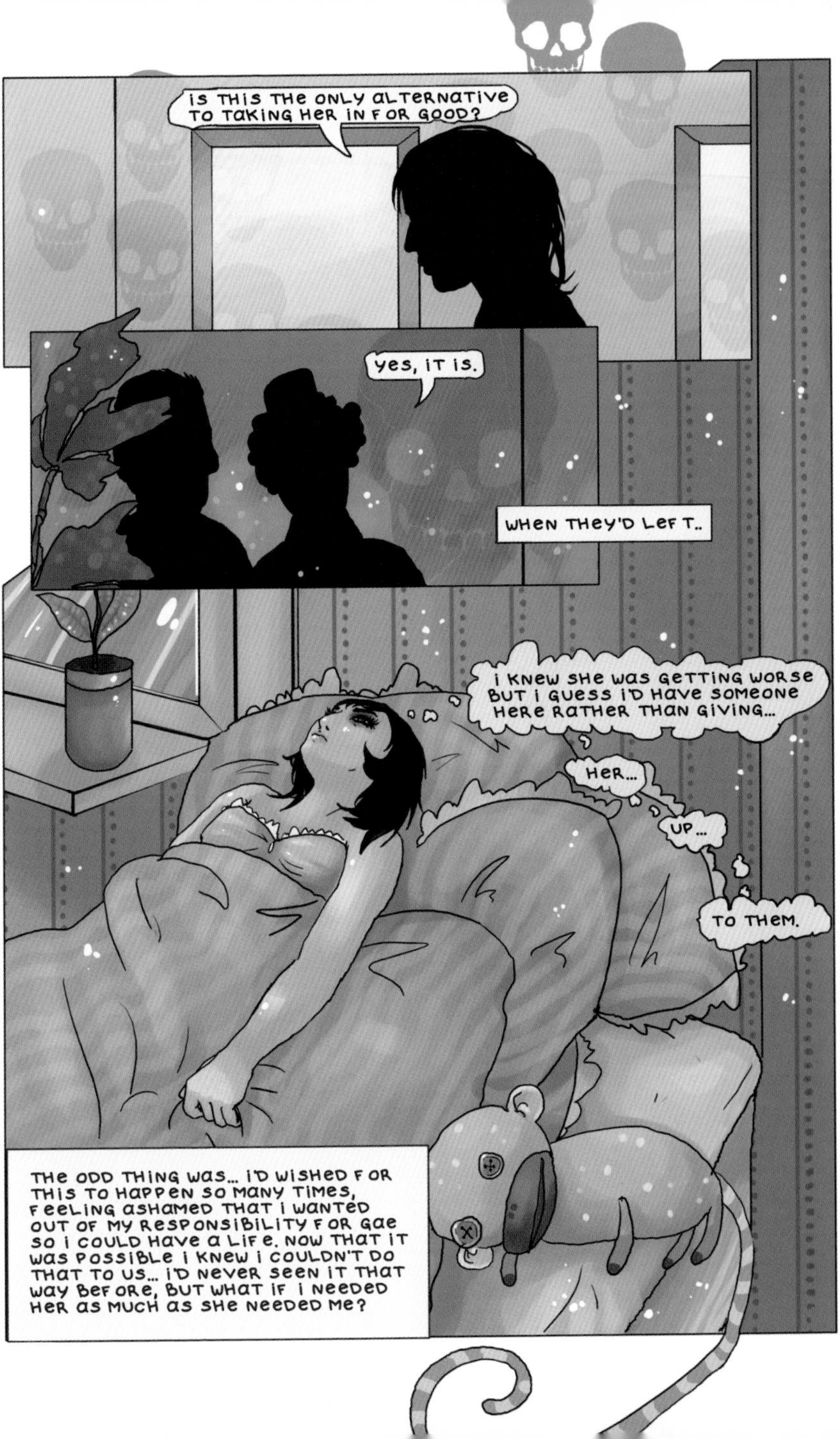
IS THIS THE ONLY ALTERNATIVE TO TAKING HER IN FOR GOOD?
YES, IT IS.
WHEN THEY'D LEFT..
I KNEW SHE WAS GETTING WORSE BUT I GUESS I'D HAVE SOMEONE HERE RATHER THAN GIVING...
HER...
UP...
TO THEM.
THE ODD THING WAS... I'D WISHED FOR THIS TO HAPPEN SO MANY TIMES, FEELING ASHAMED THAT I WANTED OUT OF MY RESPONSIBILITY FOR GAE SO I COULD HAVE A LIFE. NOW THAT IT WAS POSSIBLE I KNEW I COULDN'T DO THAT TO US... I'D NEVER SEEN IT THAT WAY BEFORE, BUT WHAT IF I NEEDED HER AS MUCH AS SHE NEEDED ME?

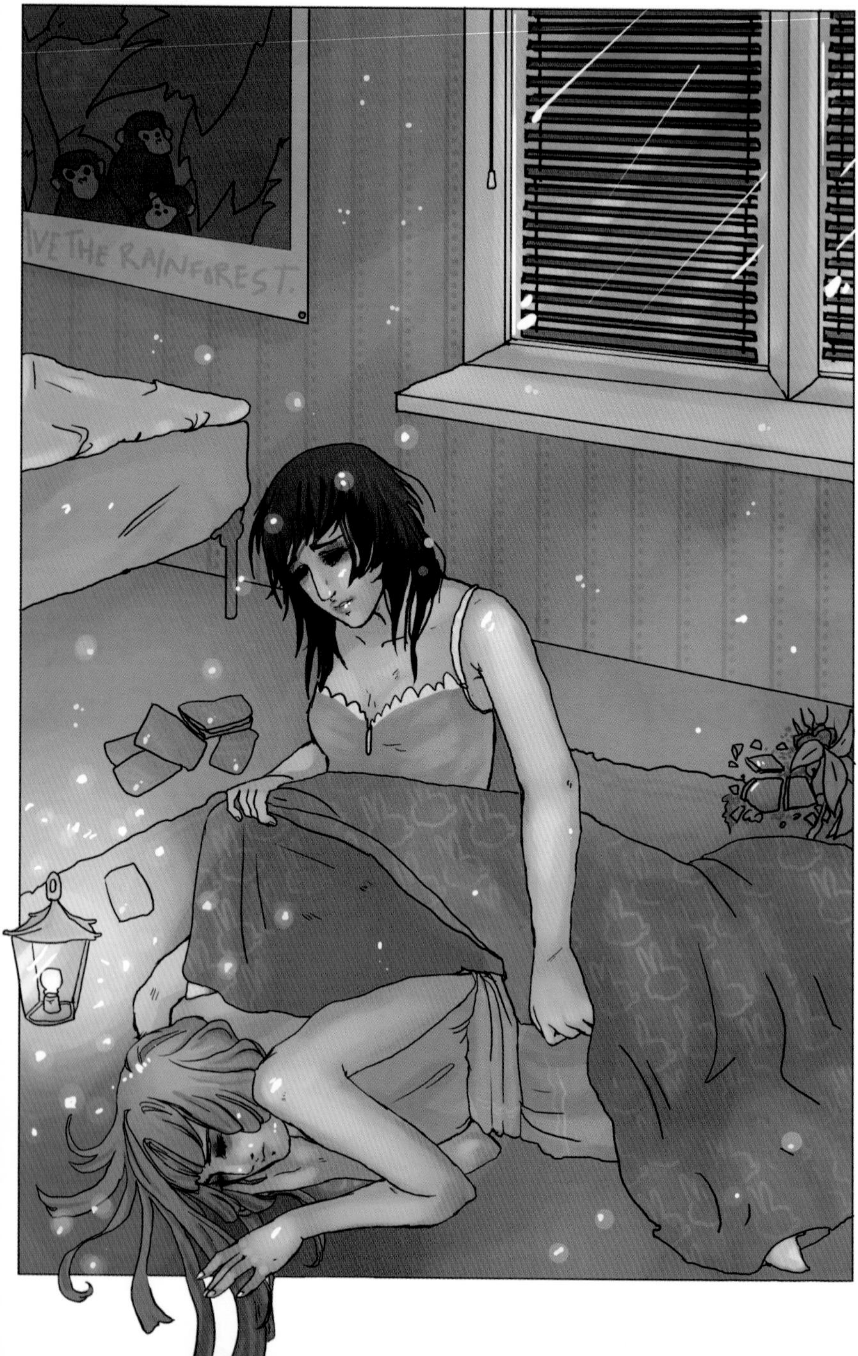
VE THE RAINFOREST.

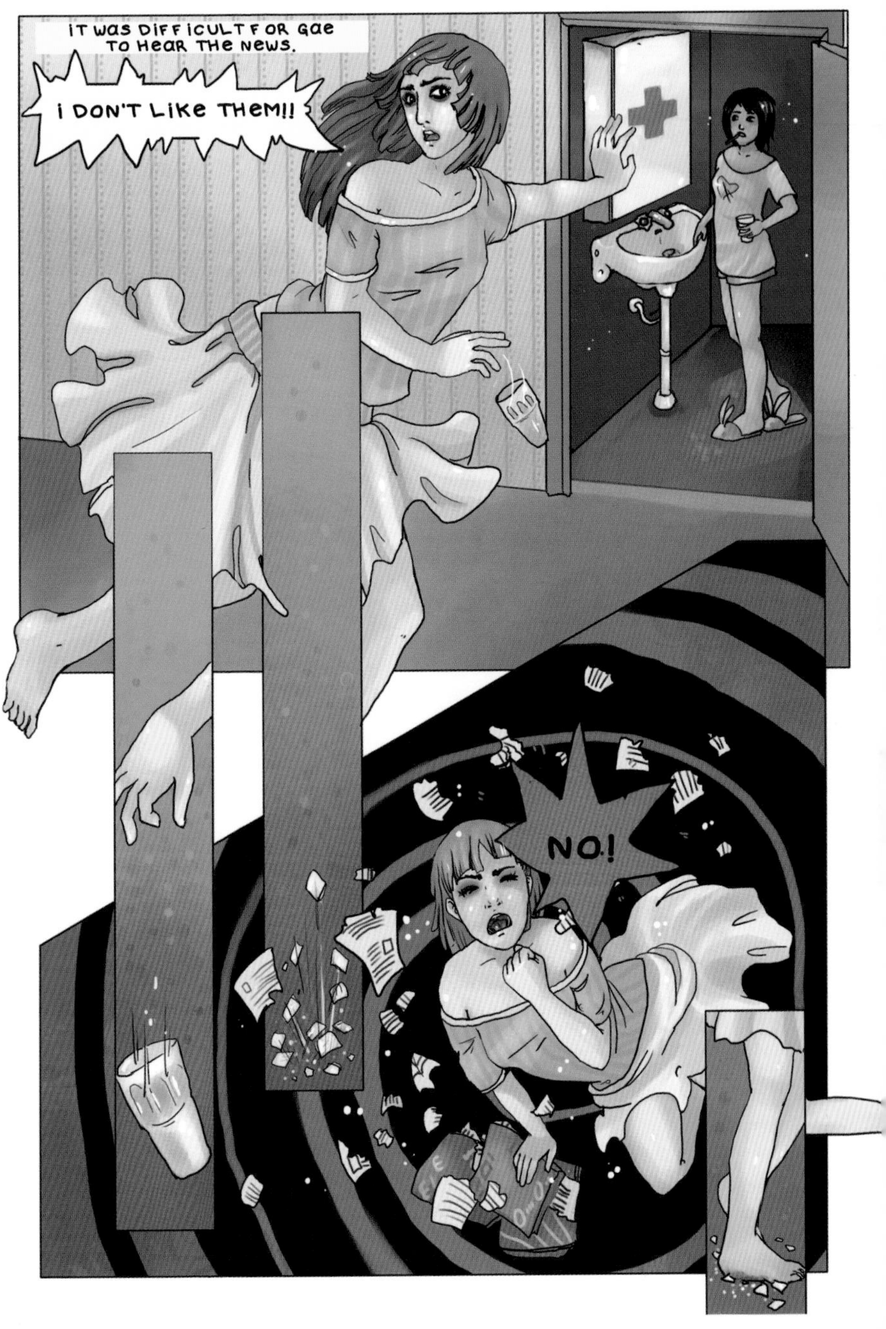
IT WAS DIFFICULT FOR GAE TO HEAR THE NEWS.
I DON'T LIKE THEM!!
NO!

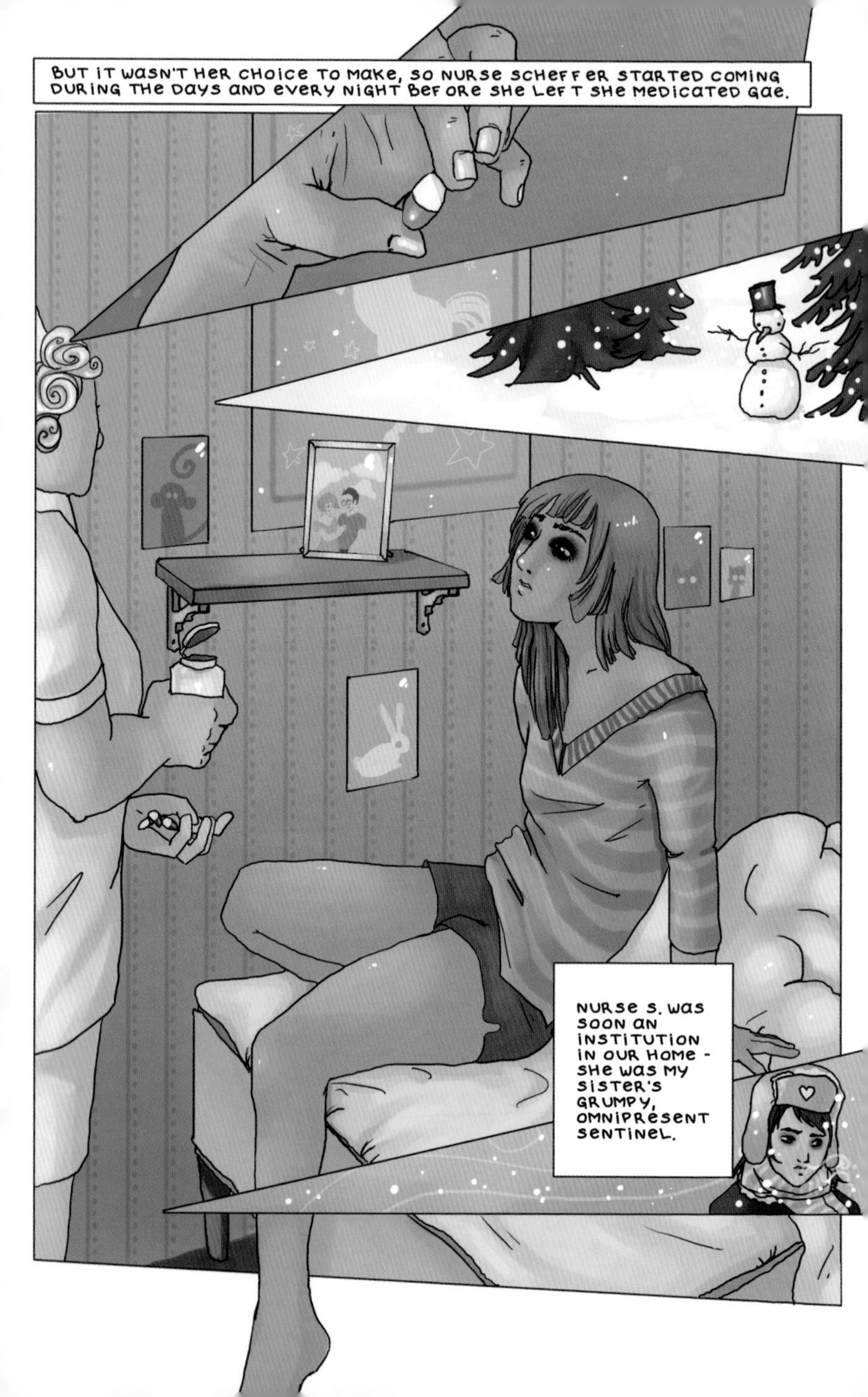
BUT IT WASN'T HER CHOICE TO MAKE, SO NURSE SCHEFFER STARTED COMING DURING THE DAYS AND EVERY NIGHT BEFORE SHE LEFT SHE MEDICATED GAE.
NURSE S. WAS SOON AN INSTITUTION IN OUR HOME - SHE WAS MY SISTER'S GRUMPY, OMNIPRESENT SENTINEL.

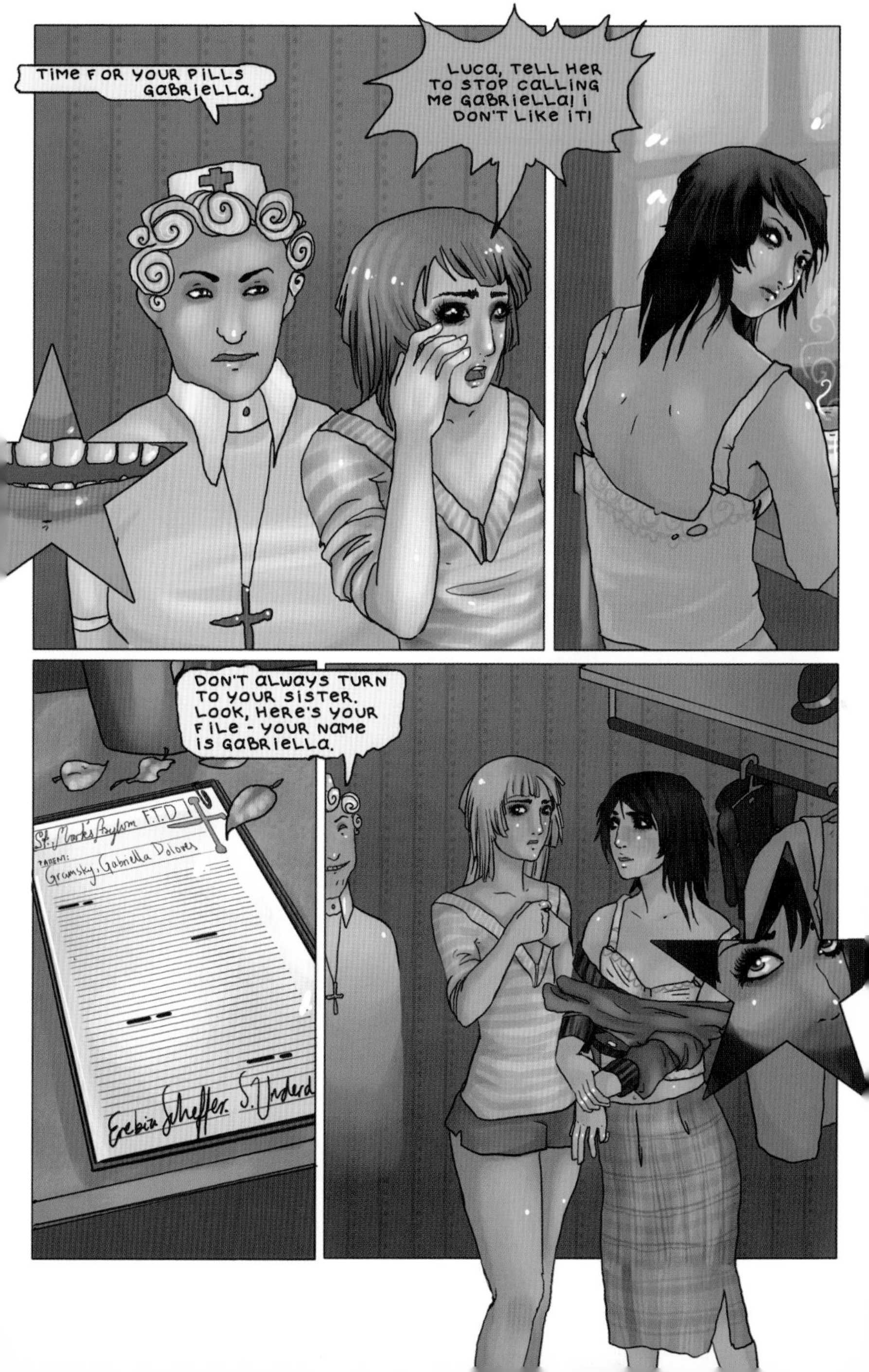
TIME FOR YOUR PILLS GABRIELLA.
LUCA, TELL HER TO STOP CALLING ME GABRIELLA! I DON'T LIKE IT!
St. Mark's Asylum F.T.D
PATIENT:
Gramsky, Gabriella Dolores
DON'T ALWAYS TURN TO YOUR SISTER. LOOK, HERE'S YOUR FILE - YOUR NAME IS GABRIELLA.

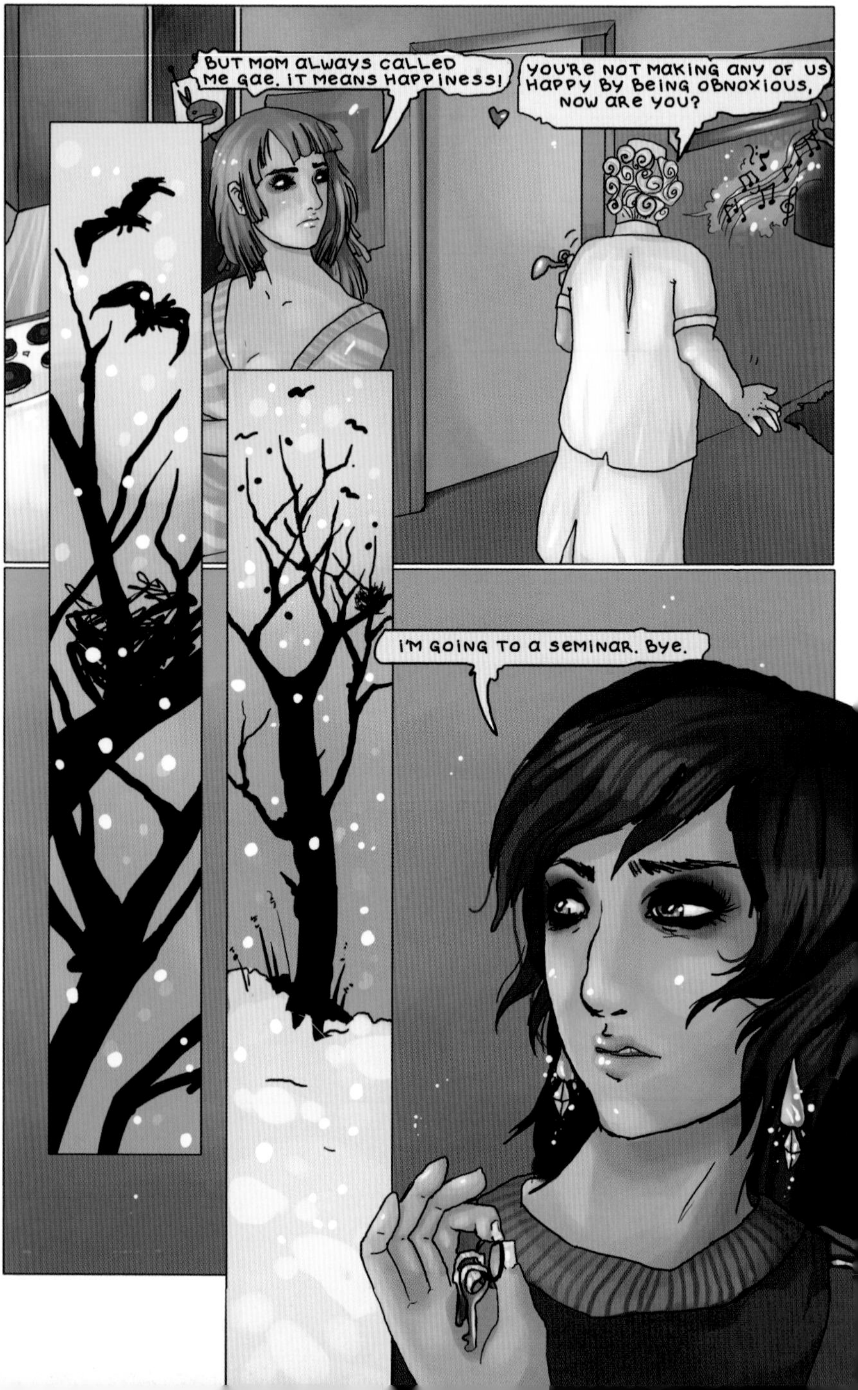
BUT MOM ALWAYS CALLED ME GAE. IT MEANS HAPPINESS!
YOU'RE NOT MAKING ANY OF US HAPPY BY BEING OBNOXIOUS, NOW ARE YOU?
I'M GOING TO A SEMINAR. BYE.

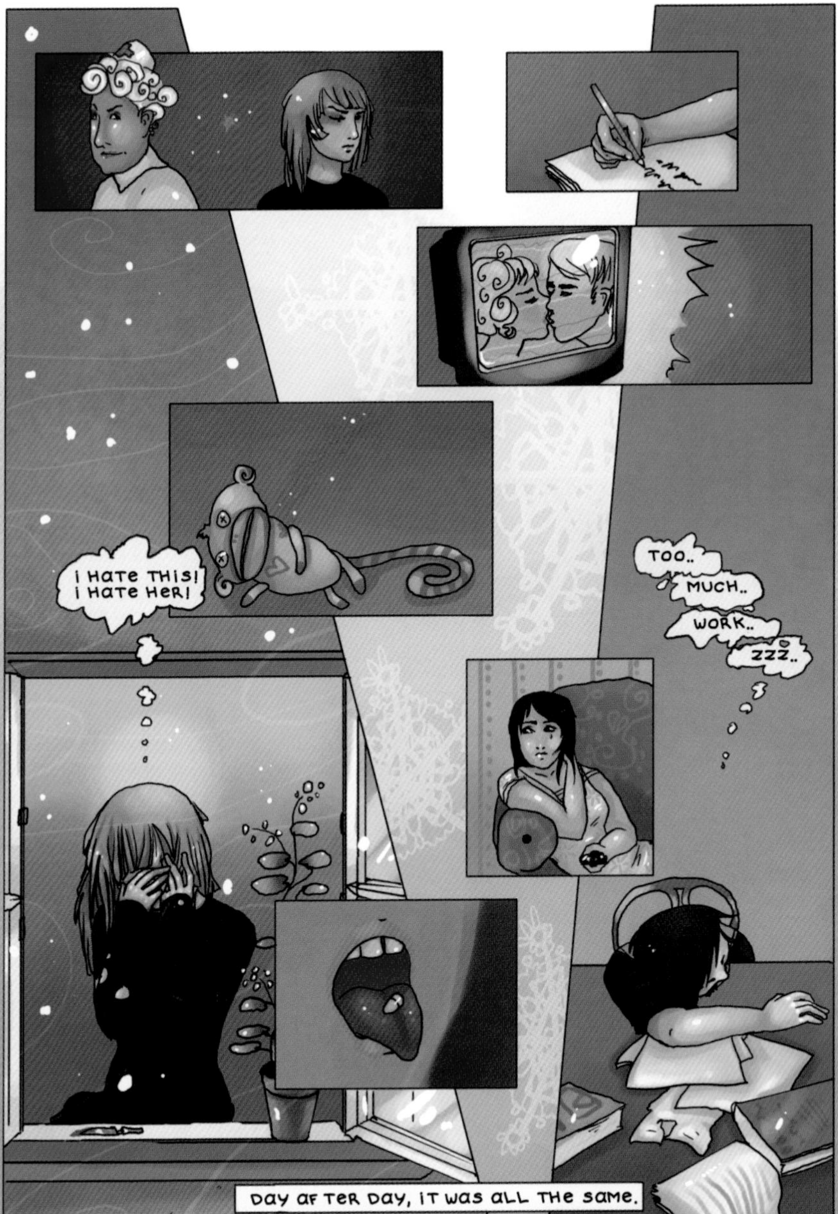
i HATE THIS! i HATE HER!
TOO..
MUCH..
WORK..
ZZZ..
DAY AFTER DAY, IT WAS ALL THE SAME.

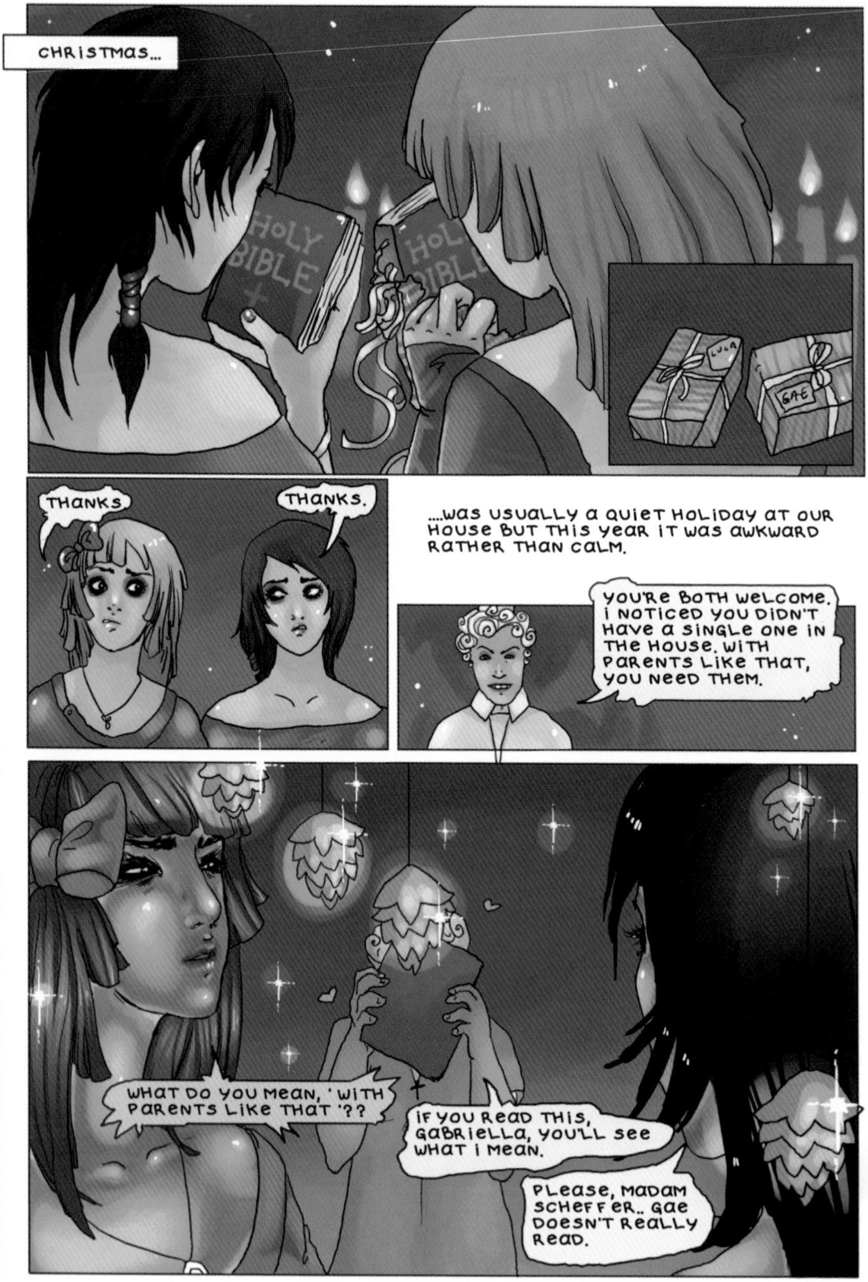
CHRISTMAS...
LULA
GAE
THANKS.
THANKS.
....WAS USUALLY A QUIET HOLIDAY AT OUR HOUSE BUT THIS YEAR IT WAS AWKWARD RATHER THAN CALM.
YOU'RE BOTH WELCOME. I NOTICED YOU DIDN'T HAVE A SINGLE ONE IN THE HOUSE. WITH PARENTS LIKE THAT, YOU NEED THEM.
WHAT DO YOU MEAN, 'WITH PARENTS LIKE THAT'??
IF YOU READ THIS, GABRIELLA, YOU'LL SEE WHAT I MEAN.
PLEASE, MADAM SCHEFFER.. GAE DOESN'T REALLY READ.

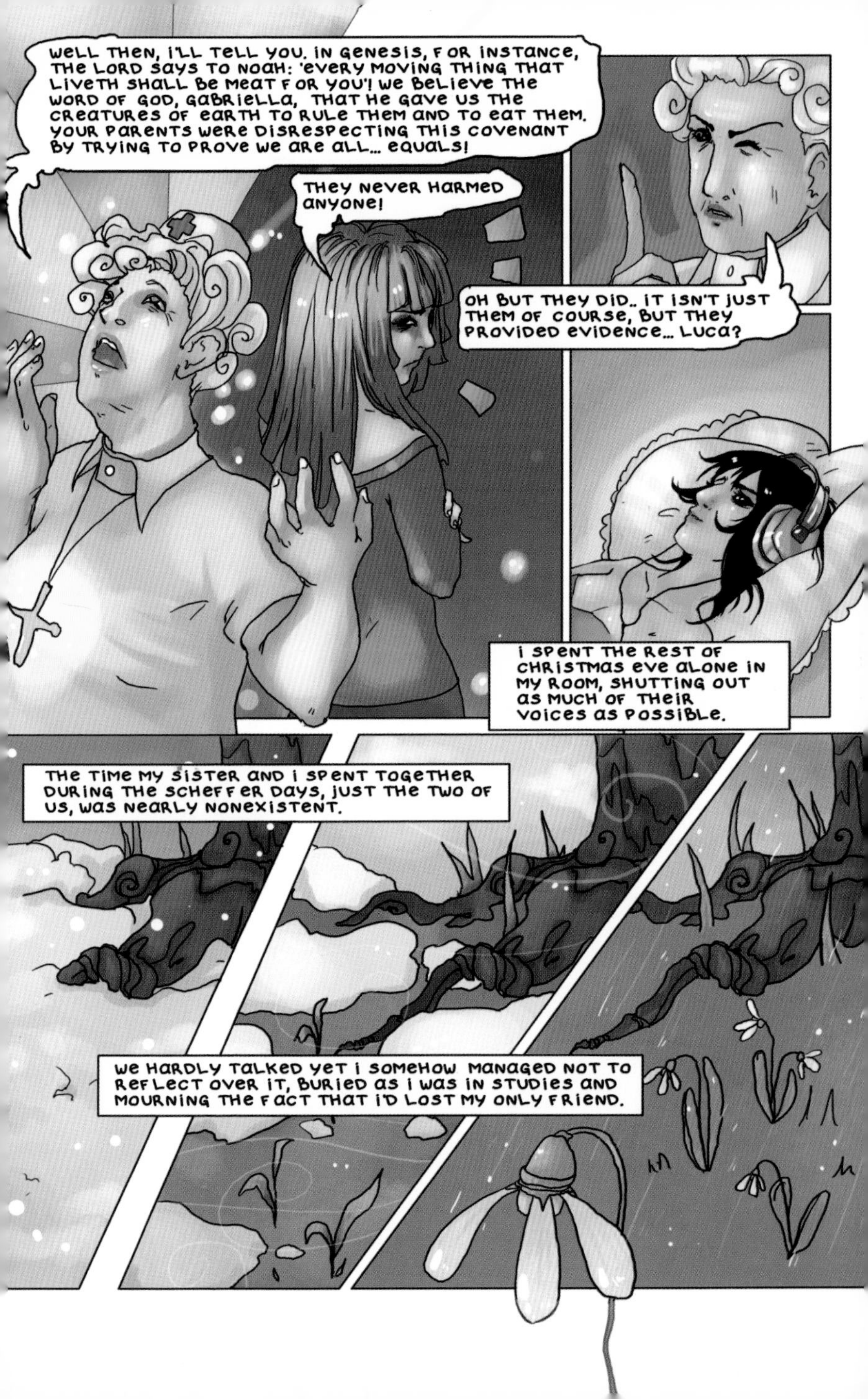
WELL THEN, I'LL TELL YOU. IN GENESIS, FOR INSTANCE, THE LORD SAYS TO NOAH: 'EVERY MOVING THING THAT LIVETH SHALL BE MEAT FOR YOU'! WE BELIEVE THE WORD OF GOD, GABRIELLA, THAT HE GAVE US THE CREATURES OF EARTH TO RULE THEM AND TO EAT THEM. YOUR PARENTS WERE DISRESPECTING THIS COVENANT BY TRYING TO PROVE WE ARE ALL... EQUALS!
THEY NEVER HARMED ANYONE!
OH BUT THEY DID.. IT ISN'T JUST THEM OF COURSE, BUT THEY PROVIDED EVIDENCE... LUCA?
I SPENT THE REST OF CHRISTMAS EVE ALONE IN MY ROOM, SHUTTING OUT AS MUCH OF THEIR VOICES AS POSSIBLE.
THE TIME MY SISTER AND I SPENT TOGETHER DURING THE SCHEFFER DAYS, JUST THE TWO OF US, WAS NEARLY NONEXISTENT.
WE HARDLY TALKED YET I SOMEHOW MANAGED NOT TO REFLECT OVER IT, BURIED AS I WAS IN STUDIES AND MOURNING THE FACT THAT I'D LOST MY ONLY FRIEND.

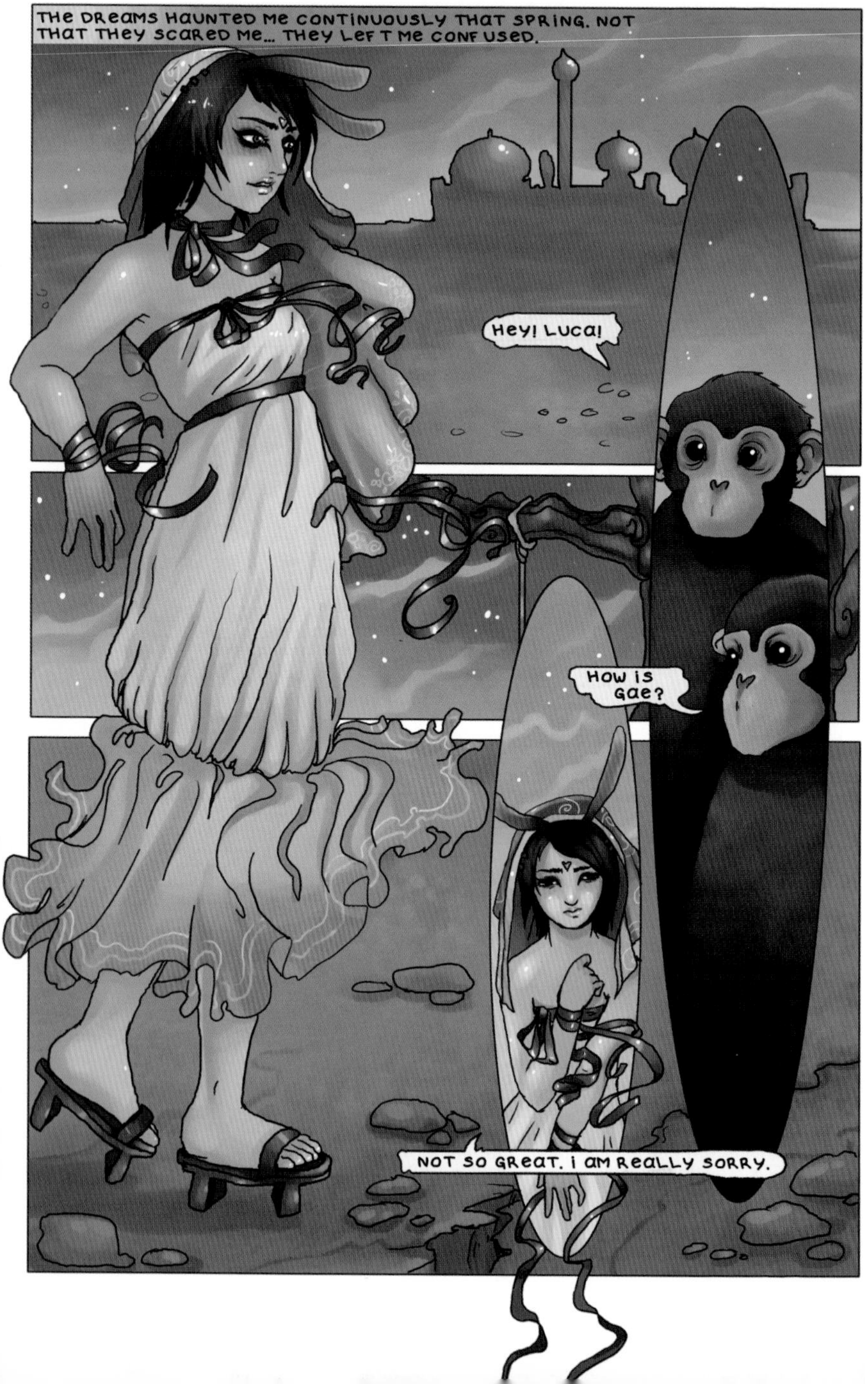
THE DREAMS HAUNTED ME CONTINUOUSLY THAT SPRING. NOT THAT THEY SCARED ME... THEY LEFT ME CONFUSED.
HEY! LUCA!
HOW IS GAE?
NOT SO GREAT. I AM REALLY SORRY.

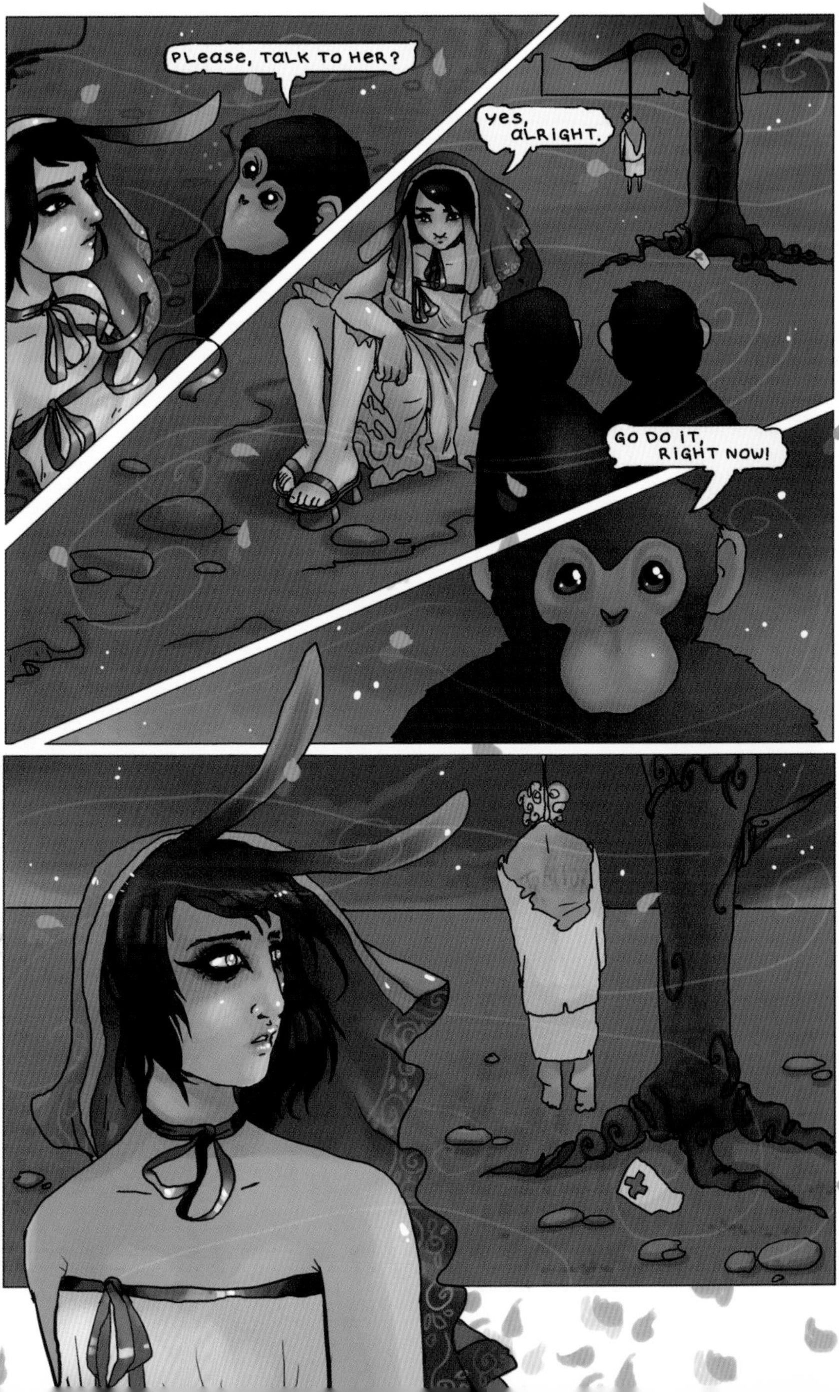
PLease, TALK TO HER?
yes, aLRIGHT.
GO DO IT, RIGHT NOW!

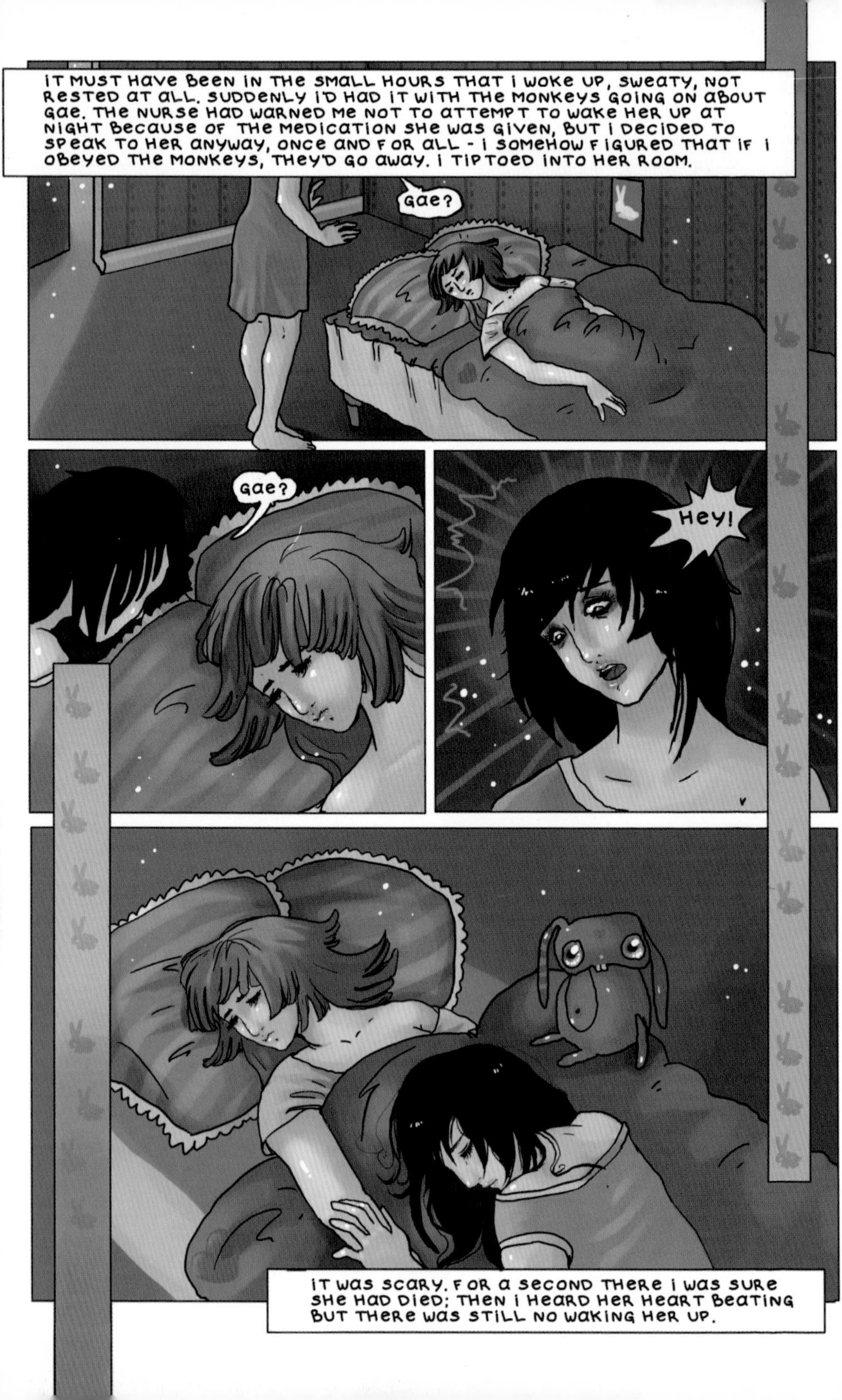
IT MUST HAVE BEEN IN THE SMALL HOURS THAT I WOKE UP, SWEATY, NOT RESTED AT ALL. SUDDENLY I'D HAD IT WITH THE MONKEYS GOING ON ABOUT GAE. THE NURSE HAD WARNED ME NOT TO ATTEMPT TO WAKE HER UP AT NIGHT BECAUSE OF THE MEDICATION SHE WAS GIVEN, BUT I DECIDED TO SPEAK TO HER ANYWAY, ONCE AND FOR ALL - I SOMEHOW FIGURED THAT IF I OBEYED THE MONKEYS, THEY'D GO AWAY. I TIPTOED INTO HER ROOM.
GAE?
GAE?
HEY!
IT WAS SCARY. FOR A SECOND THERE I WAS SURE SHE HAD DIED; THEN I HEARD HER HEART BEATING BUT THERE WAS STILL NO WAKING HER UP.

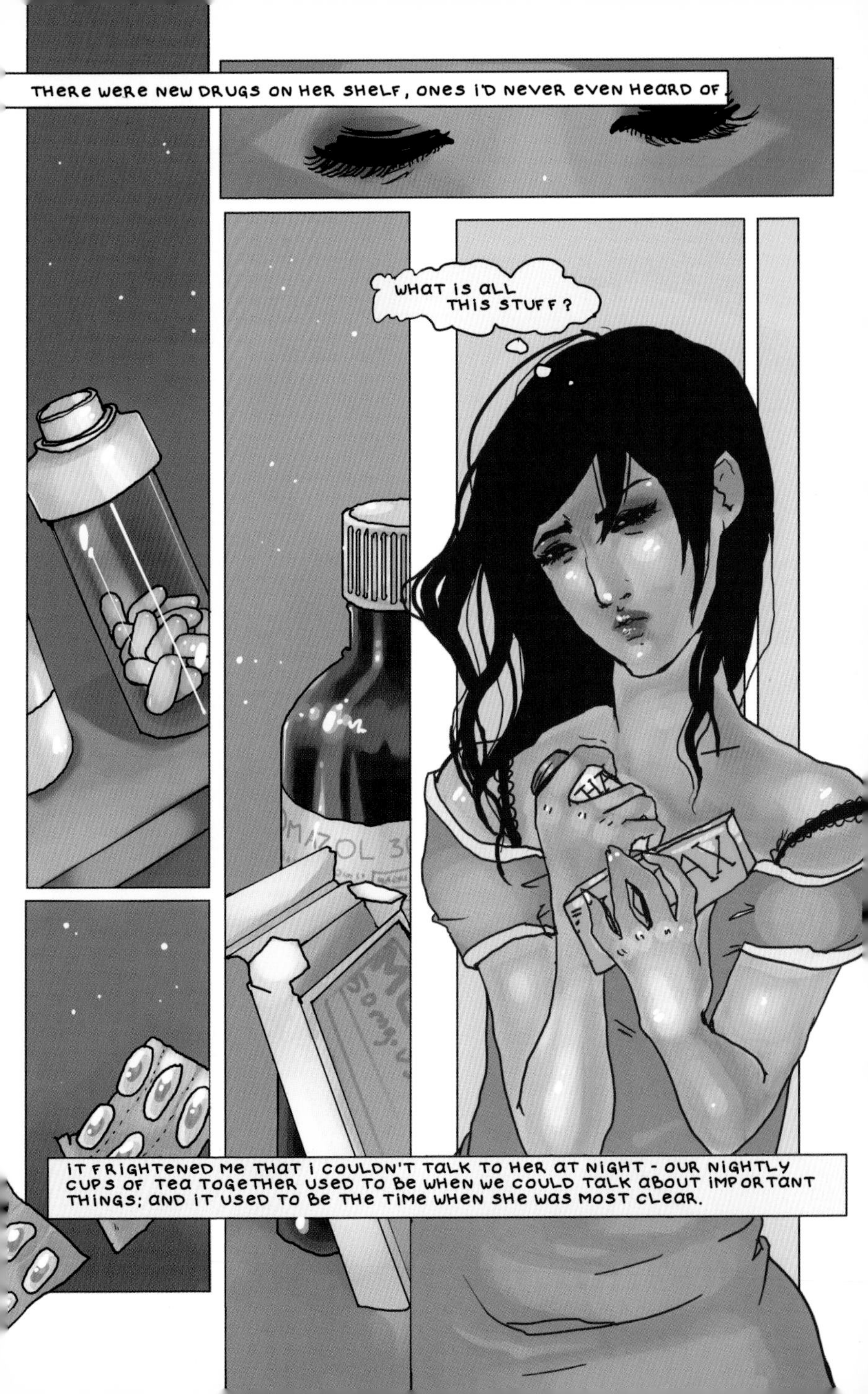
THERE WERE NEW DRUGS ON HER SHELF, ONES I'D NEVER EVEN HEARD OF.
WHAT IS ALL THIS STUFF?
IT FRIGHTENED ME THAT I COULDN'T TALK TO HER AT NIGHT - OUR NIGHTLY CUPS OF TEA TOGETHER USED TO BE WHEN WE COULD TALK ABOUT IMPORTANT THINGS; AND IT USED TO BE THE TIME WHEN SHE WAS MOST CLEAR.

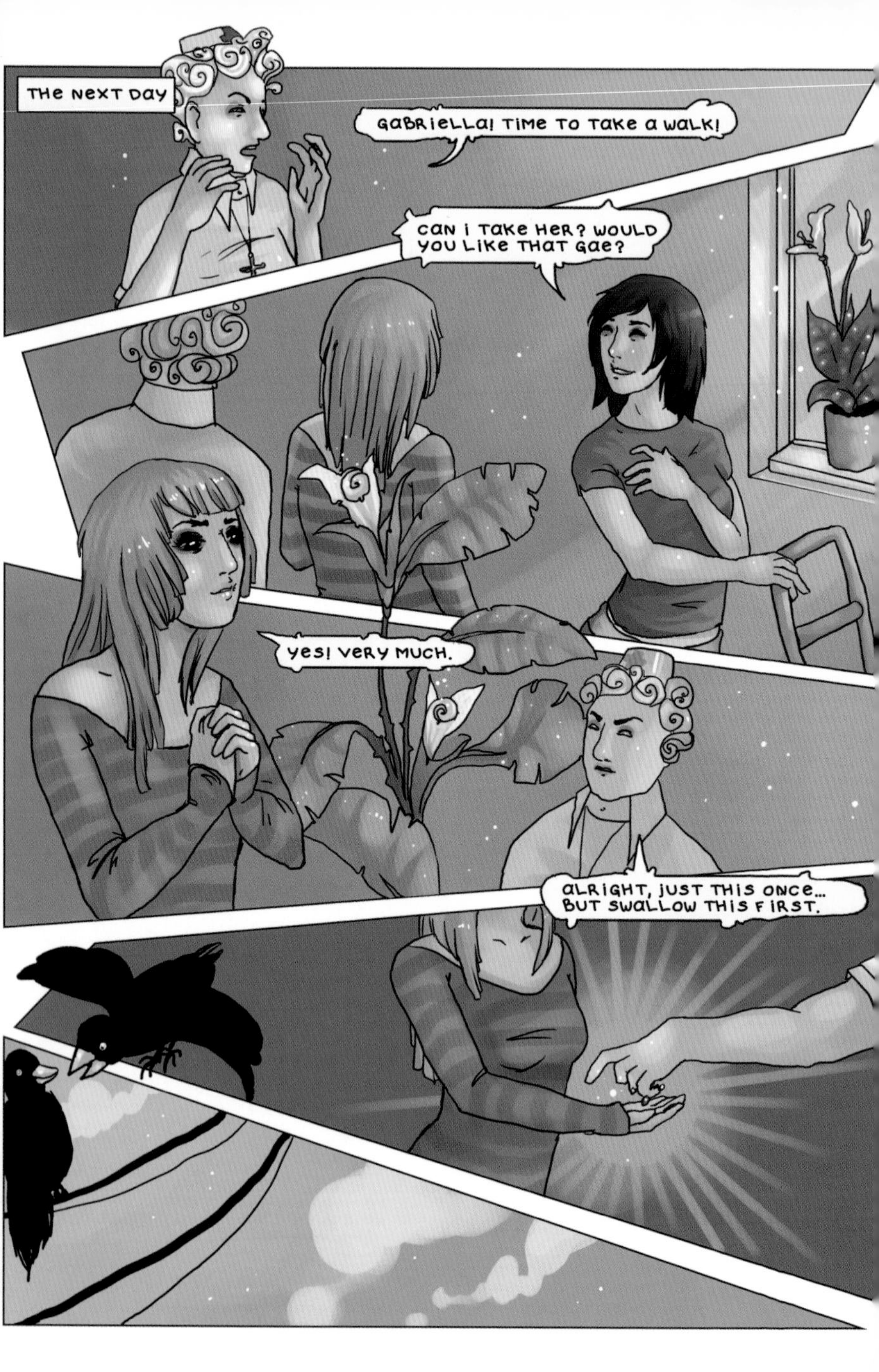
THE NEXT DAY
GABRIELLA! TIME TO TAKE A WALK!
CAN I TAKE HER? WOULD YOU LIKE THAT GAE?
YES! VERY MUCH.
ALRIGHT, JUST THIS ONCE... BUT SWALLOW THIS FIRST.

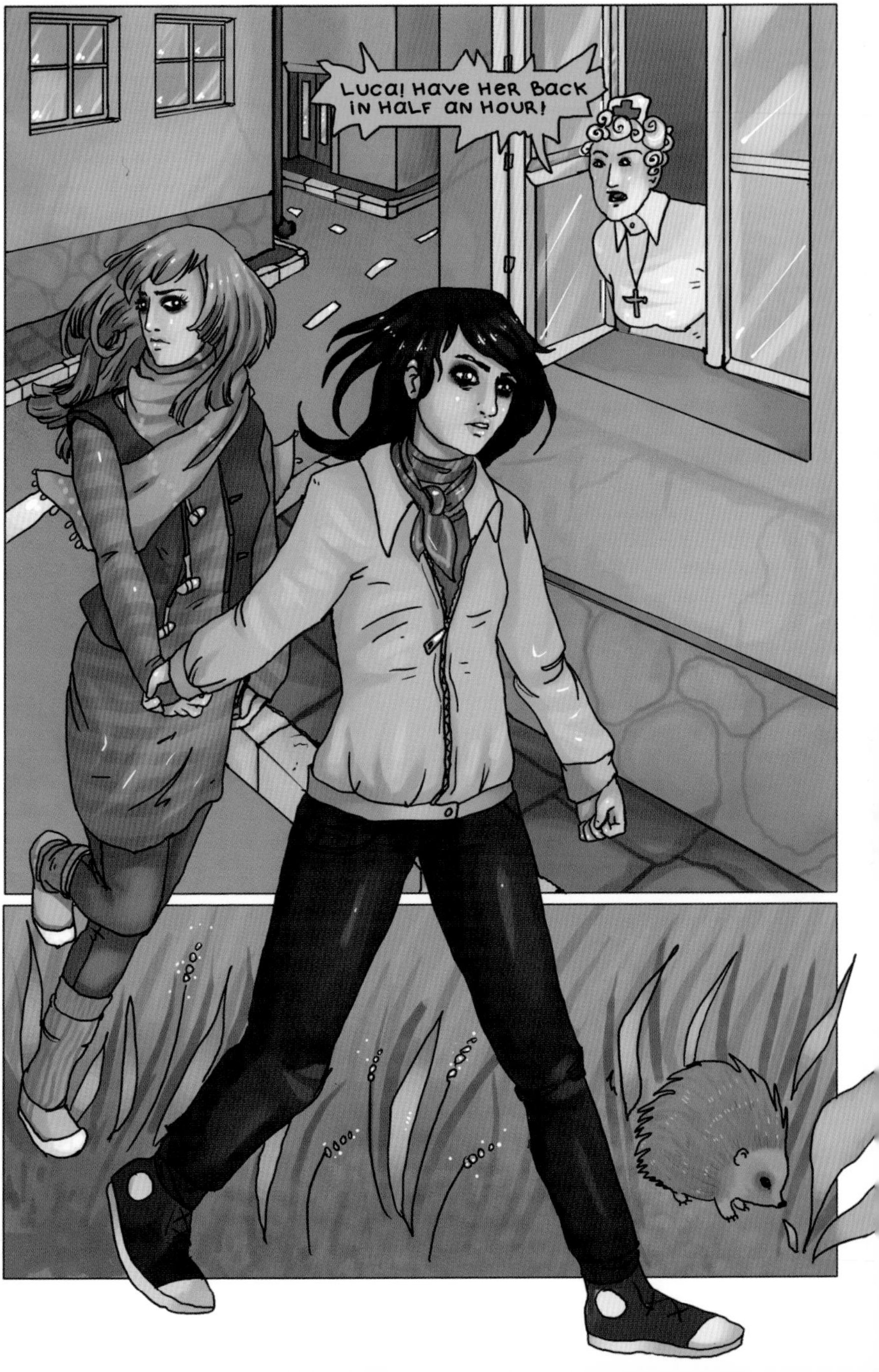
Luca! Have Her Back in HALF an HOUR!

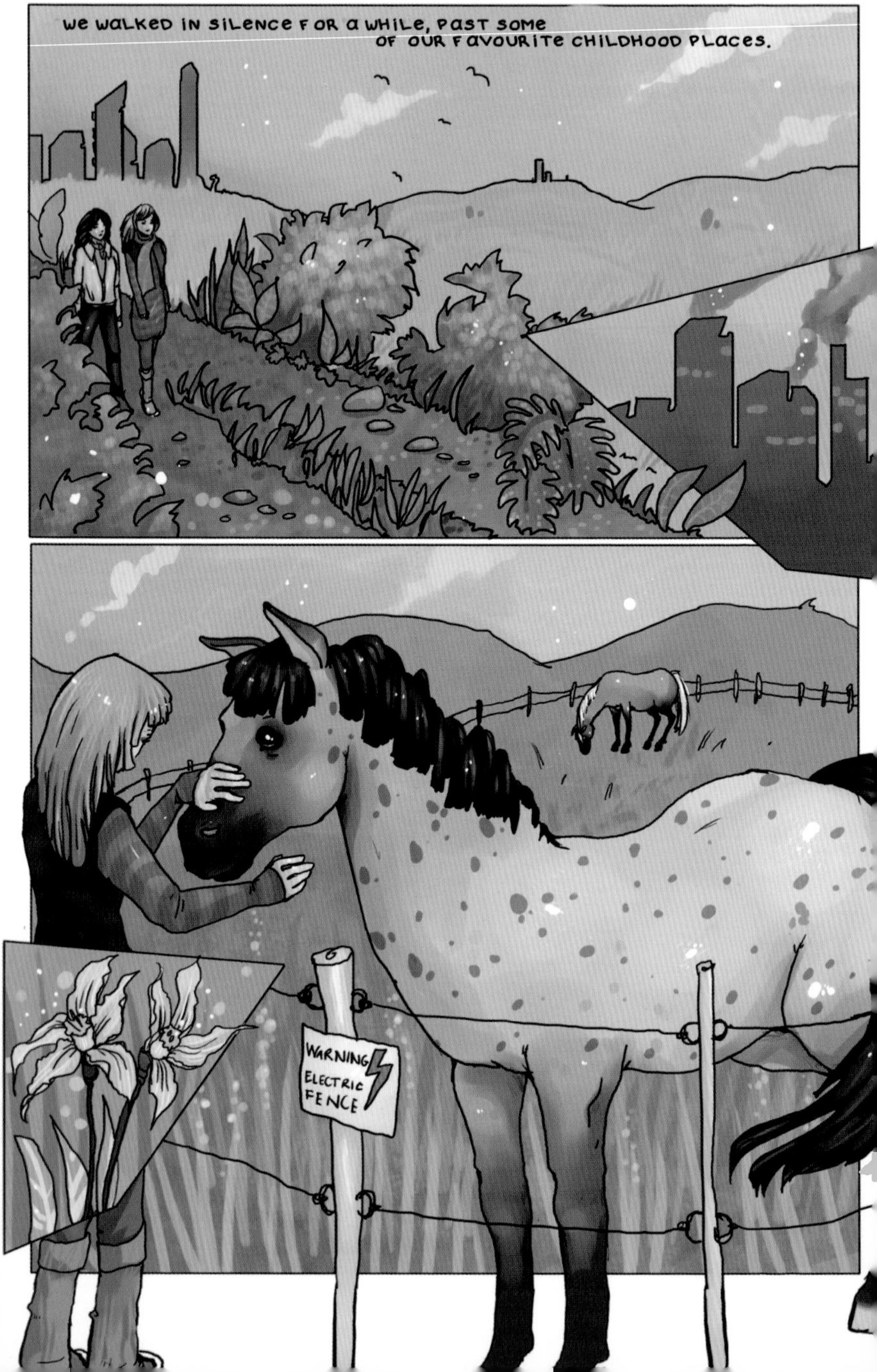
we walked in silence for a while, past some of our favourite childhood places.
WARNING ELECTRIC FENCE

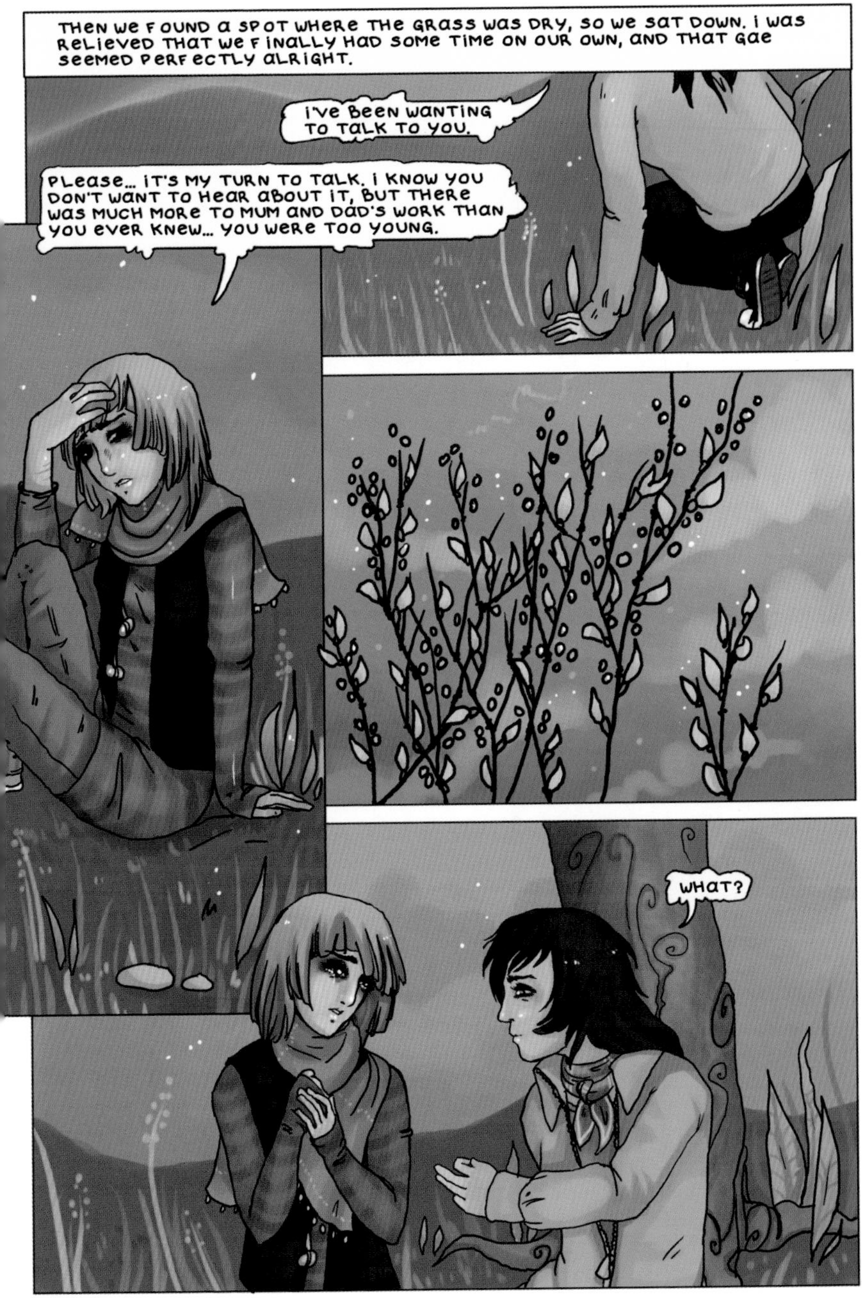
THEN WE FOUND A SPOT WHERE THE GRASS WAS DRY, SO WE SAT DOWN. I WAS RELIEVED THAT WE FINALLY HAD SOME TIME ON OUR OWN, AND THAT GAE SEEMED PERFECTLY ALRIGHT.
I'VE BEEN WANTING TO TALK TO YOU.
PLEASE... IT'S MY TURN TO TALK. I KNOW YOU DON'T WANT TO HEAR ABOUT IT, BUT THERE WAS MUCH MORE TO MUM AND DAD'S WORK THAN YOU EVER KNEW... YOU WERE TOO YOUNG.
WHAT?

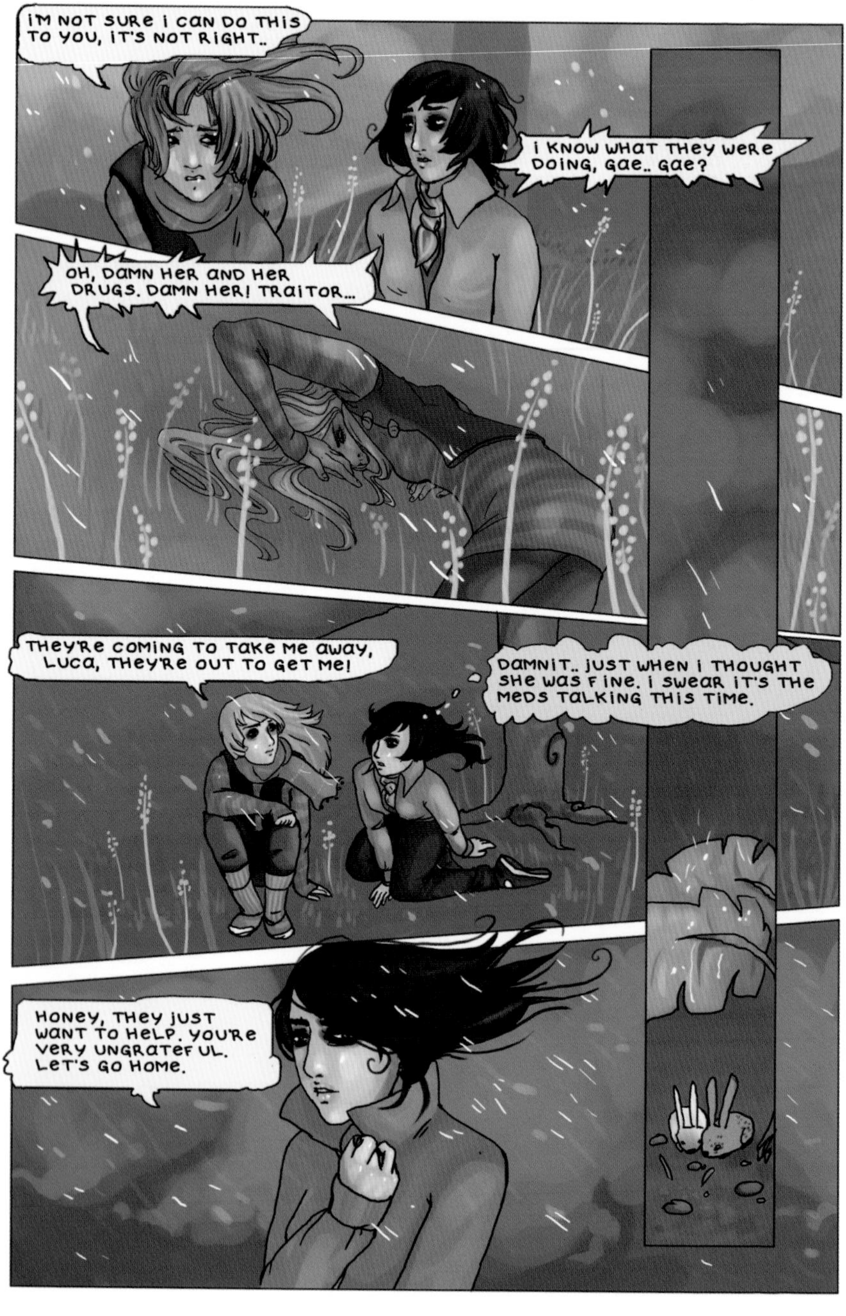
I'M NOT SURE I CAN DO THIS TO YOU, IT'S NOT RIGHT..
I KNOW WHAT THEY WERE DOING, GAE.. GAE?
OH, DAMN HER AND HER DRUGS. DAMN HER! TRAITOR...
THEY'RE COMING TO TAKE ME AWAY, LUCA, THEY'RE OUT TO GET ME!
DAMNIT.. JUST WHEN I THOUGHT SHE WAS FINE. I SWEAR IT'S THE MEDS TALKING THIS TIME.
HONEY, THEY JUST WANT TO HELP. YOU'RE VERY UNGRATEFUL. LET'S GO HOME.

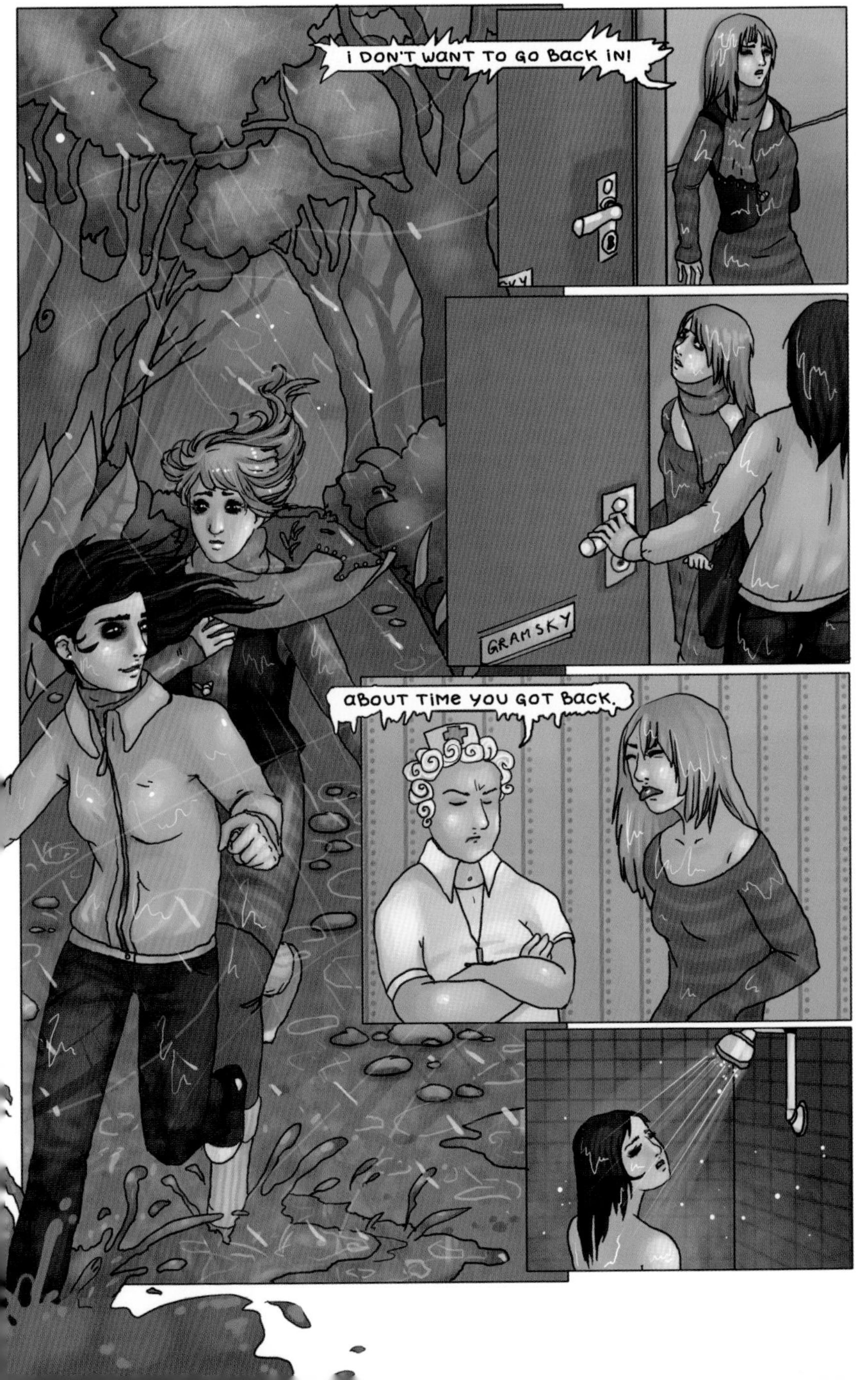
I DON'T WANT TO GO BACK IN!
GRAMSKY
ABOUT TIME YOU GOT BACK.

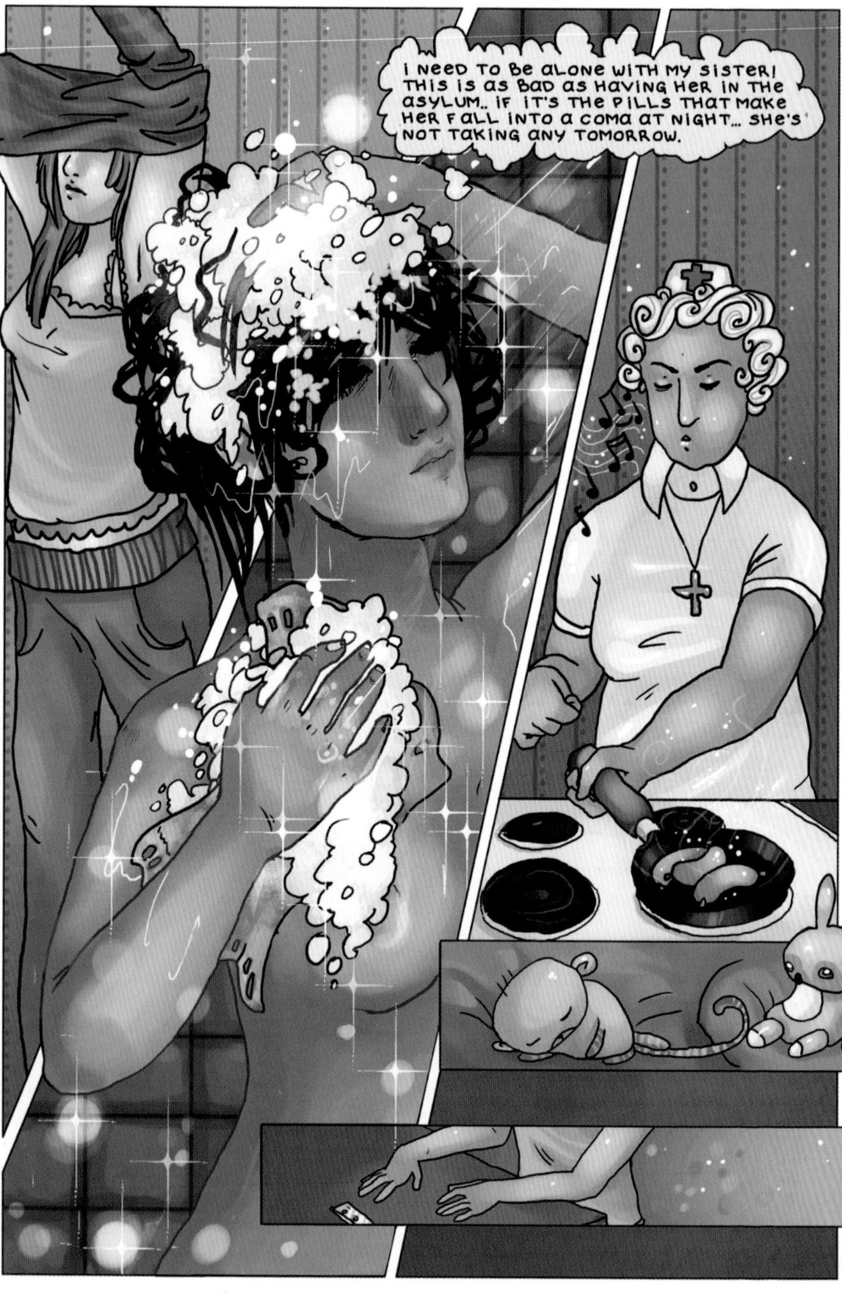
I NEED TO BE ALONE WITH MY SISTER! THIS IS AS BAD AS HAVING HER IN THE ASYLUM.. IF IT'S THE PILLS THAT MAKE HER FALL INTO A COMA AT NIGHT... SHE'S NOT TAKING ANY TOMORROW.

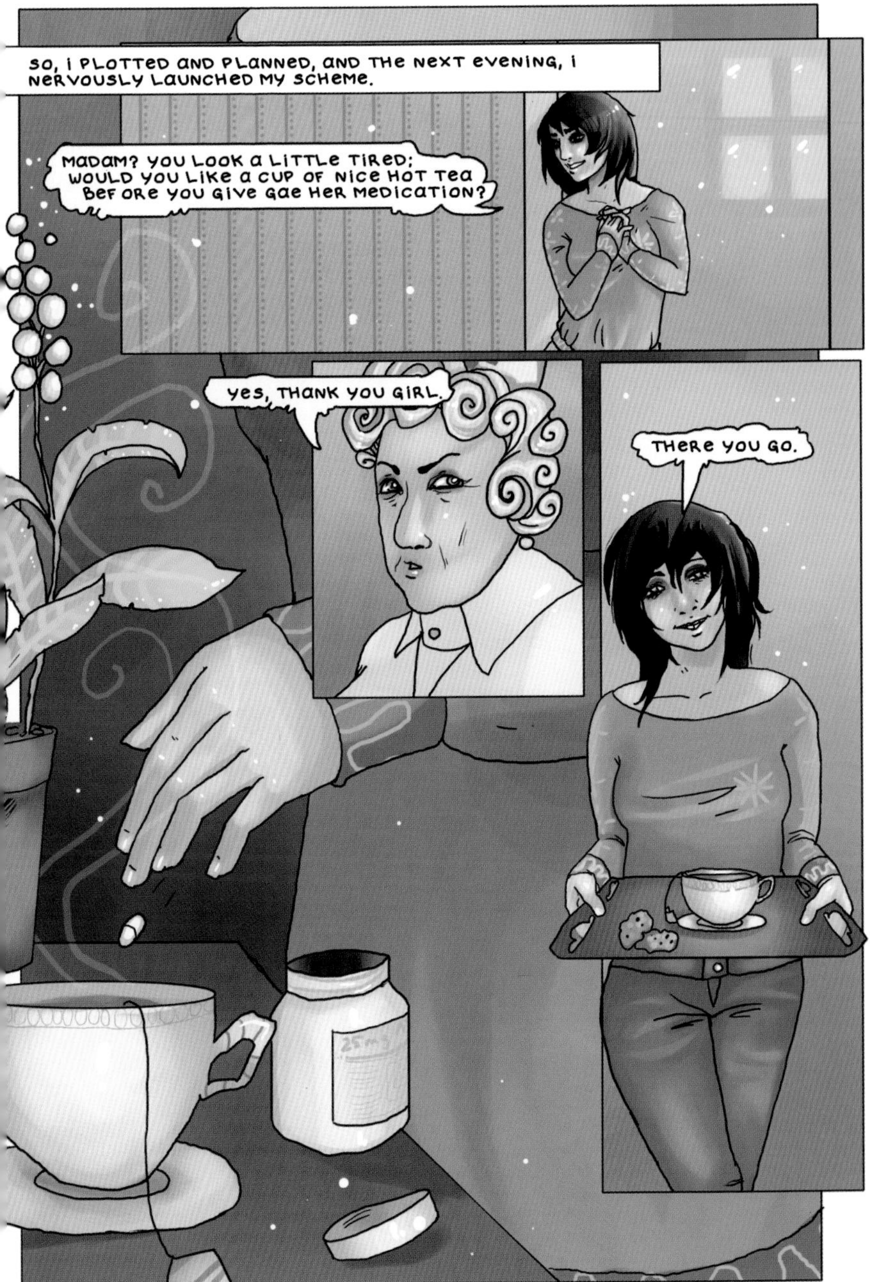
SO, I PLOTTED AND PLANNED, AND THE NEXT EVENING, I NERVOUSLY LAUNCHED MY SCHEME.
MADAM? YOU LOOK A LITTLE TIRED; WOULD YOU LIKE A CUP OF NICE HOT TEA BEFORE YOU GIVE GAE HER MEDICATION?
YES, THANK YOU GIRL.
THERE YOU GO.
25mg

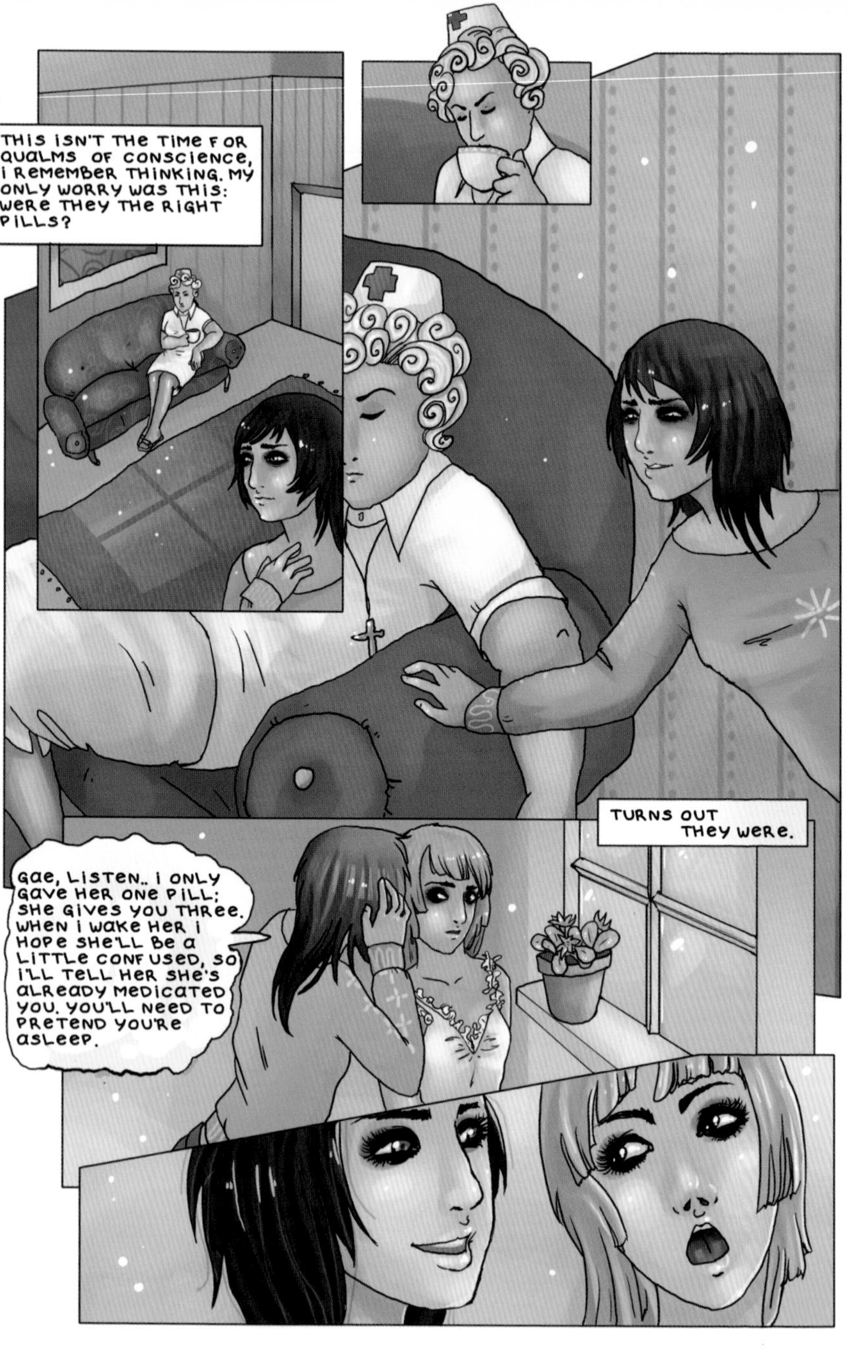
THIS ISN'T THE TIME FOR QUALMS OF CONSCIENCE, I REMEMBER THINKING. MY ONLY WORRY WAS THIS: WERE THEY THE RIGHT PILLS?
TURNS OUT THEY WERE.
GAE, LISTEN.. I ONLY GAVE HER ONE PILL; SHE GIVES YOU THREE. WHEN I WAKE HER I HOPE SHE'LL BE A LITTLE CONFUSED, SO I'LL TELL HER SHE'S ALREADY MEDICATED YOU. YOU'LL NEED TO PRETEND YOU'RE ASLEEP.

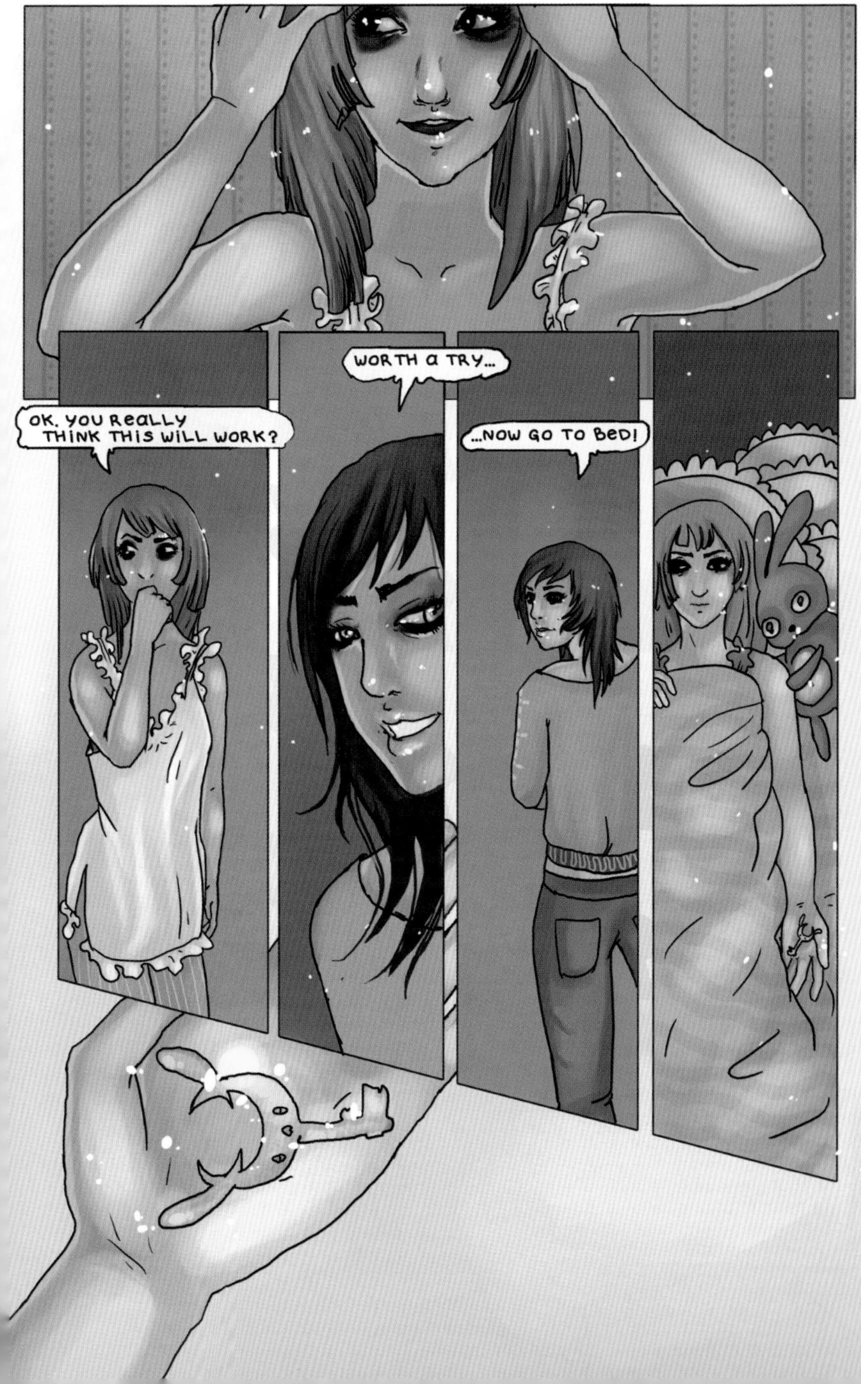
OK. YOU REALLY THINK THIS WILL WORK?
WORTH A TRY...
...NOW GO TO BED!

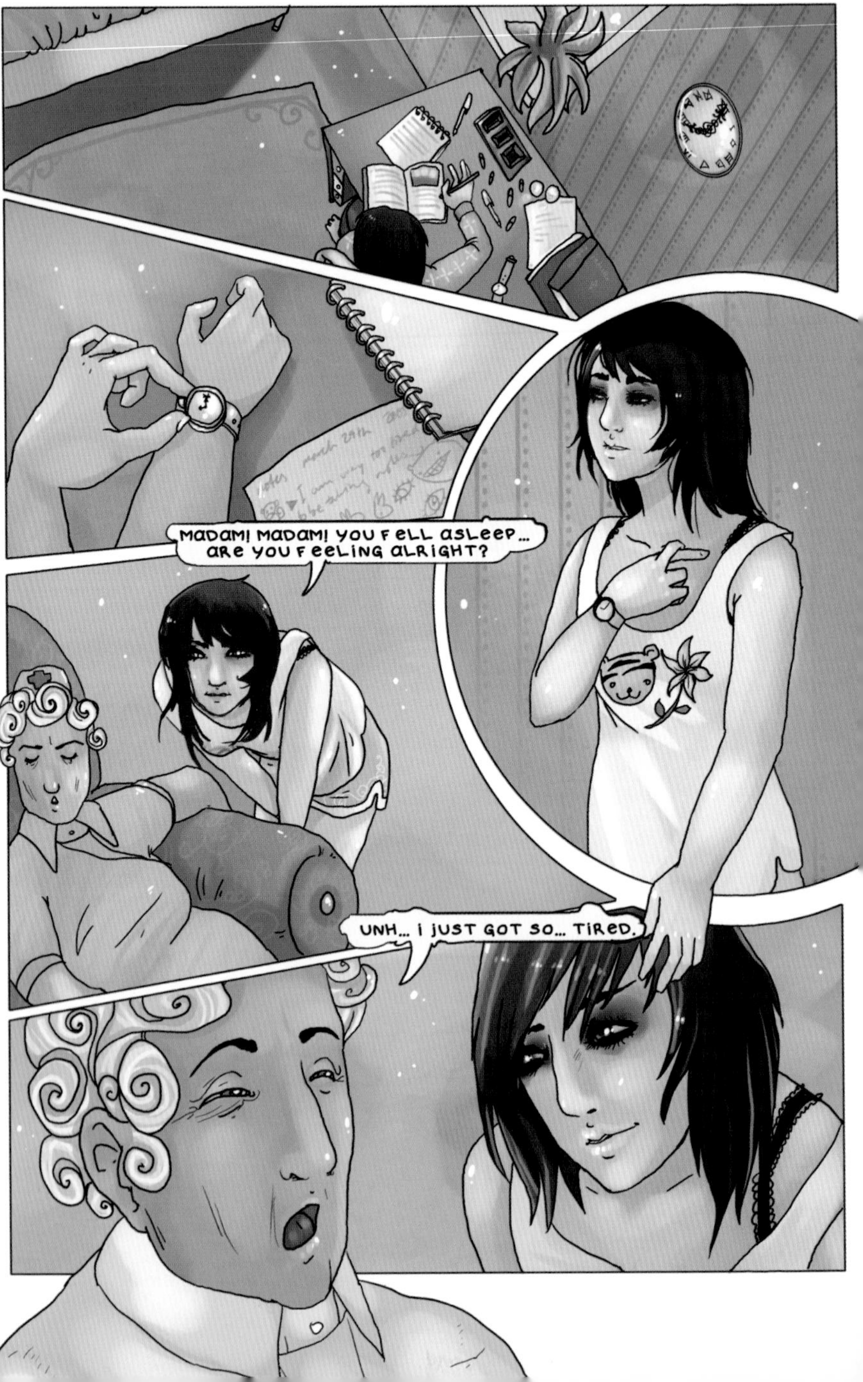
MADAM! MADAM! YOU FELL ASLEEP... ARE YOU FEELING ALRIGHT?
UNH... I JUST GOT SO... TIRED.

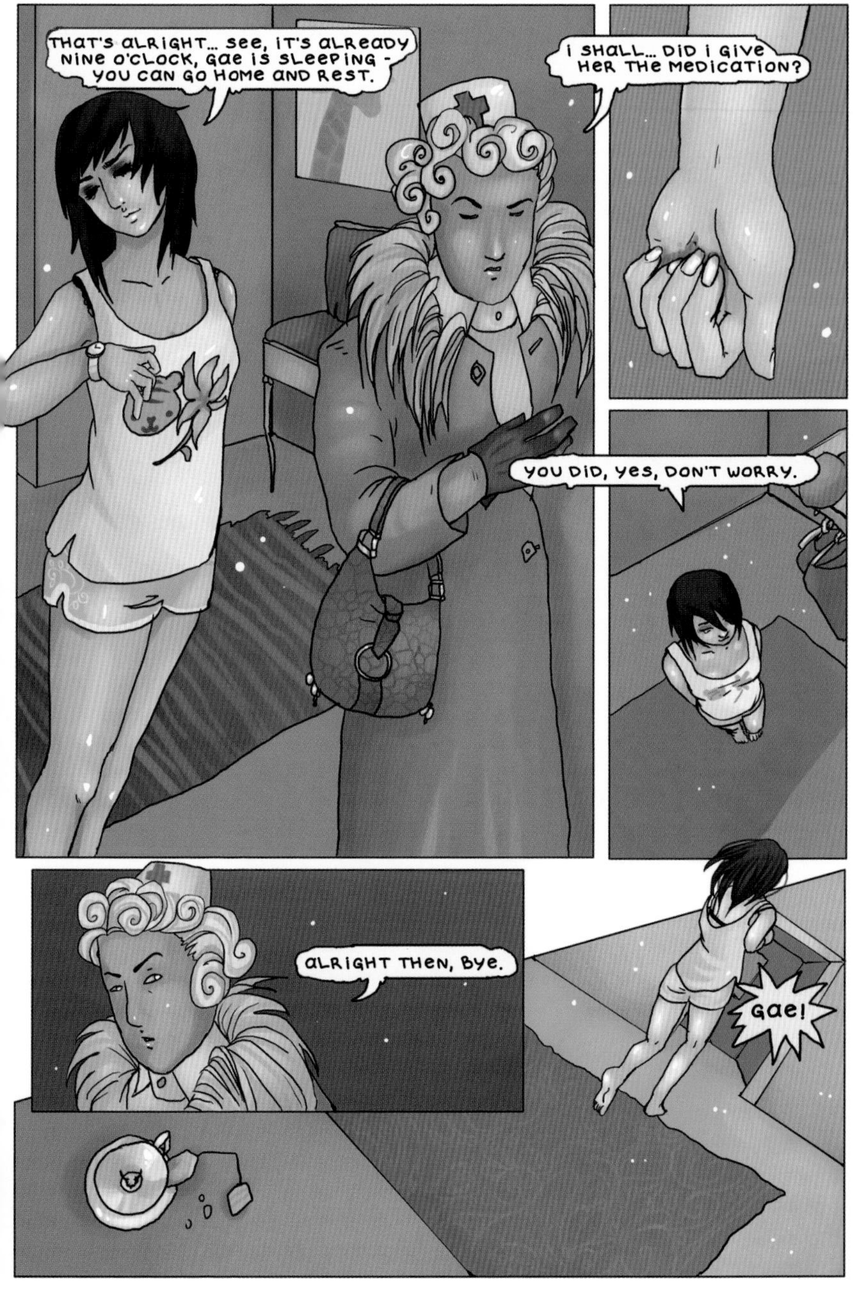
THAT'S ALRIGHT... SEE, IT'S ALREADY NINE O'CLOCK, GAE IS SLEEPING - YOU CAN GO HOME AND REST.
I SHALL... DID I GIVE HER THE MEDICATION?
YOU DID, YES, DON'T WORRY.
ALRIGHT THEN, BYE.
GAE!

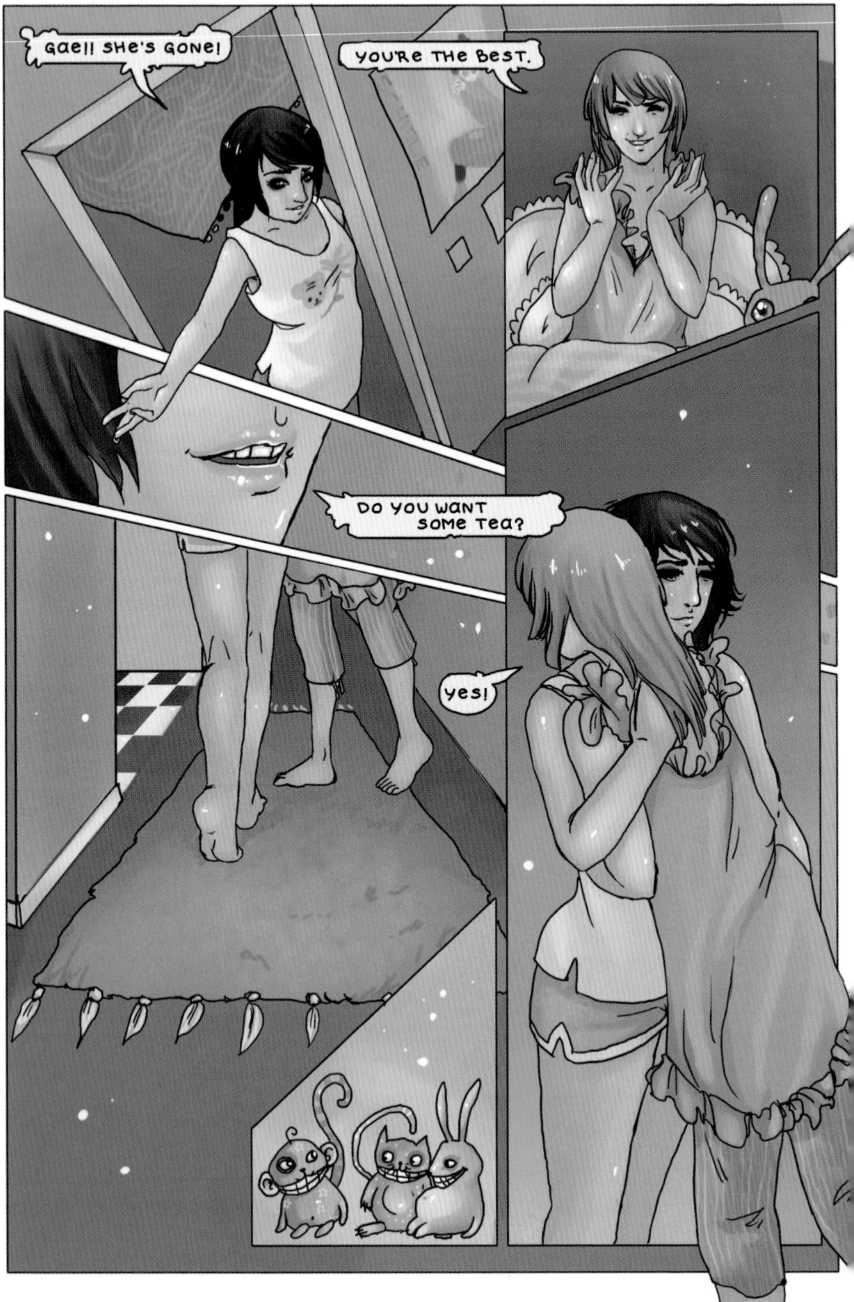
Gael! SHE'S GONE!
YOU'RE THE BEST.
DO YOU WANT some Tea?
yes!

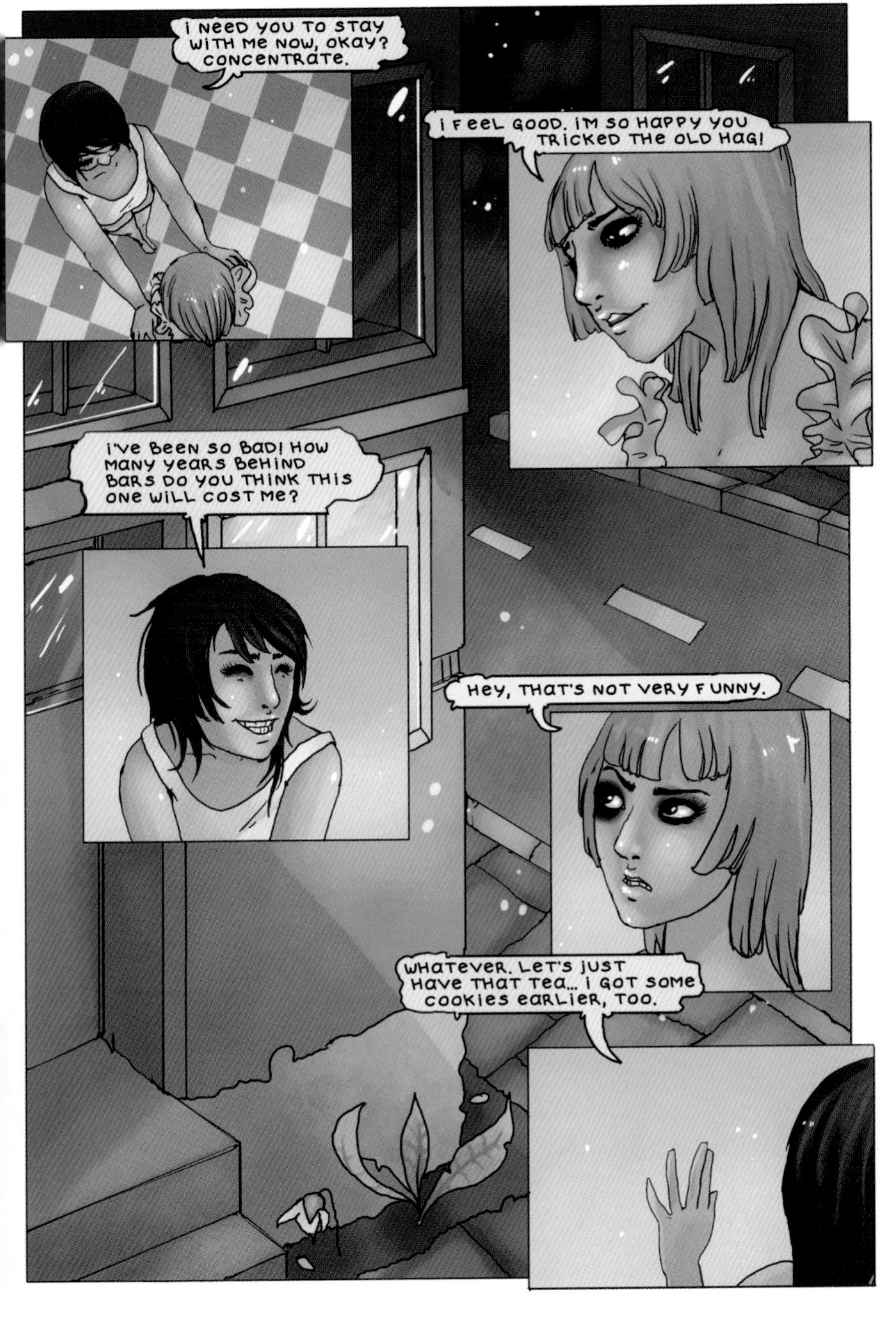
i NEED YOU TO STAY WITH ME NOW, OKAY? CONCENTRATE.
i FEEL GOOD. iM SO HAPPY YOU TRICKED THE OLD HAG!
i'VE BEEN SO BAD! HOW MANY YEARS BEHIND BARS DO YOU THINK THIS ONE WILL COST ME?
HEY, THAT'S NOT VERY FUNNY.
WHATEVER. LET'S JUST HAVE THAT TEA... i GOT SOME COOKIES EARLIER, TOO.

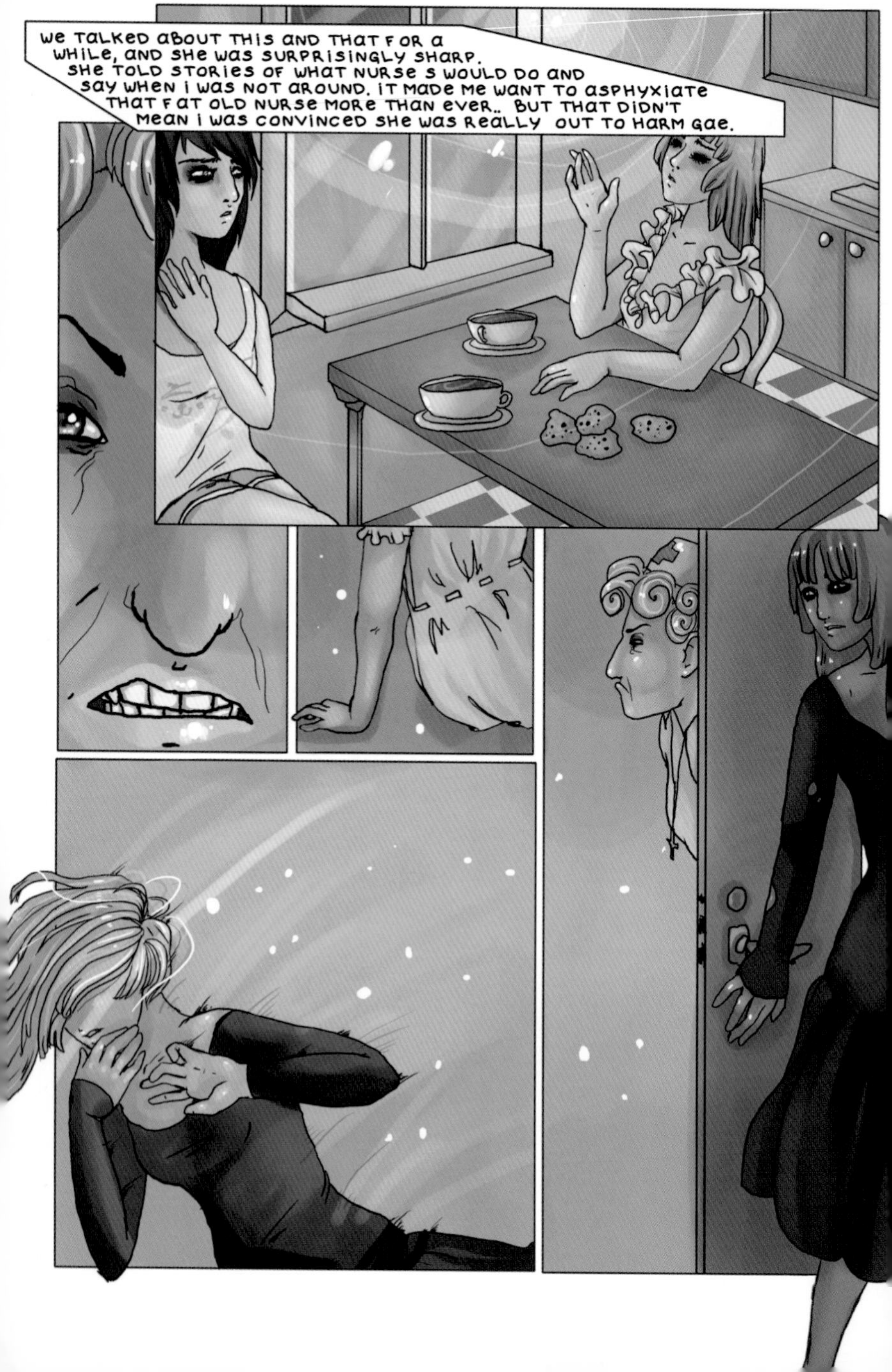
WE TALKED ABOUT THIS AND THAT FOR A WHILE, AND SHE WAS SURPRISINGLY SHARP. SHE TOLD STORIES OF WHAT NURSE S WOULD DO AND SAY WHEN I WAS NOT AROUND. IT MADE ME WANT TO ASPHYXIATE THAT FAT OLD NURSE MORE THAN EVER.. BUT THAT DIDN'T MEAN I WAS CONVINCED SHE WAS REALLY OUT TO HARM GAE.

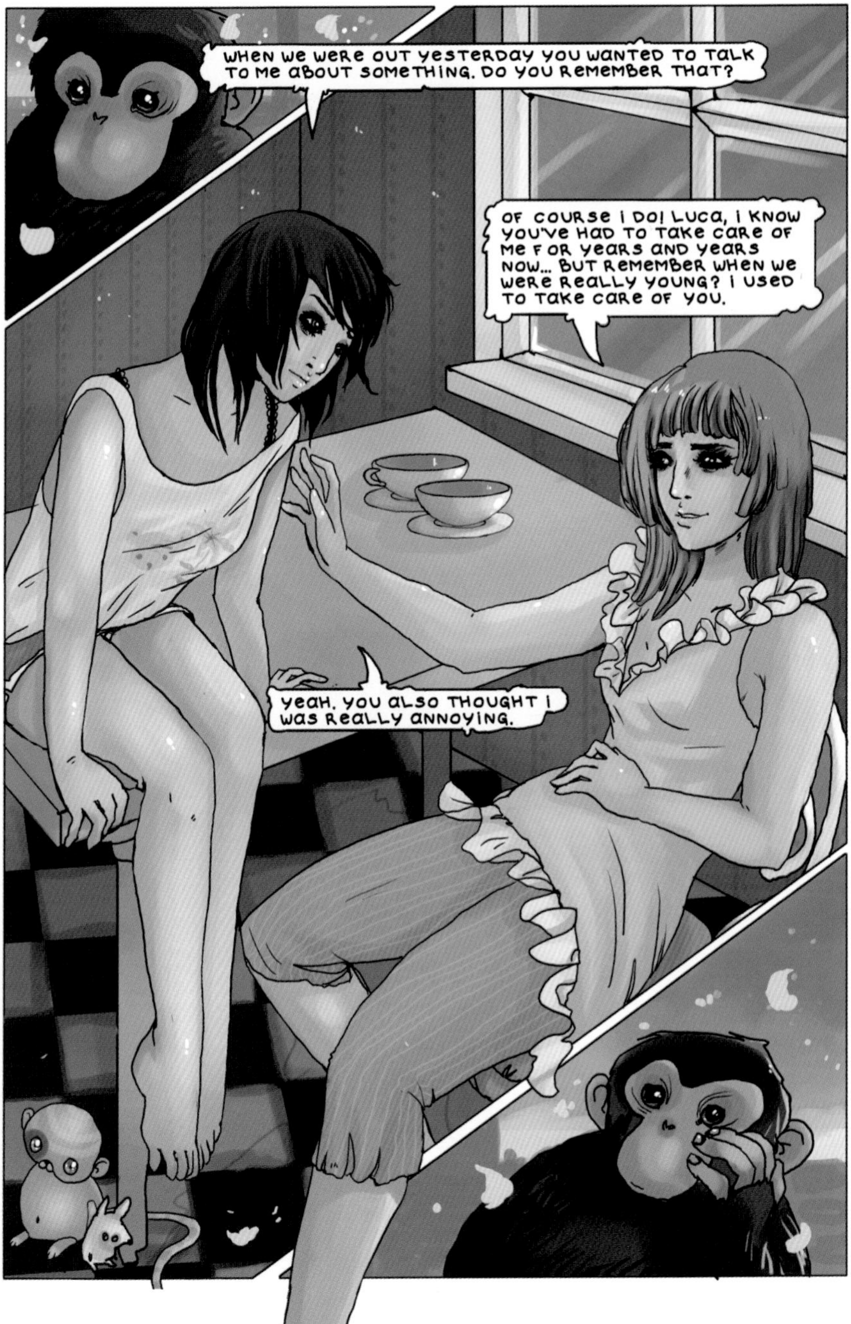
WHEN WE WERE OUT YESTERDAY YOU WANTED TO TALK TO ME ABOUT SOMETHING. DO YOU REMEMBER THAT?
OF COURSE I DO! LUCA, I KNOW YOU'VE HAD TO TAKE CARE OF ME FOR YEARS AND YEARS NOW... BUT REMEMBER WHEN WE WERE REALLY YOUNG? I USED TO TAKE CARE OF YOU.
YEAH. YOU ALSO THOUGHT I WAS REALLY ANNOYING.

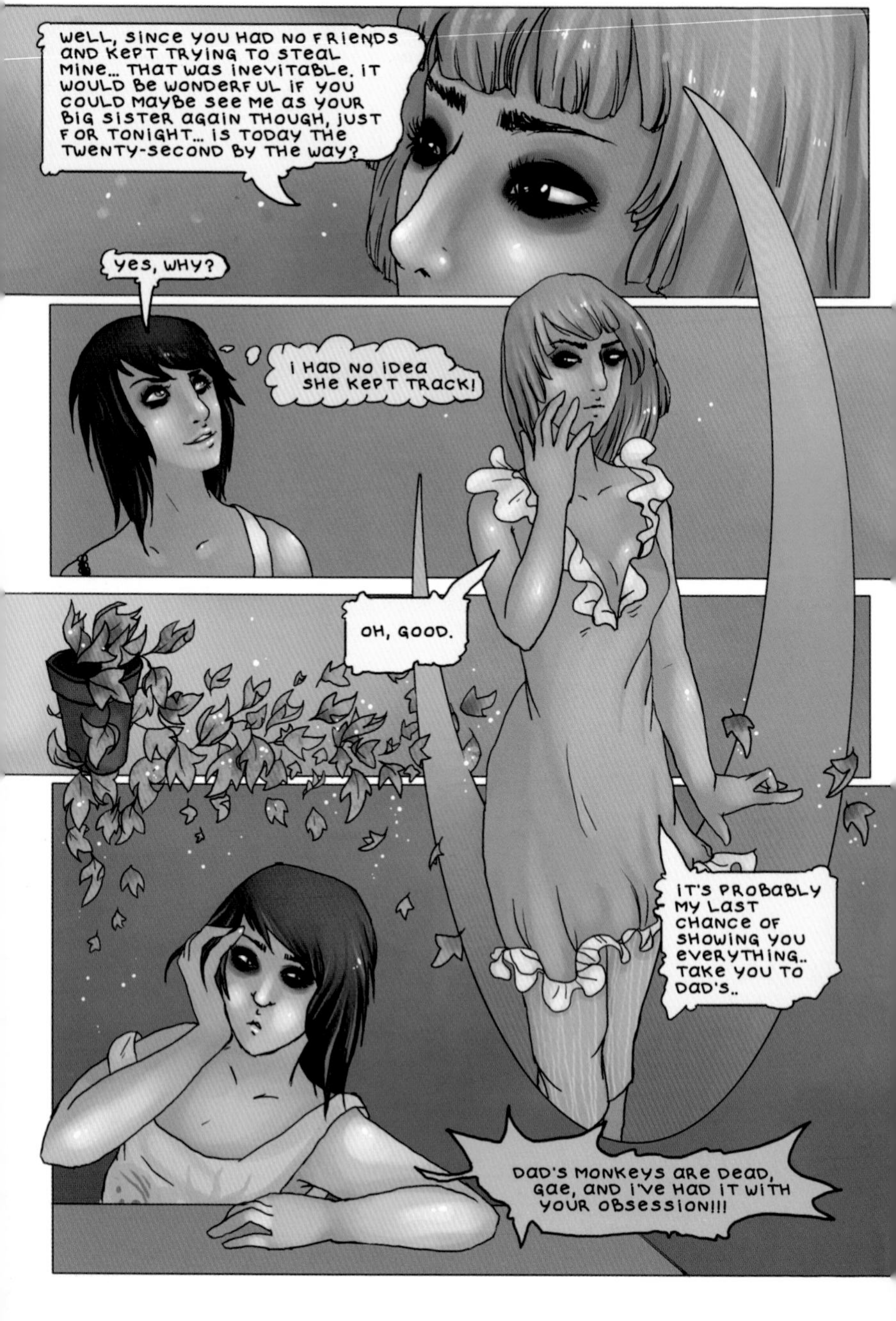
WELL, SINCE YOU HAD NO FRIENDS AND KEPT TRYING TO STEAL MINE... THAT WAS INEVITABLE. IT WOULD BE WONDERFUL IF YOU COULD MAYBE SEE ME AS YOUR BIG SISTER AGAIN THOUGH, JUST FOR TONIGHT... IS TODAY THE TWENTY-SECOND BY THE WAY?
YES, WHY?
I HAD NO IDEA SHE KEPT TRACK!
OH, GOOD.
IT'S PROBABLY MY LAST CHANCE OF SHOWING YOU EVERYTHING.. TAKE YOU TO DAD'S..
DAD'S MONKEYS ARE DEAD, GAE, AND I'VE HAD IT WITH YOUR OBSESSION!!!

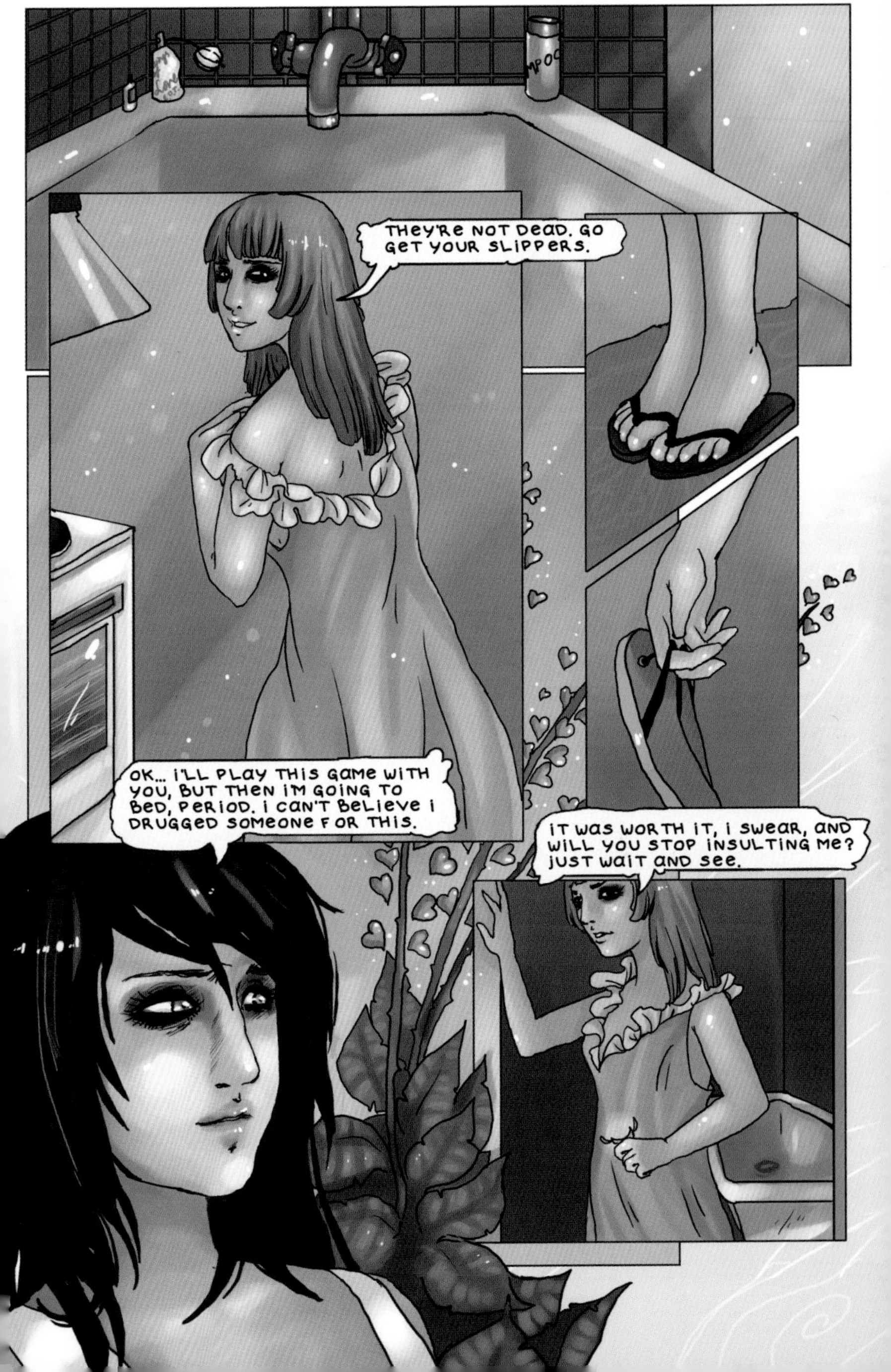
THEY'RE NOT DEAD. GO GET YOUR SLIPPERS.
OK... I'LL PLAY THIS GAME WITH YOU, BUT THEN I'M GOING TO BED, PERIOD. I CAN'T BELIEVE I DRUGGED SOMEONE FOR THIS.
IT WAS WORTH IT, I SWEAR, AND WILL YOU STOP INSULTING ME? JUST WAIT AND SEE.

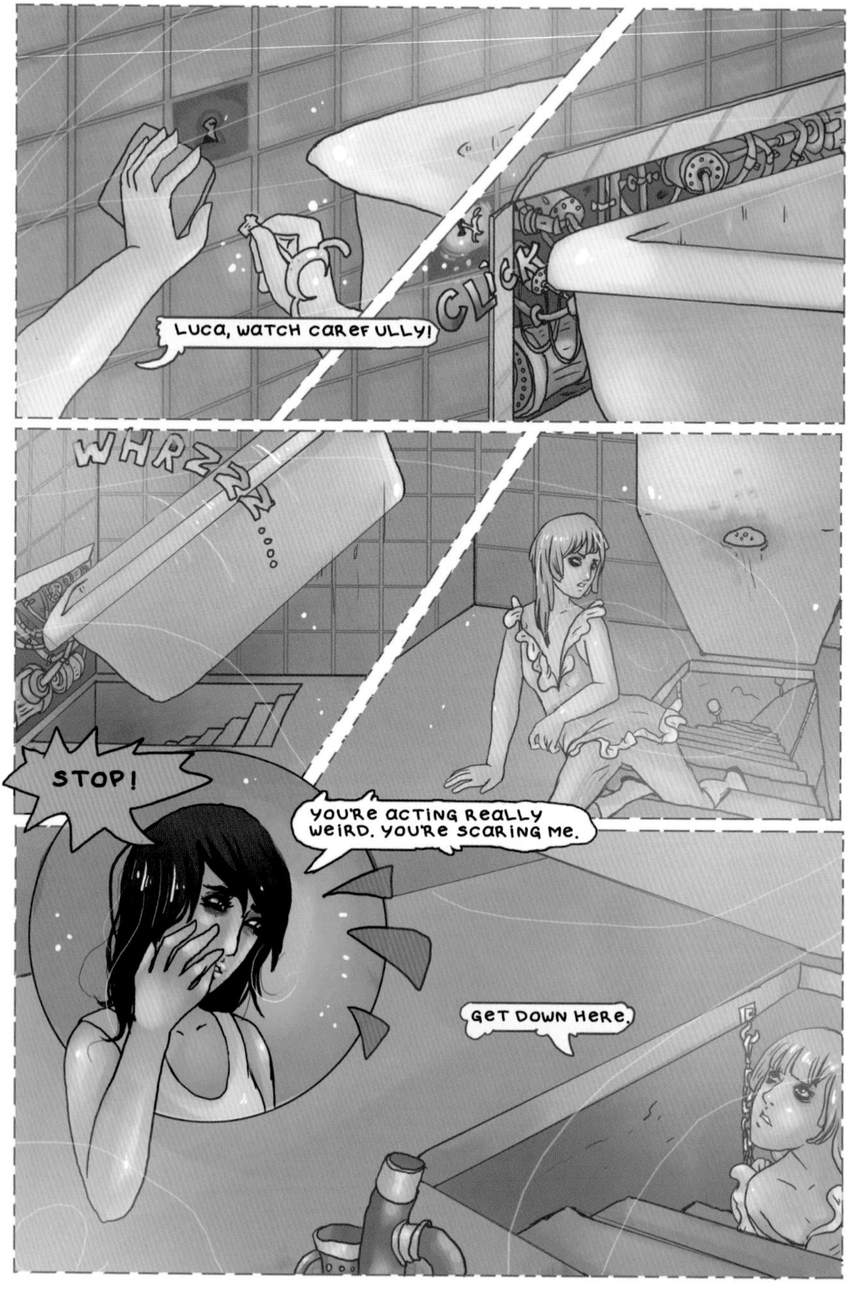
CLICK
LUCA, WATCH CAREFULLY!
WHRZZZ
STOP!
YOU'RE ACTING REALLY WEIRD. YOU'RE SCARING ME.
GET DOWN HERE.

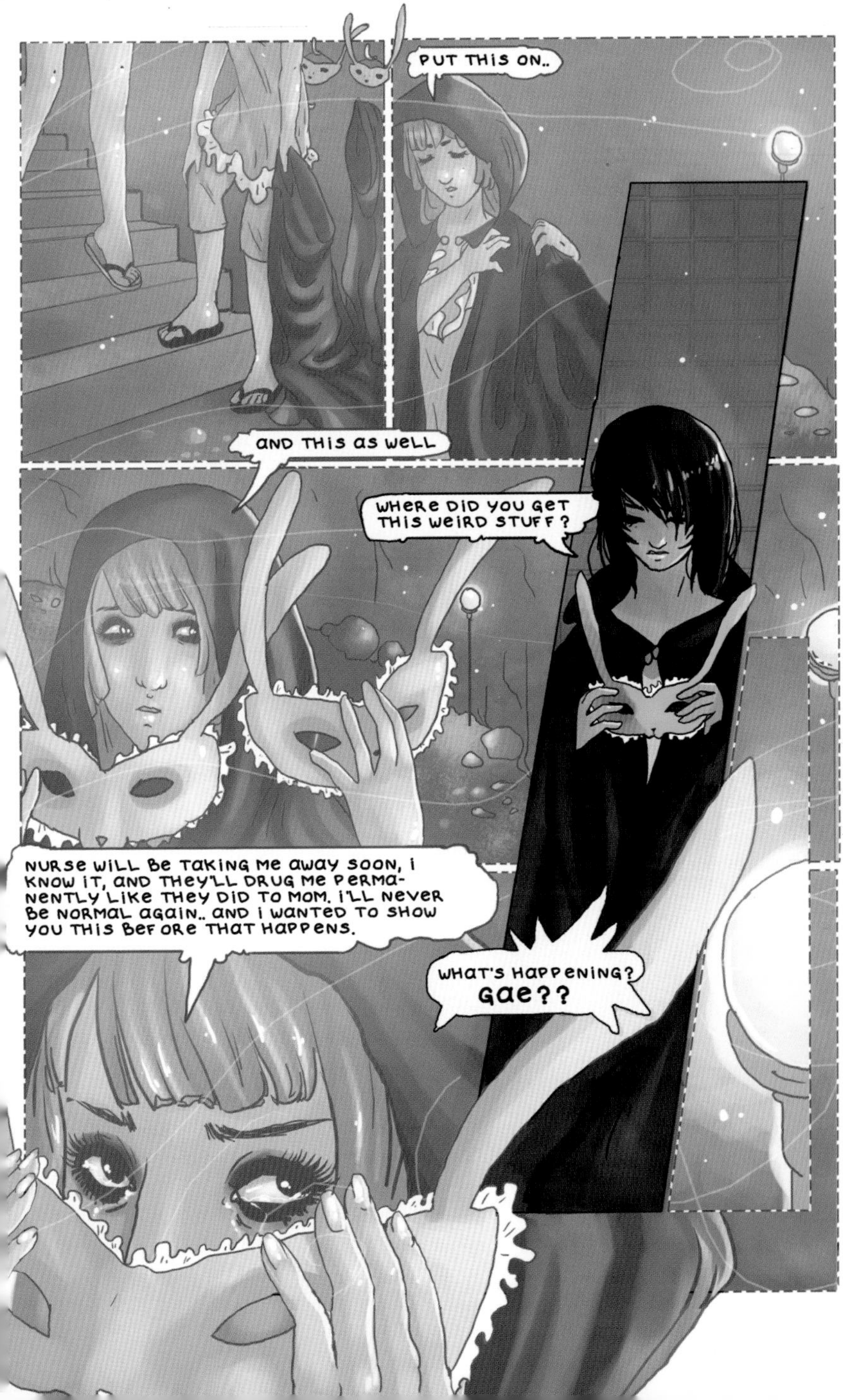
PUT THIS ON..
AND THIS AS WELL
WHERE DID YOU GET THIS WEIRD STUFF?
NURSE WILL BE TAKING ME AWAY SOON, I KNOW IT, AND THEY'LL DRUG ME PERMANENTLY LIKE THEY DID TO MOM. I'LL NEVER BE NORMAL AGAIN.. AND I WANTED TO SHOW YOU THIS BEFORE THAT HAPPENS.
WHAT'S HAPPENING? GAE??

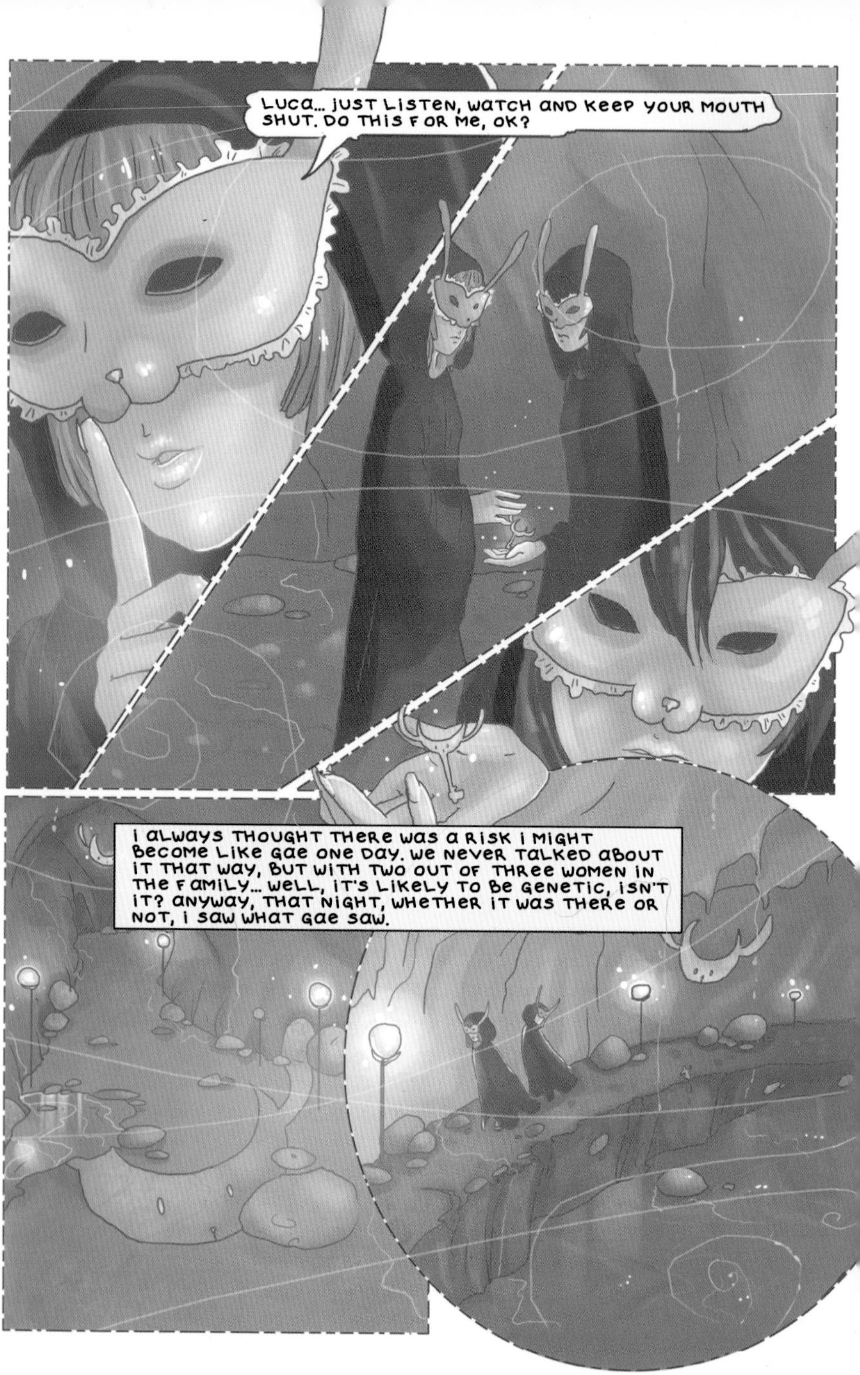
LUCA... JUST LISTEN, WATCH AND KEEP YOUR MOUTH SHUT. DO THIS FOR ME, OK?
I ALWAYS THOUGHT THERE WAS A RISK I MIGHT BECOME LIKE GAE ONE DAY. WE NEVER TALKED ABOUT IT THAT WAY, BUT WITH TWO OUT OF THREE WOMEN IN THE FAMILY... WELL, IT'S LIKELY TO BE GENETIC, ISN'T IT? ANYWAY, THAT NIGHT, WHETHER IT WAS THERE OR NOT, I SAW WHAT GAE SAW.

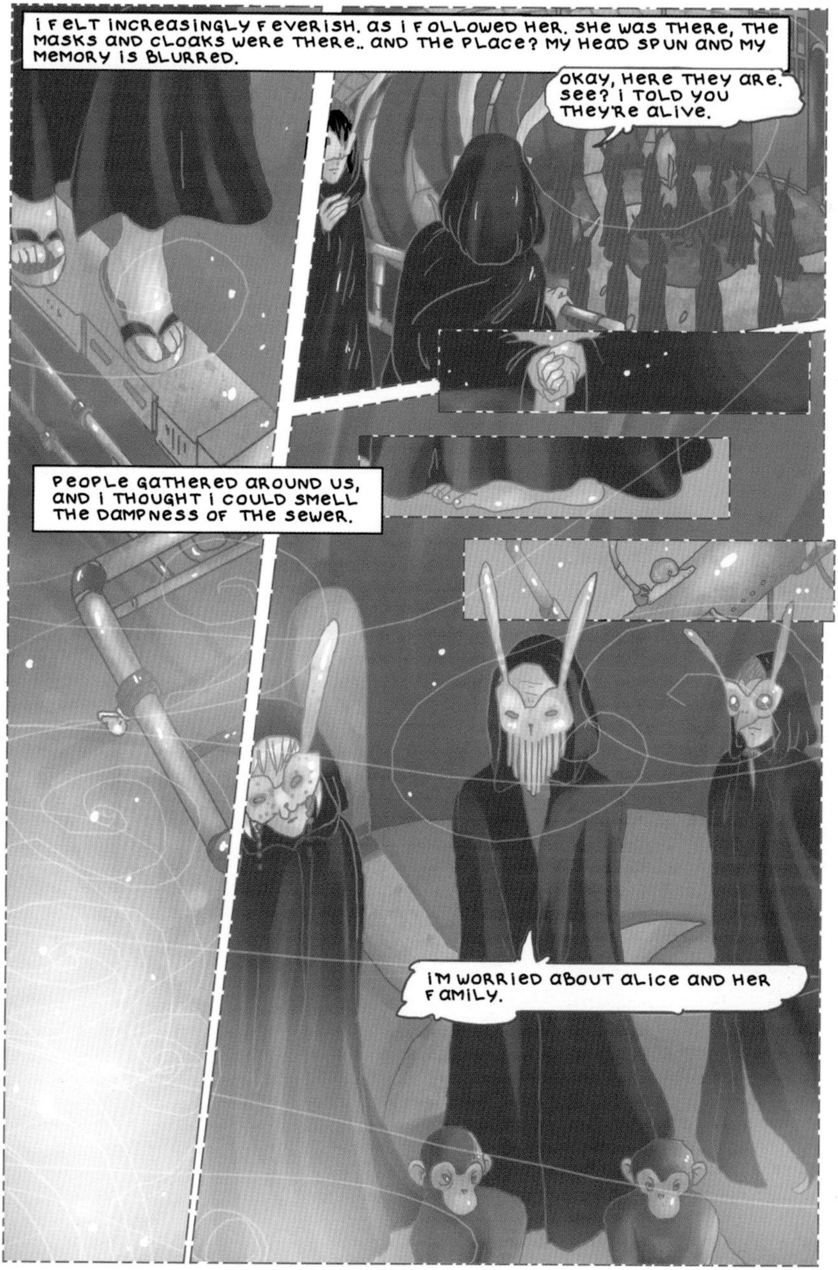
I FELT INCREASINGLY FEVERISH. AS I FOLLOWED HER. SHE WAS THERE, THE MASKS AND CLOAKS WERE THERE.. AND THE PLACE? MY HEAD SPUN AND MY MEMORY IS BLURRED.
OKAY, HERE THEY ARE. SEE? I TOLD YOU THEY'RE ALIVE.
PEOPLE GATHERED AROUND US, AND I THOUGHT I COULD SMELL THE DAMPNESS OF THE SEWER.
I'M WORRIED ABOUT ALICE AND HER FAMILY.

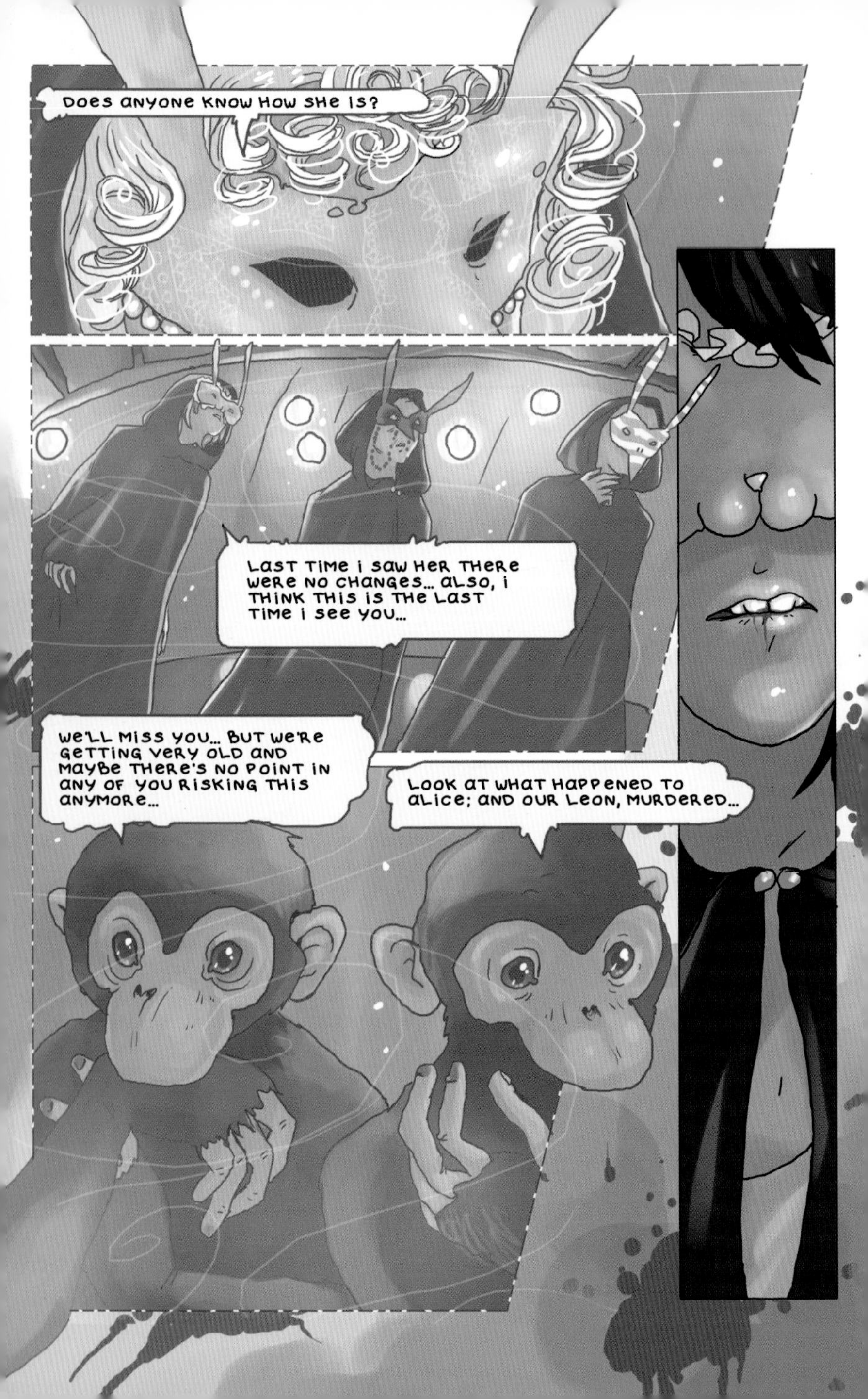
DOES ANYONE KNOW HOW SHE IS?
LAST TIME I SAW HER THERE WERE NO CHANGES... ALSO, I THINK THIS IS THE LAST TIME I SEE YOU...
WE'LL MISS YOU... BUT WE'RE GETTING VERY OLD AND MAYBE THERE'S NO POINT IN ANY OF YOU RISKING THIS ANYMORE...
LOOK AT WHAT HAPPENED TO ALICE; AND OUR LEON, MURDERED...

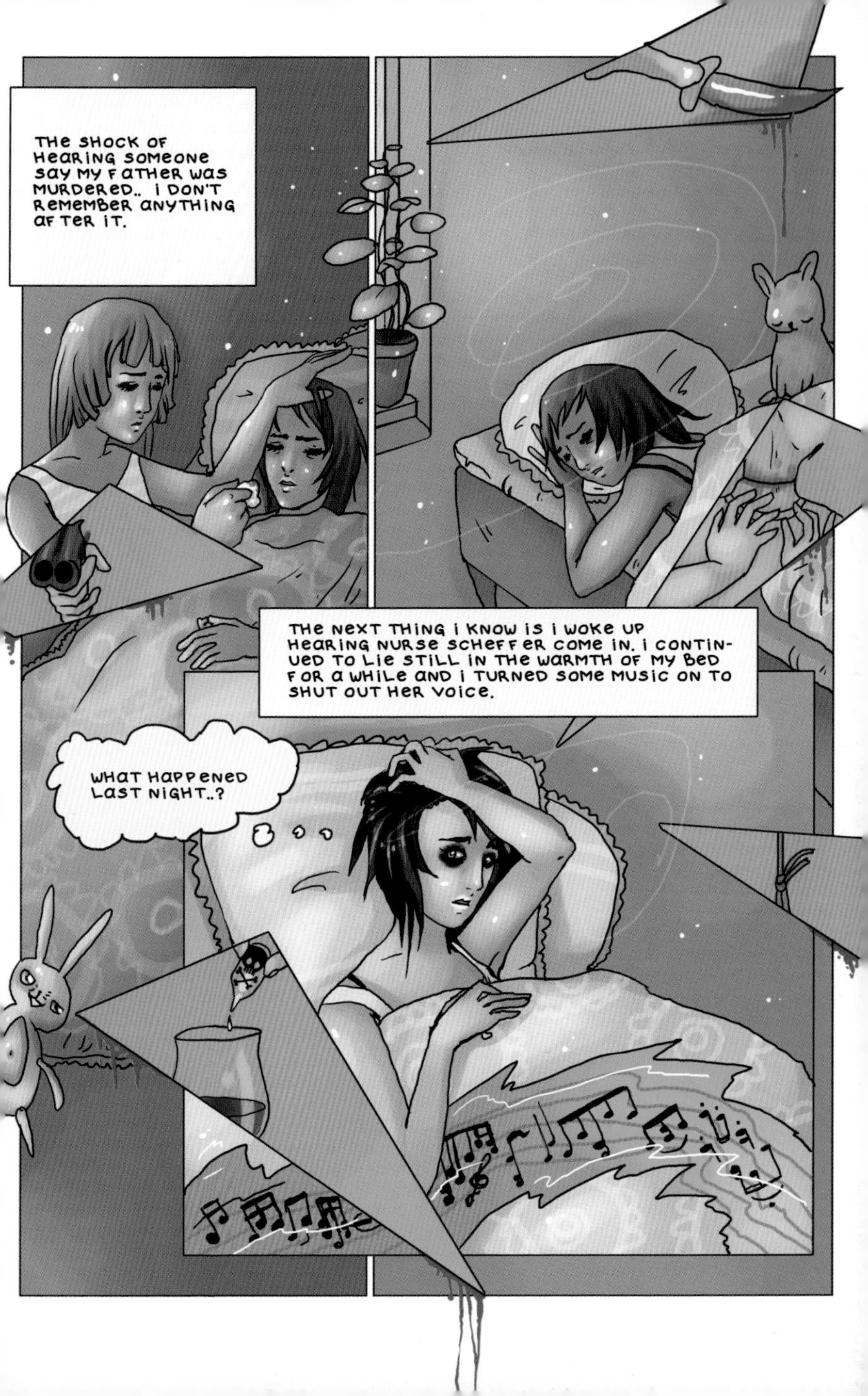
THE SHOCK OF HEARING SOMEONE SAY MY FATHER WAS MURDERED.. I DON'T REMEMBER ANYTHING AFTER IT.
THE NEXT THING I KNOW IS I WOKE UP HEARING NURSE SCHEFFER COME IN. I CONTINUED TO LIE STILL IN THE WARMTH OF MY BED FOR A WHILE AND I TURNED SOME MUSIC ON TO SHUT OUT HER VOICE.
WHAT HAPPENED LAST NIGHT..?

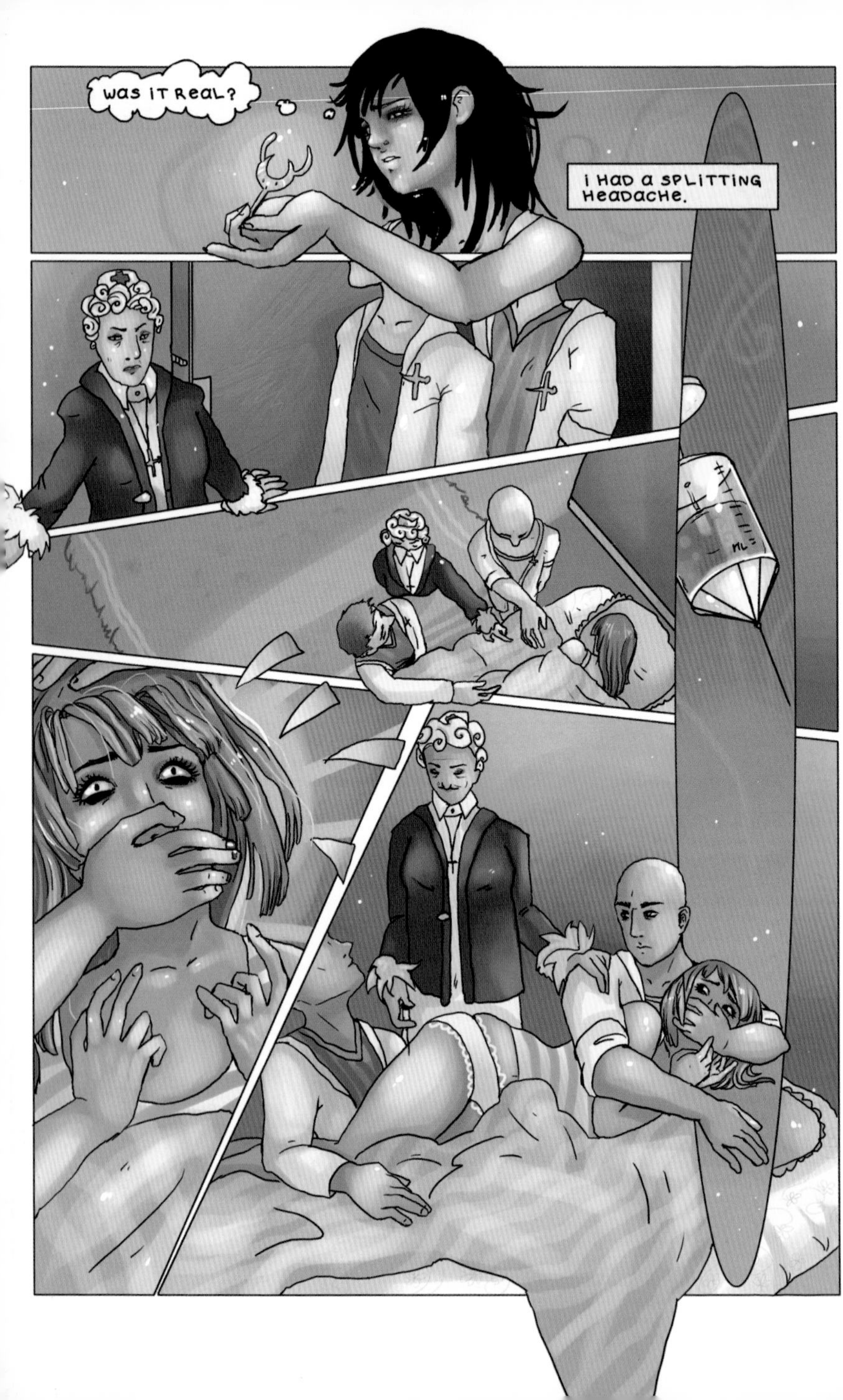
was it real?
i had a splitting headache.
ML

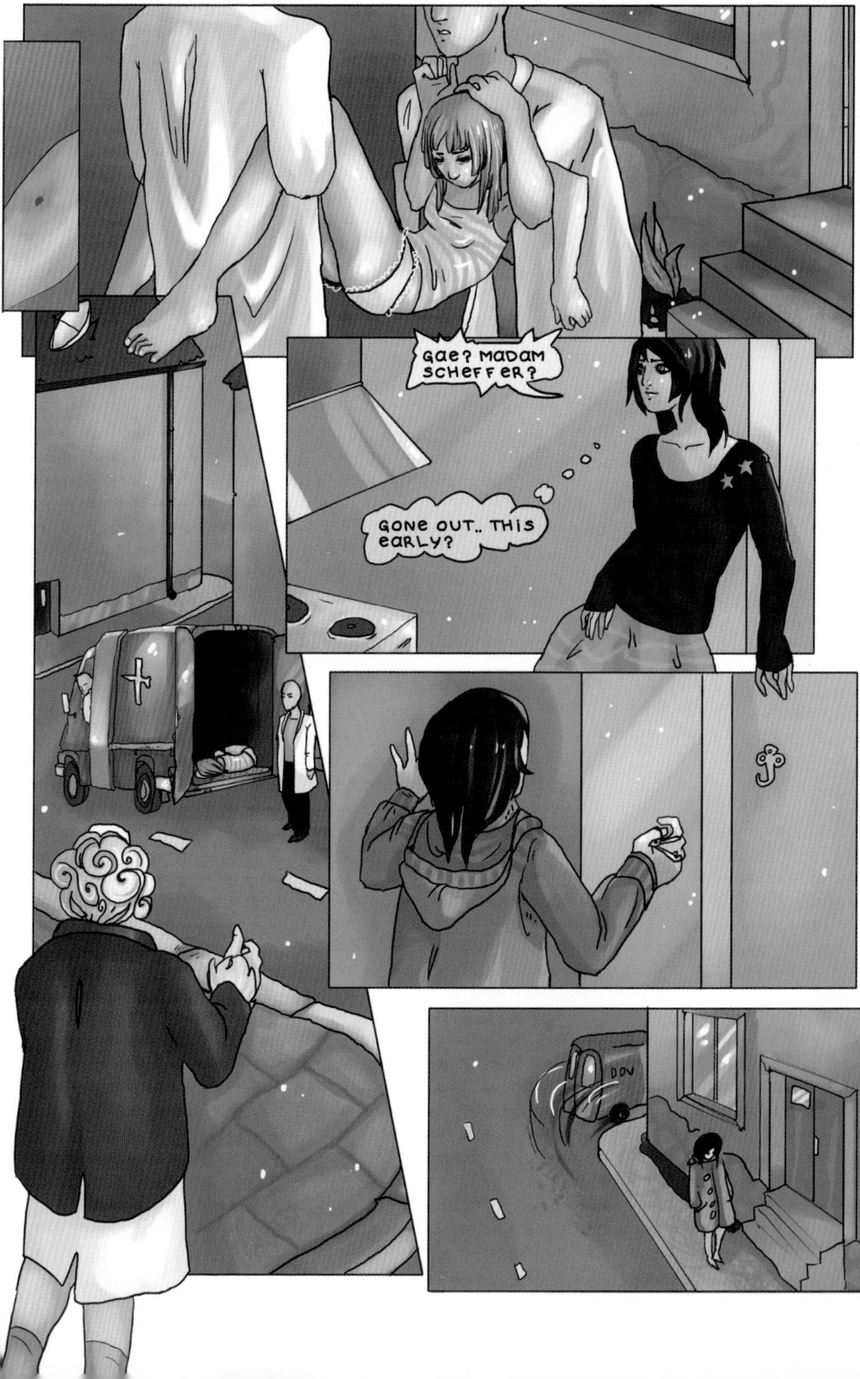
GAE? MADAM SCHEFFER?
GONE OUT.. THIS EARLY?
DOV

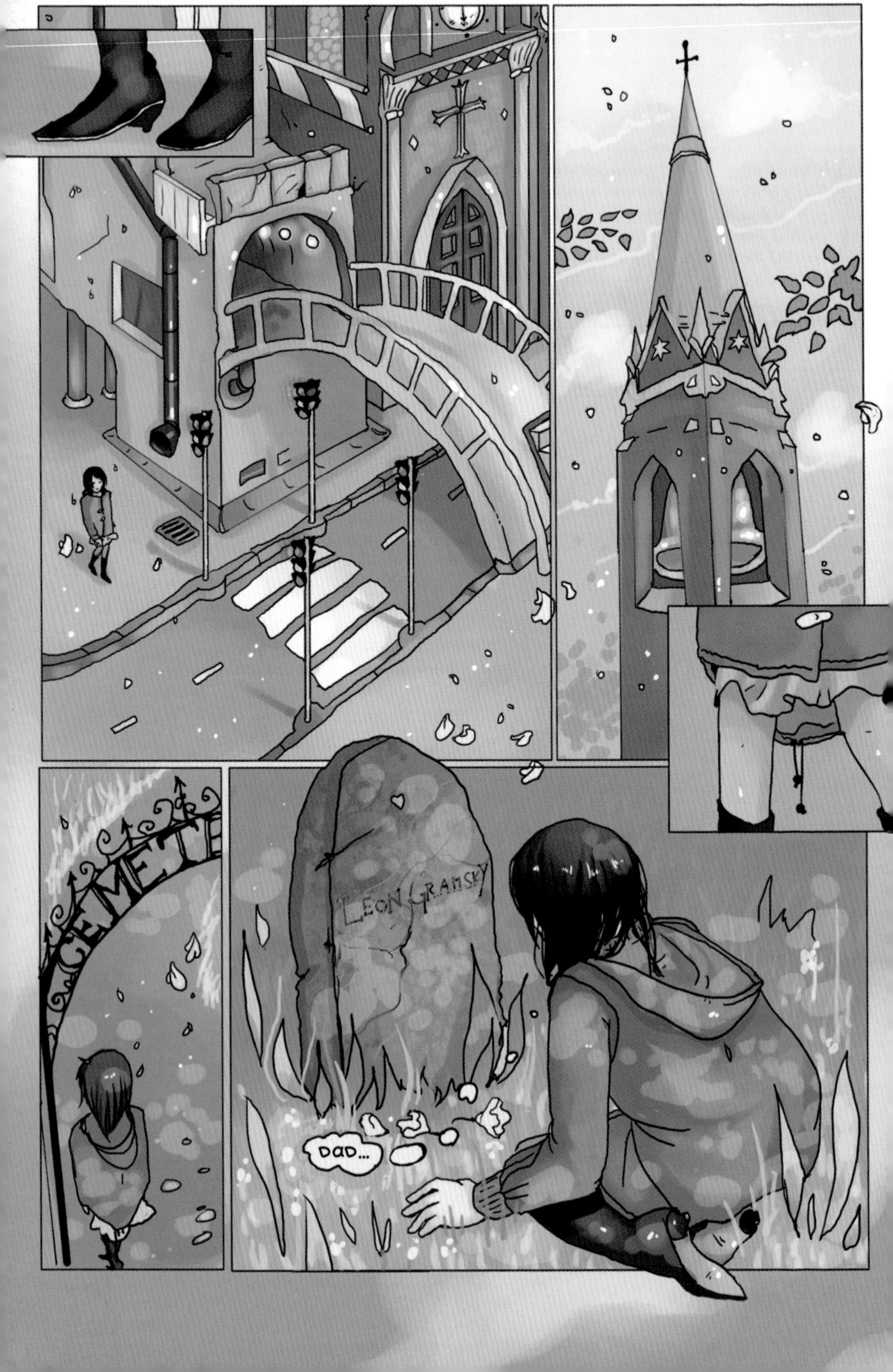
LEON GRAMSKY
DAD...

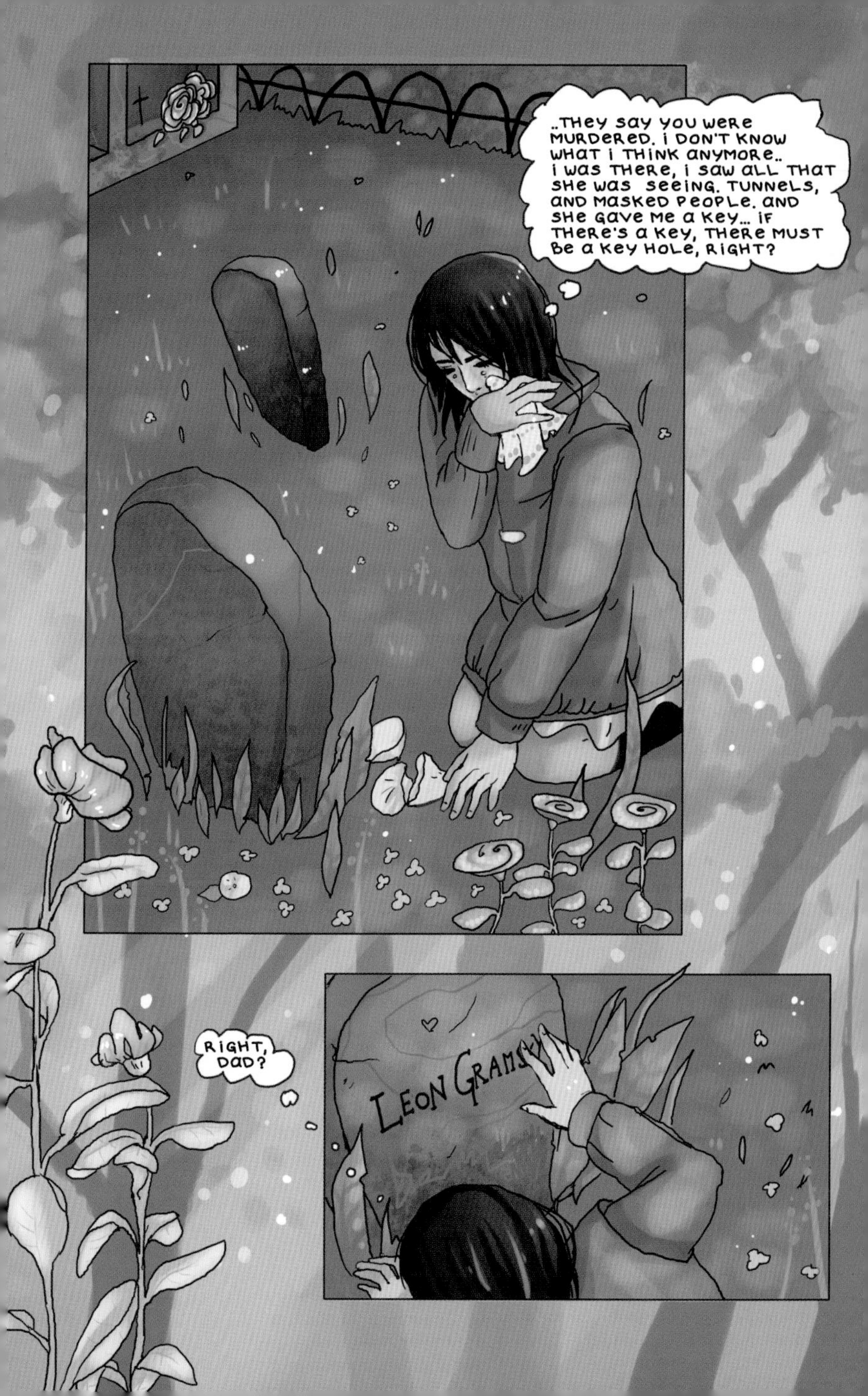
..THEY SAY YOU WERE MURDERED. I DON'T KNOW WHAT I THINK ANYMORE.. I WAS THERE, I SAW ALL THAT SHE WAS SEEING. TUNNELS, AND MASKED PEOPLE. AND SHE GAVE ME A KEY... IF THERE'S A KEY, THERE MUST BE A KEY HOLE, RIGHT?
RIGHT, DAD?
LEON GRAMSKY

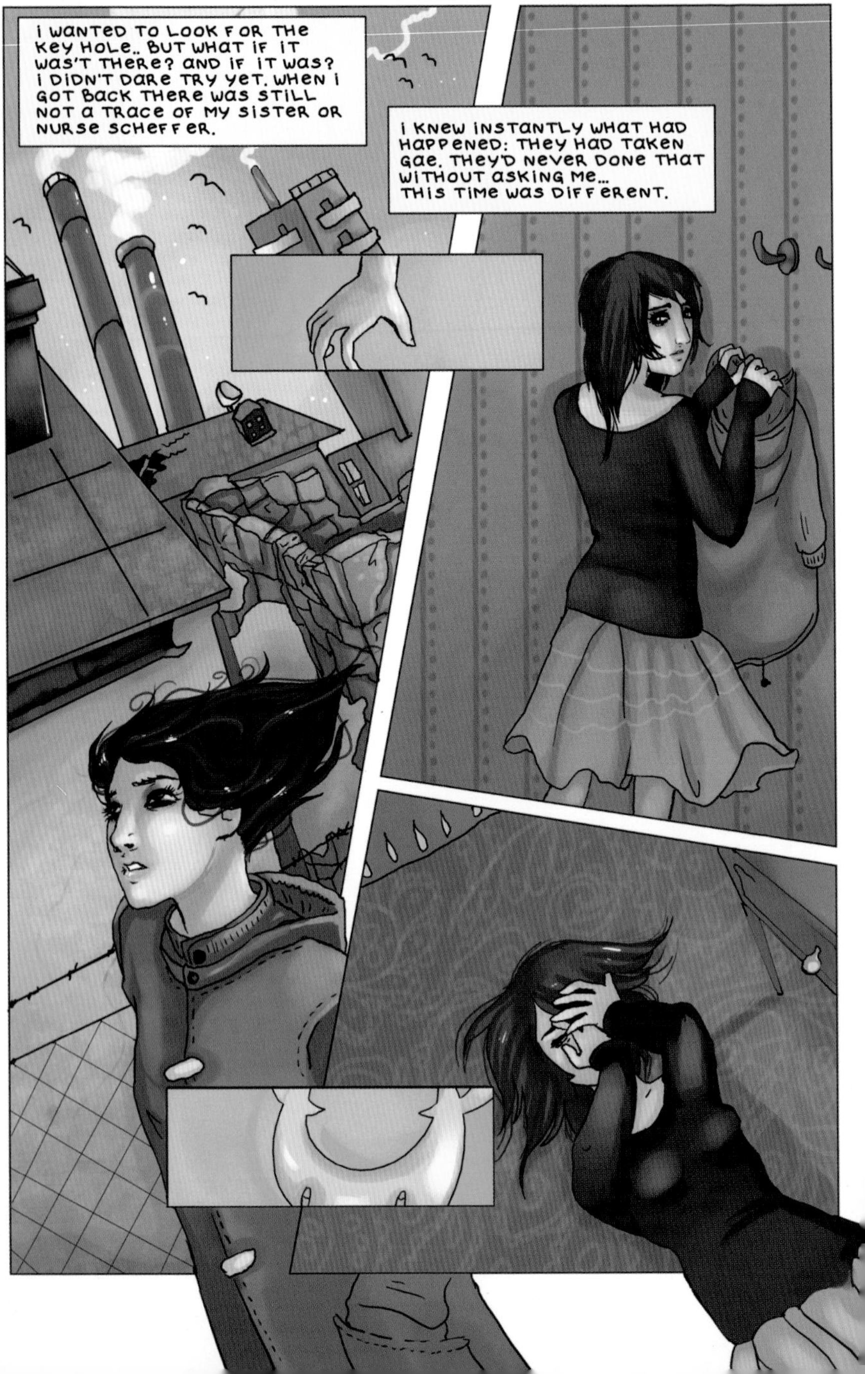
i WANTED TO LOOK FOR THE KEY HOLE.. BUT WHAT IF IT WAS'T THERE? AND IF IT WAS? i DIDN'T DARE TRY YET. WHEN i GOT BACK THERE WAS STILL NOT A TRACE OF MY SISTER OR NURSE SCHEFFER.
i KNEW INSTANTLY WHAT HAD HAPPENED: THEY HAD TAKEN GAE. THEY'D NEVER DONE THAT WITHOUT ASKING ME... THIS TIME WAS DIFFERENT.

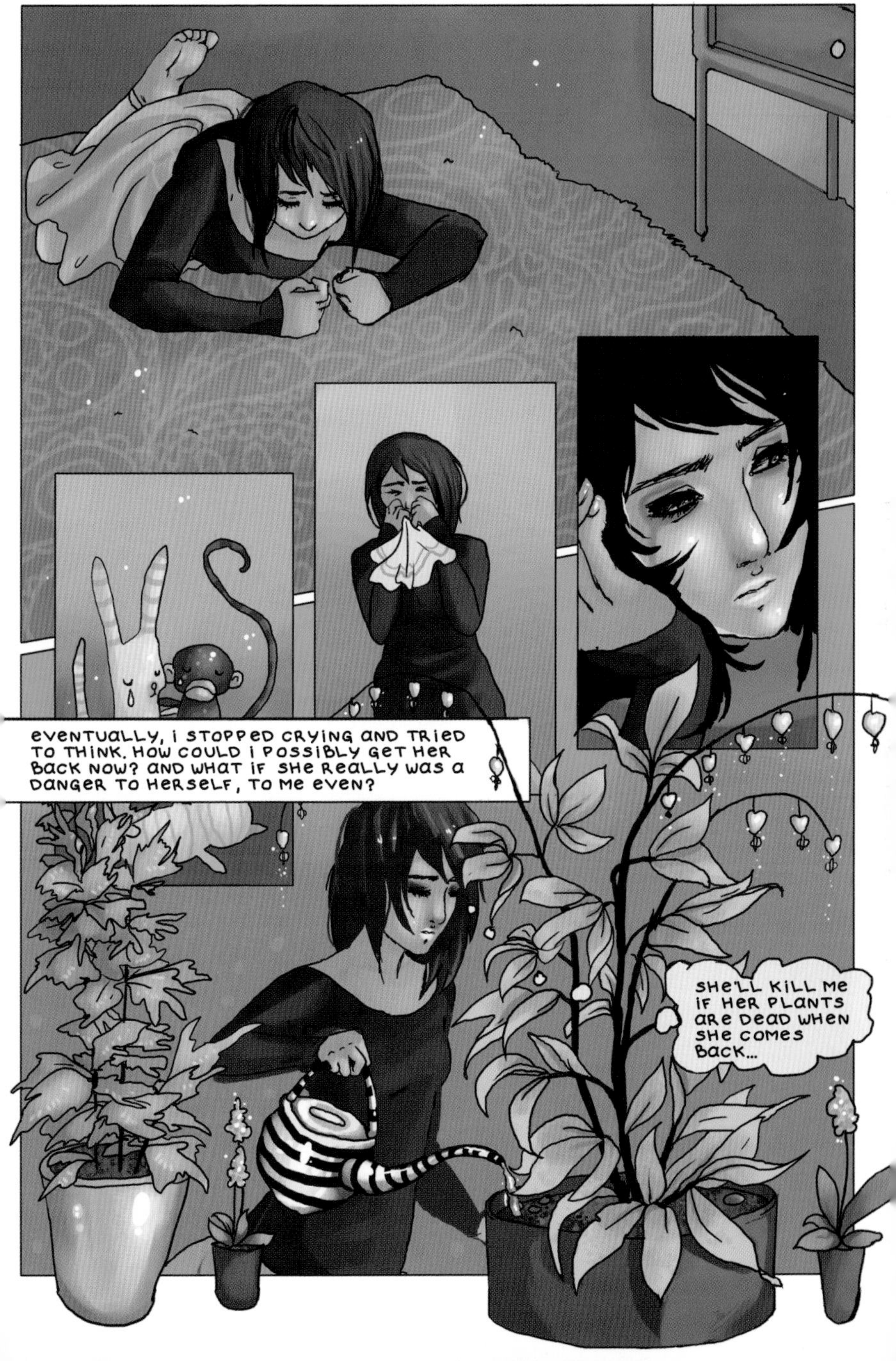
EVENTUALLY, I STOPPED CRYING AND TRIED TO THINK. HOW COULD I POSSIBLY GET HER BACK NOW? AND WHAT IF SHE REALLY WAS A DANGER TO HERSELF, TO ME EVEN?
SHE'LL KILL ME IF HER PLANTS ARE DEAD WHEN SHE COMES BACK...

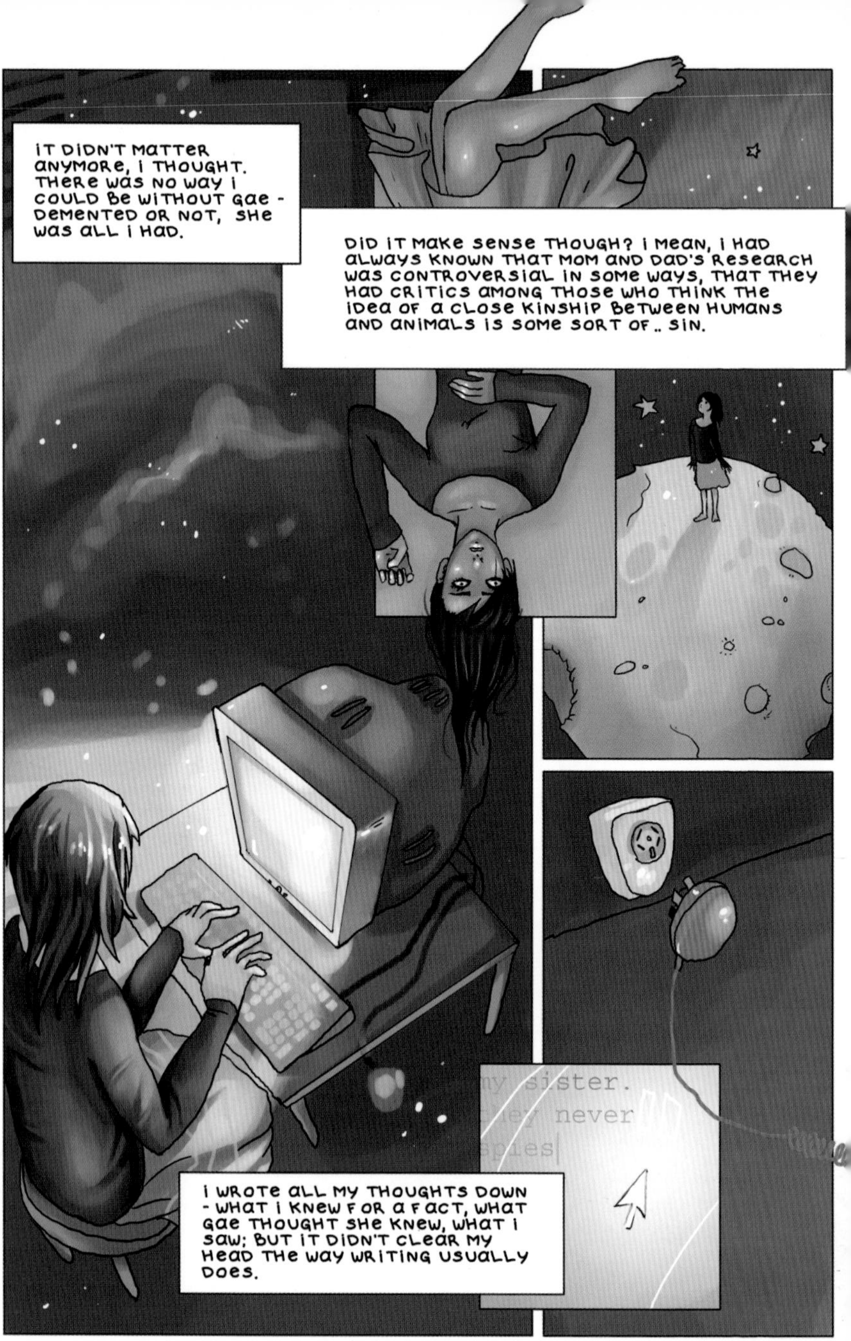
IT DIDN'T MATTER ANYMORE, I THOUGHT. THERE WAS NO WAY I COULD BE WITHOUT GAE - DEMENTED OR NOT, SHE WAS ALL I HAD.
DID IT MAKE SENSE THOUGH? I MEAN, I HAD ALWAYS KNOWN THAT MOM AND DAD'S RESEARCH WAS CONTROVERSIAL IN SOME WAYS, THAT THEY HAD CRITICS AMONG THOSE WHO THINK THE IDEA OF A CLOSE KINSHIP BETWEEN HUMANS AND ANIMALS IS SOME SORT OF .. SIN.
my sister.
never
spies
I WROTE ALL MY THOUGHTS DOWN - WHAT I KNEW FOR A FACT, WHAT GAE THOUGHT SHE KNEW, WHAT I SAW; BUT IT DIDN'T CLEAR MY HEAD THE WAY WRITING USUALLY DOES.

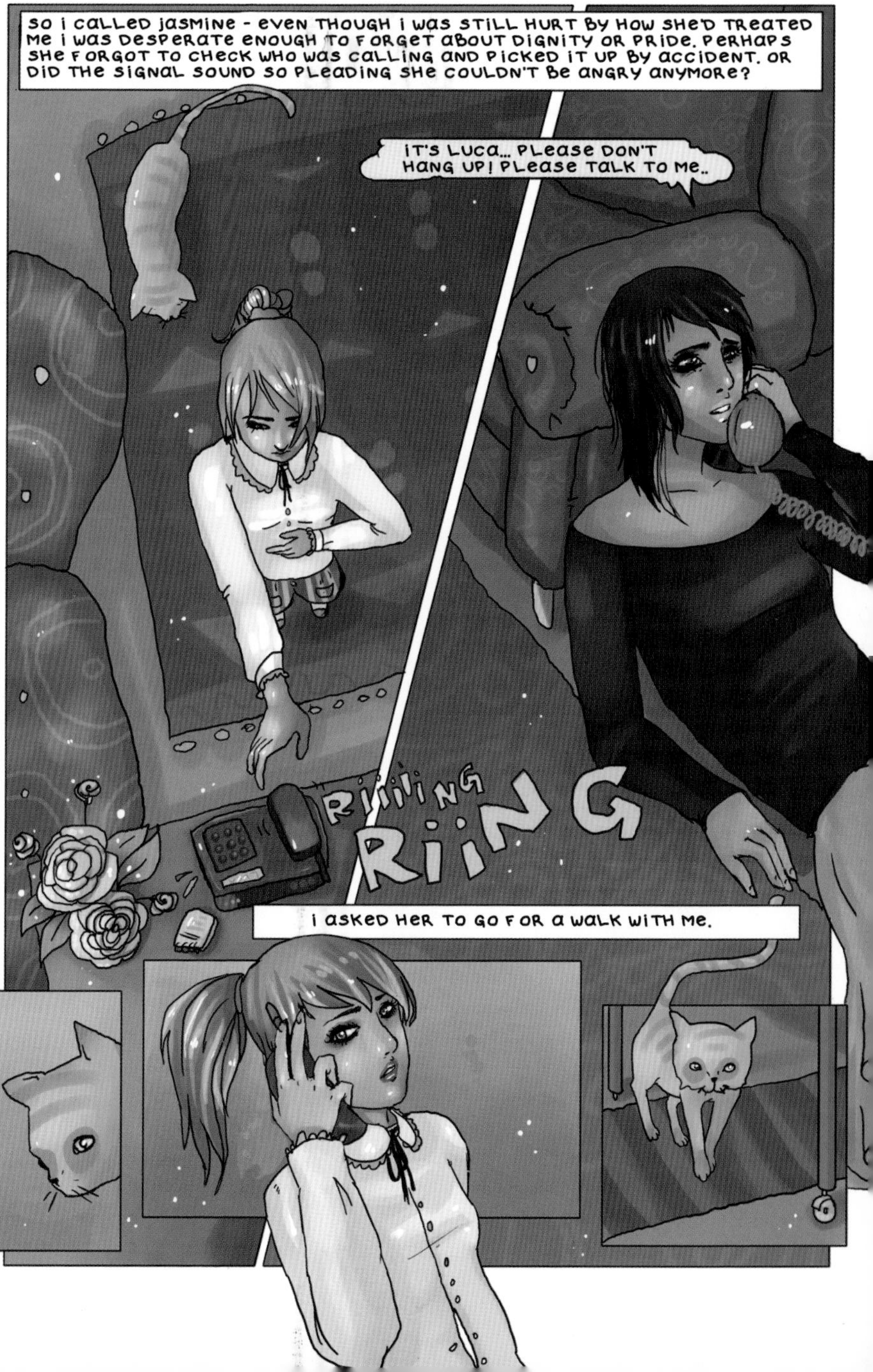
so i called jasmine - even though i was still hurt by how she'd treated me i was desperate enough to forget about dignity or pride. perhaps she forgot to check who was calling and picked it up by accident. or did the signal sound so pleading she couldn't be angry anymore?
it's luca... please don't hang up! please talk to me..
riiiing
riiing
i asked her to go for a walk with me.

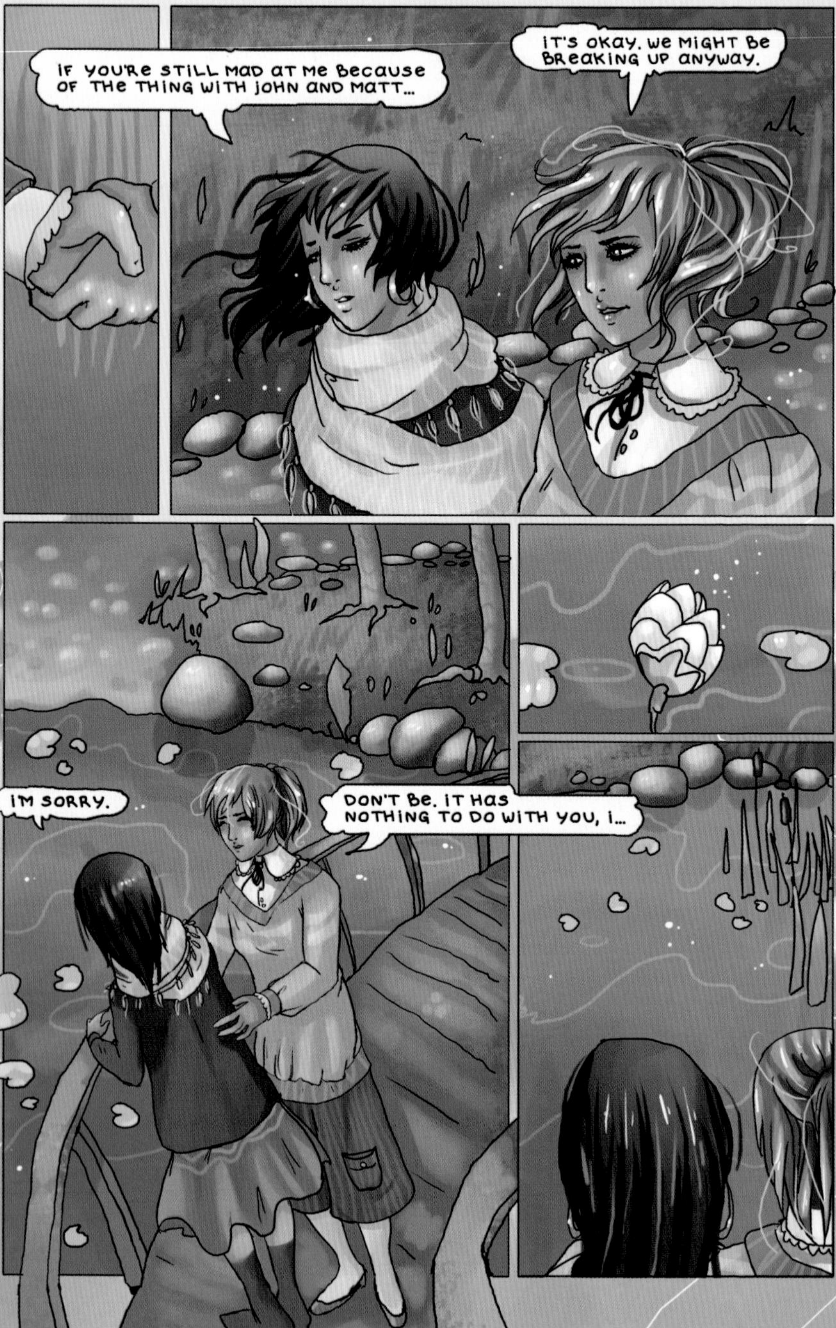
IF YOU'RE STILL MAD AT ME BECAUSE OF THE THING WITH JOHN AND MATT...
IT'S OKAY. WE MIGHT BE BREAKING UP ANYWAY.
IM SORRY.
DON'T BE. IT HAS NOTHING TO DO WITH YOU, I...

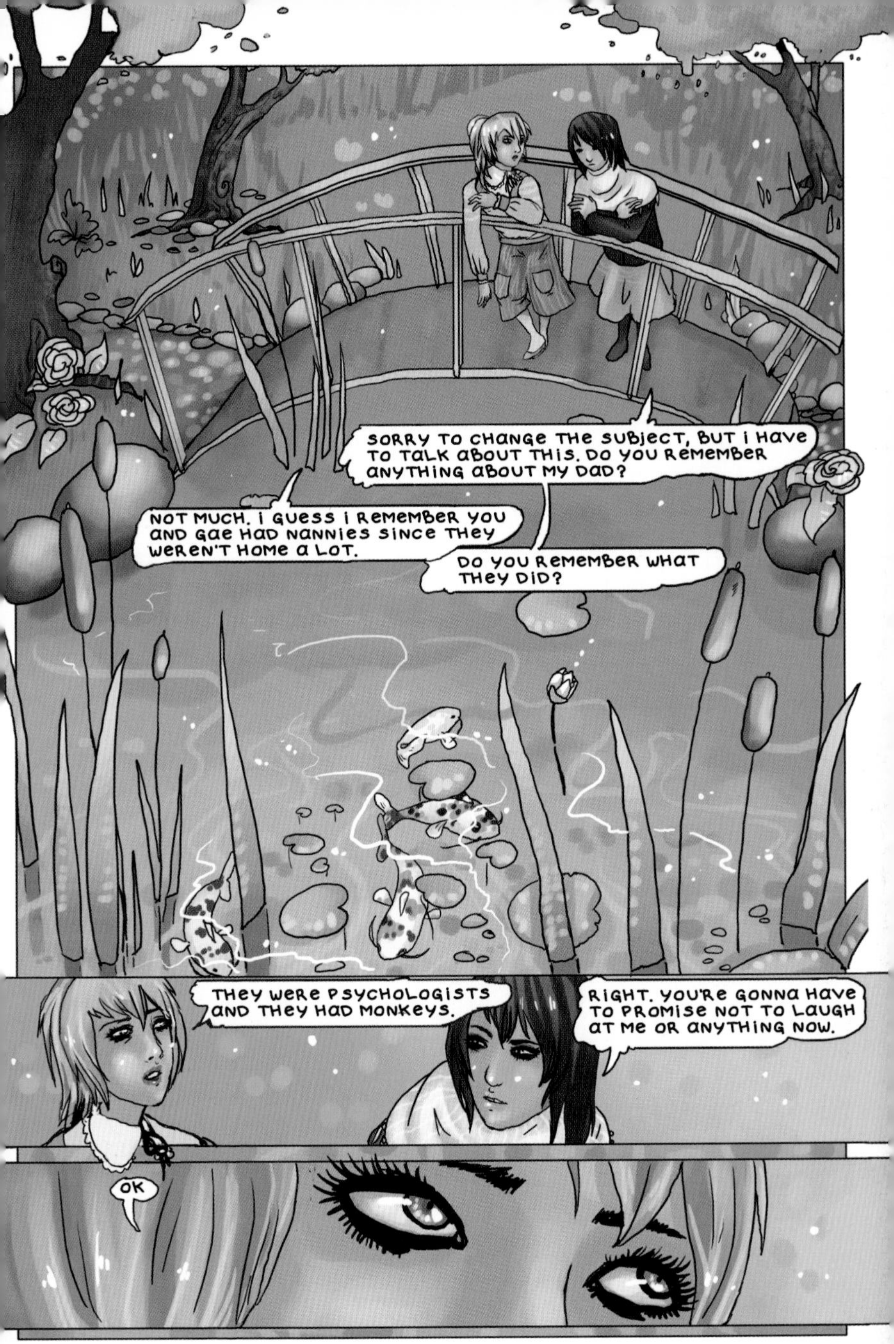
SORRY TO CHANGE THE SUBJECT, BUT I HAVE TO TALK ABOUT THIS. DO YOU REMEMBER ANYTHING ABOUT MY DAD?
NOT MUCH. I GUESS I REMEMBER YOU AND GAE HAD NANNIES SINCE THEY WEREN'T HOME A LOT.
DO YOU REMEMBER WHAT THEY DID?
THEY WERE PSYCHOLOGISTS AND THEY HAD MONKEYS.
RIGHT. YOU'RE GONNA HAVE TO PROMISE NOT TO LAUGH AT ME OR ANYTHING NOW.
OK

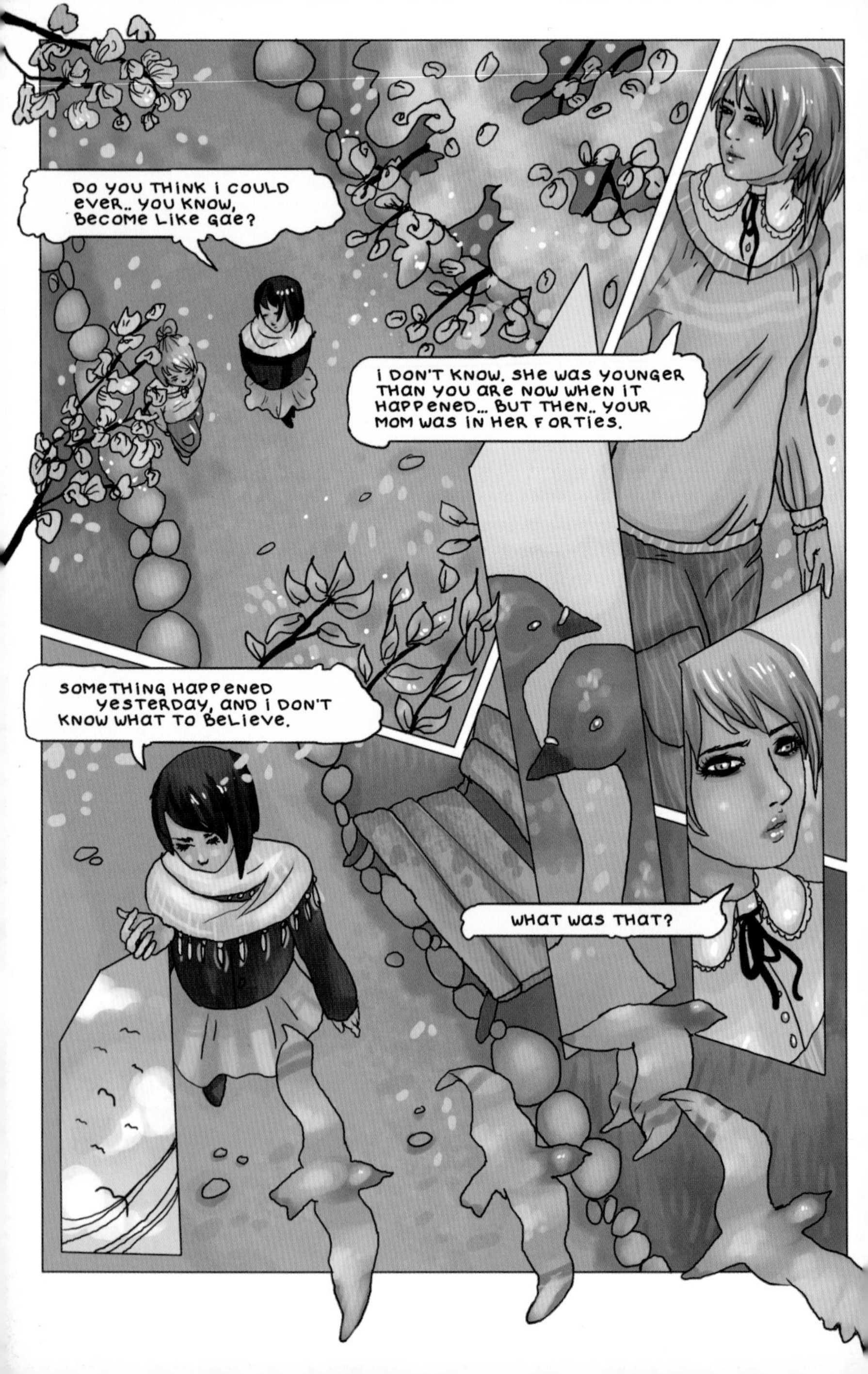
DO YOU THINK i COULD ever.. YOU KNOW, Become LIKE Gae?
i DON'T KNOW. SHE WaS YOUNGER THAN YOU are NOW WHEN IT Happened... BUT THEN.. YOUR MOM WaS IN HER FORTies.
SOMeTHING Happened yesterday, and i DON'T KNOW WHAT TO BeLieve.
WHAT WaS THAT?

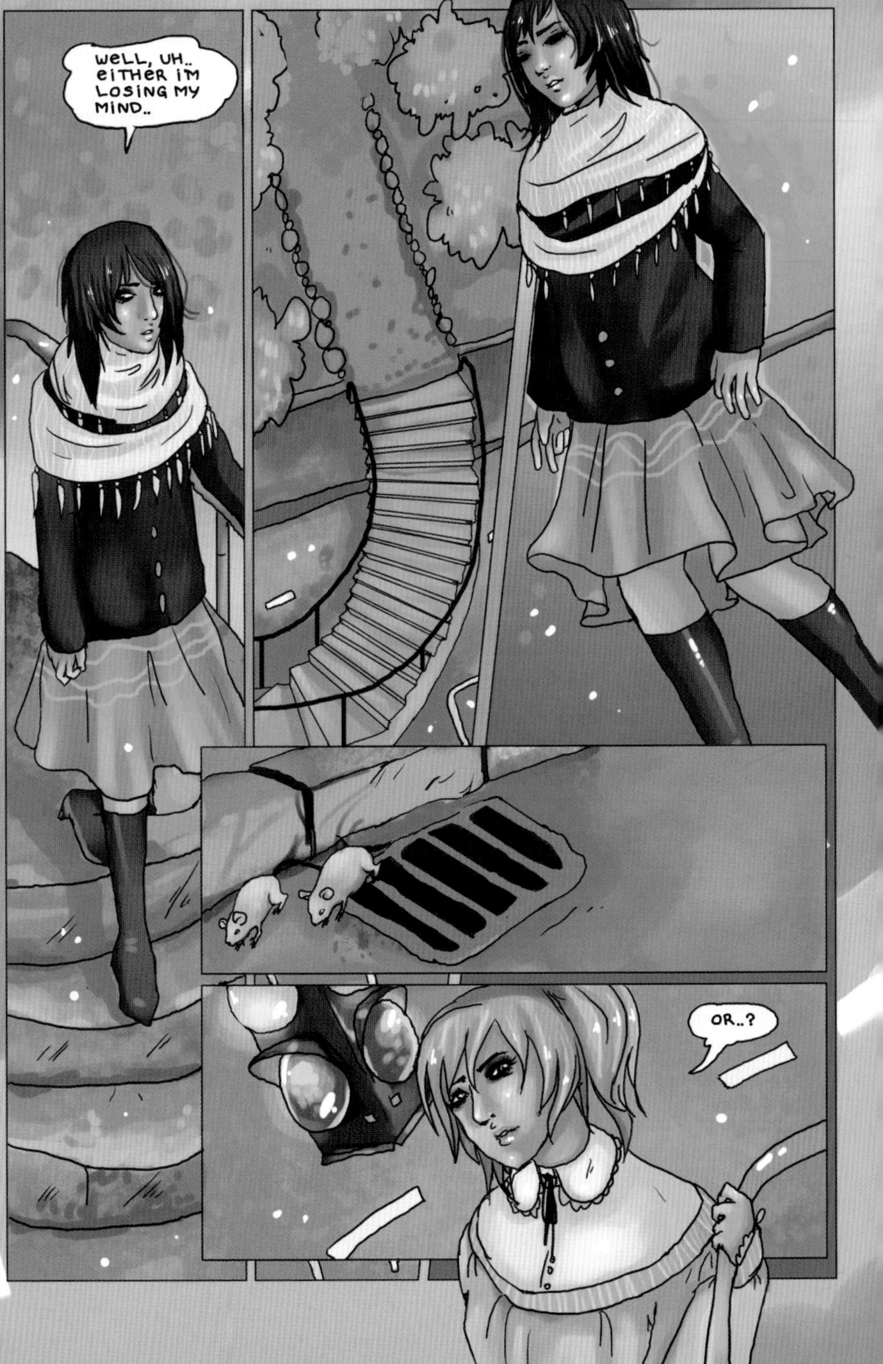
WELL, UH..
EITHER IM
LOSING MY
MIND..
OR..?

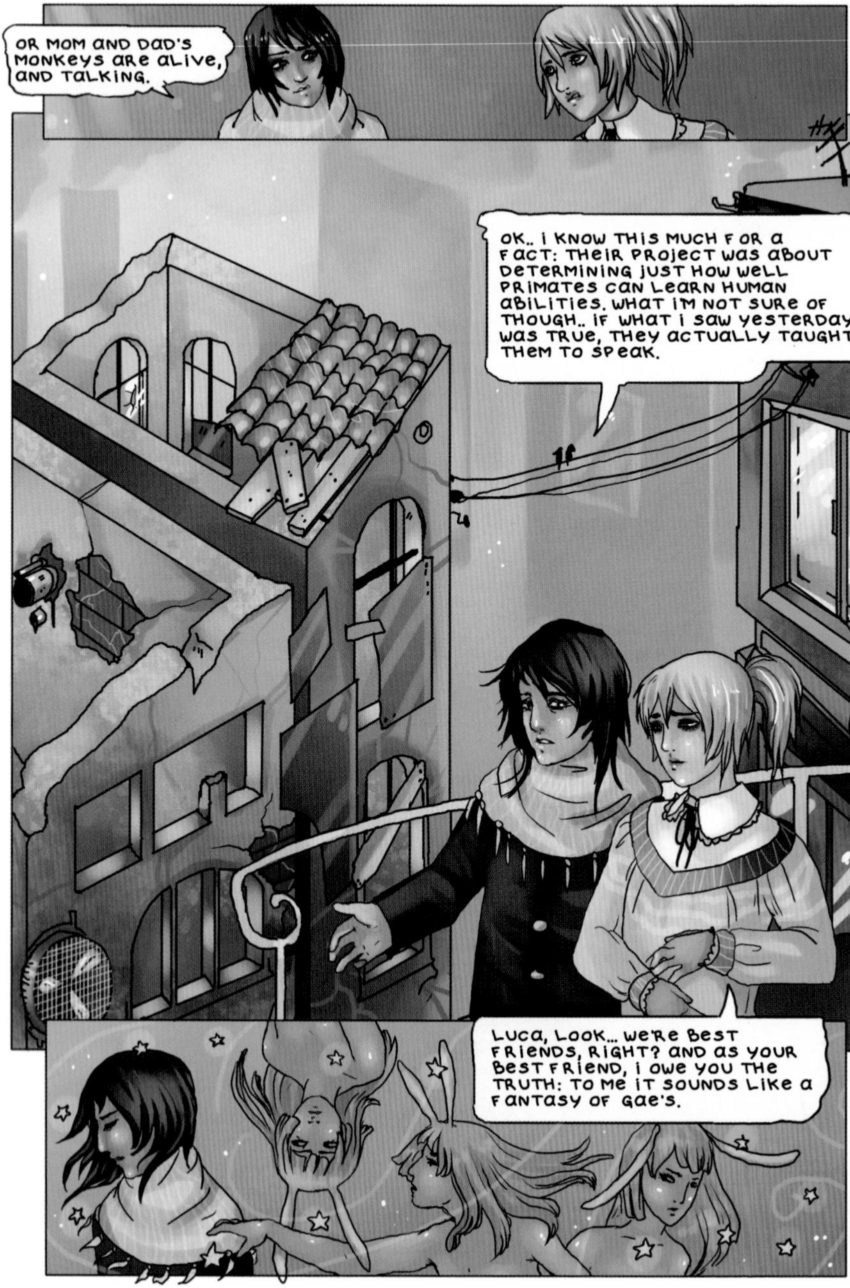
OR MOM AND DAD'S MONKEYS ARE ALIVE, AND TALKING.
OK.. I KNOW THIS MUCH FOR A FACT: THEIR PROJECT WAS ABOUT DETERMINING JUST HOW WELL PRIMATES CAN LEARN HUMAN ABILITIES. WHAT I'M NOT SURE OF THOUGH.. IF WHAT I SAW YESTERDAY WAS TRUE, THEY ACTUALLY TAUGHT THEM TO SPEAK.
LUCA, LOOK... WE'RE BEST FRIENDS, RIGHT? AND AS YOUR BEST FRIEND, I OWE YOU THE TRUTH: TO ME IT SOUNDS LIKE A FANTASY OF GAE'S.

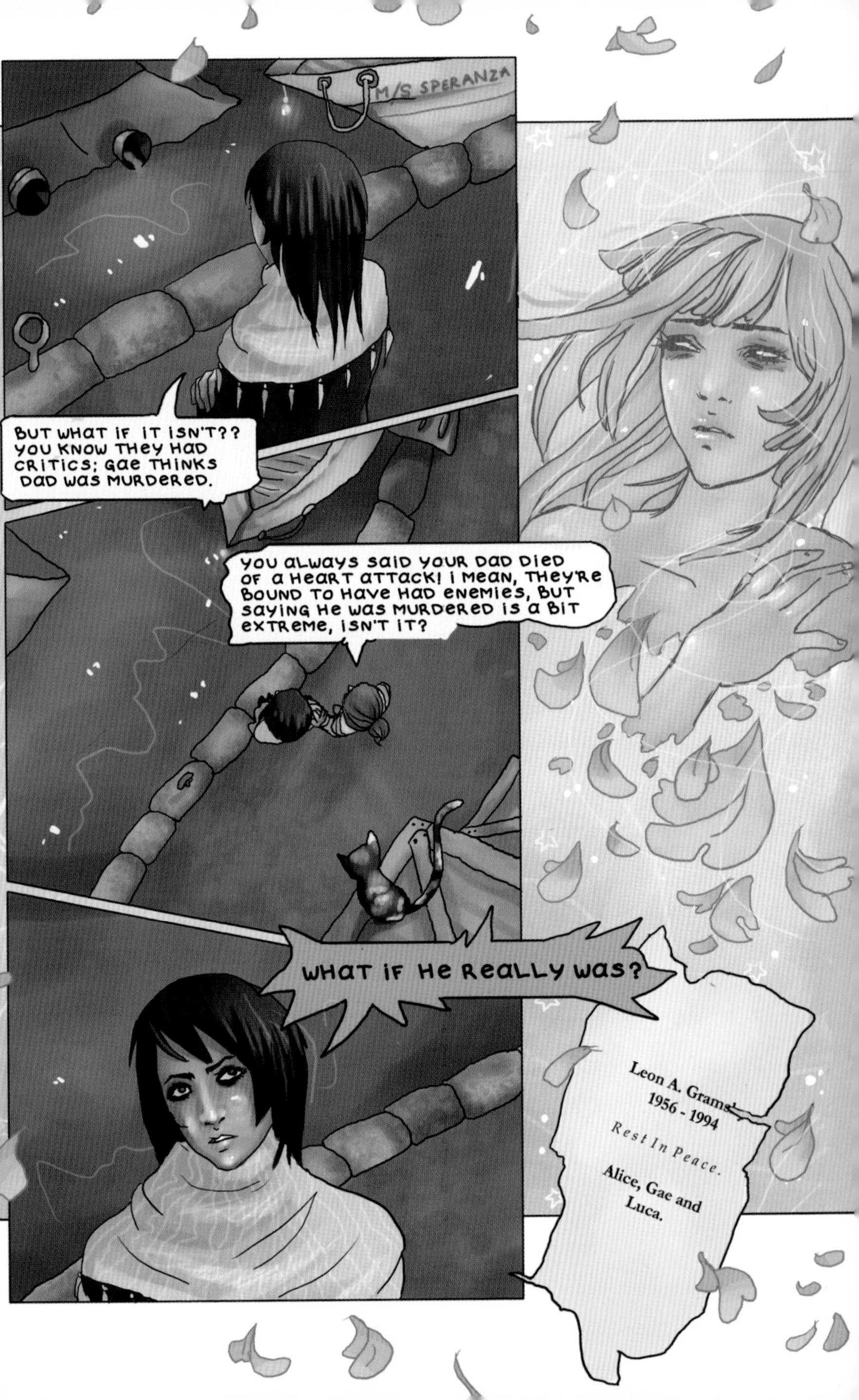
M/S SPERANZA
BUT WHAT IF IT ISN'T?? YOU KNOW THEY HAD CRITICS; GAE THINKS DAD WAS MURDERED.
YOU ALWAYS SAID YOUR DAD DIED OF A HEART ATTACK! I MEAN, THEY'RE BOUND TO HAVE HAD ENEMIES, BUT SAYING HE WAS MURDERED IS A BIT EXTREME, ISN'T IT?
WHAT IF HE REALLY WAS?
Leon A. Grams
1956 - 1994
Rest In Peace.
Alice, Gae and Luca.

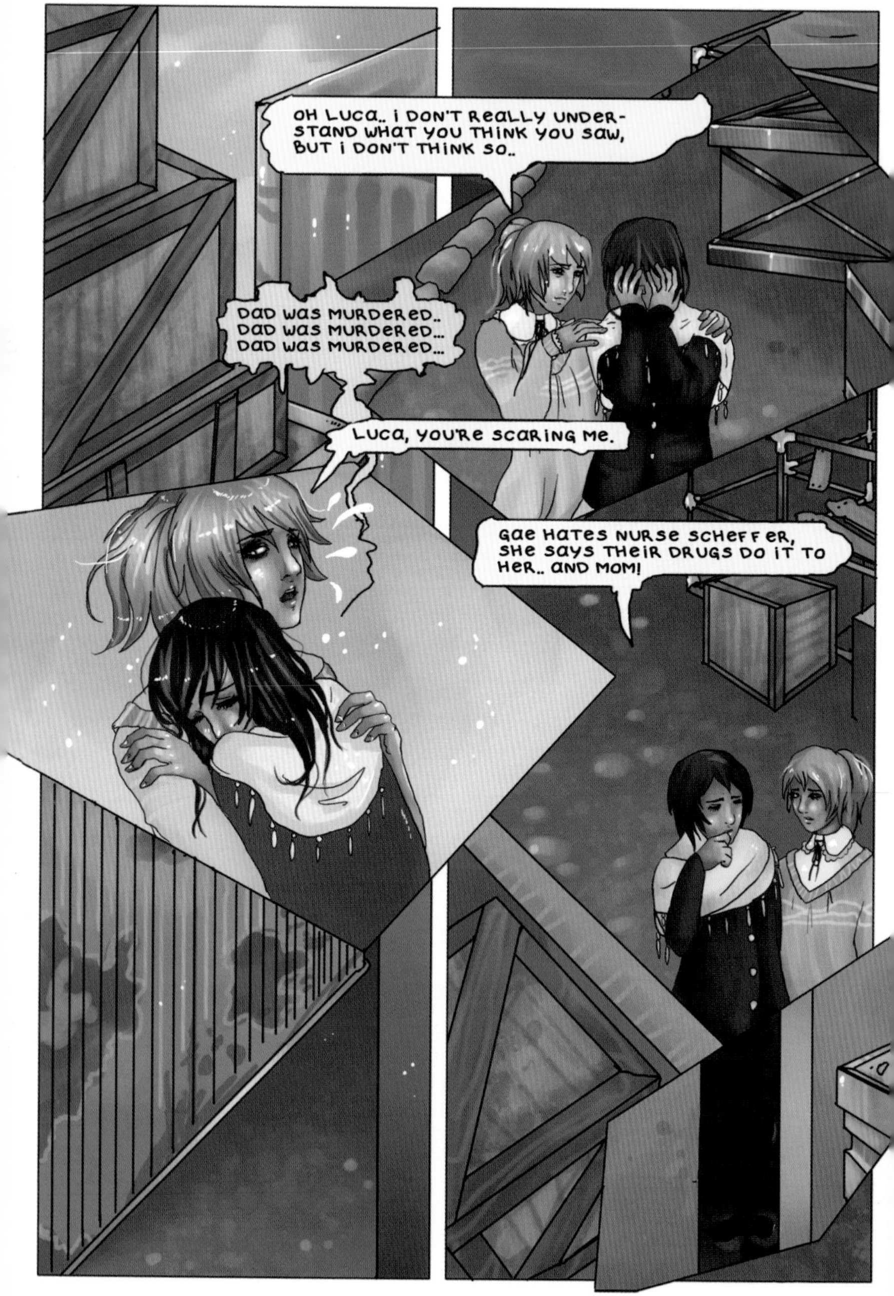
OH LUCA.. I DON'T REALLY UNDER-STAND WHAT YOU THINK YOU SAW, BUT I DON'T THINK SO..
DAD WAS MURDERED.. DAD WAS MURDERED... DAD WAS MURDERED...
LUCA, YOU'RE SCARING ME.
GAE HATES NURSE SCHEFFER, SHE SAYS THEIR DRUGS DO IT TO HER.. AND MOM!

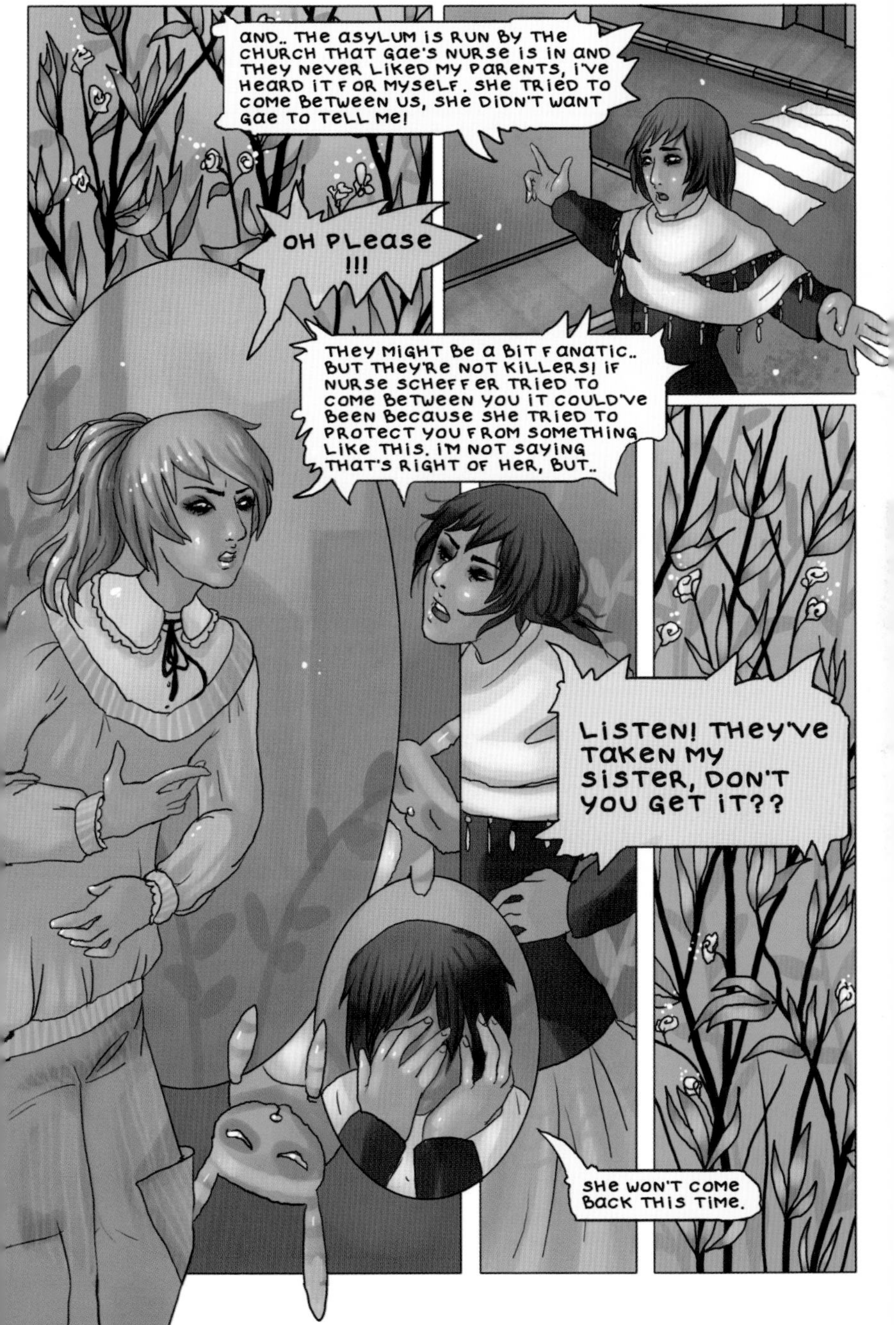
AND.. THE ASYLUM IS RUN BY THE CHURCH THAT GAE'S NURSE IS IN AND THEY NEVER LIKED MY PARENTS, I'VE HEARD IT FOR MYSELF. SHE TRIED TO COME BETWEEN US, SHE DIDN'T WANT GAE TO TELL ME!
OH PLEASE !!!
THEY MIGHT BE A BIT FANATIC.. BUT THEY'RE NOT KILLERS! IF NURSE SCHEFFER TRIED TO COME BETWEEN YOU IT COULD'VE BEEN BECAUSE SHE TRIED TO PROTECT YOU FROM SOMETHING LIKE THIS. I'M NOT SAYING THAT'S RIGHT OF HER, BUT..
LISTEN! THEY'VE TAKEN MY SISTER, DON'T YOU GET IT??
SHE WON'T COME BACK THIS TIME.

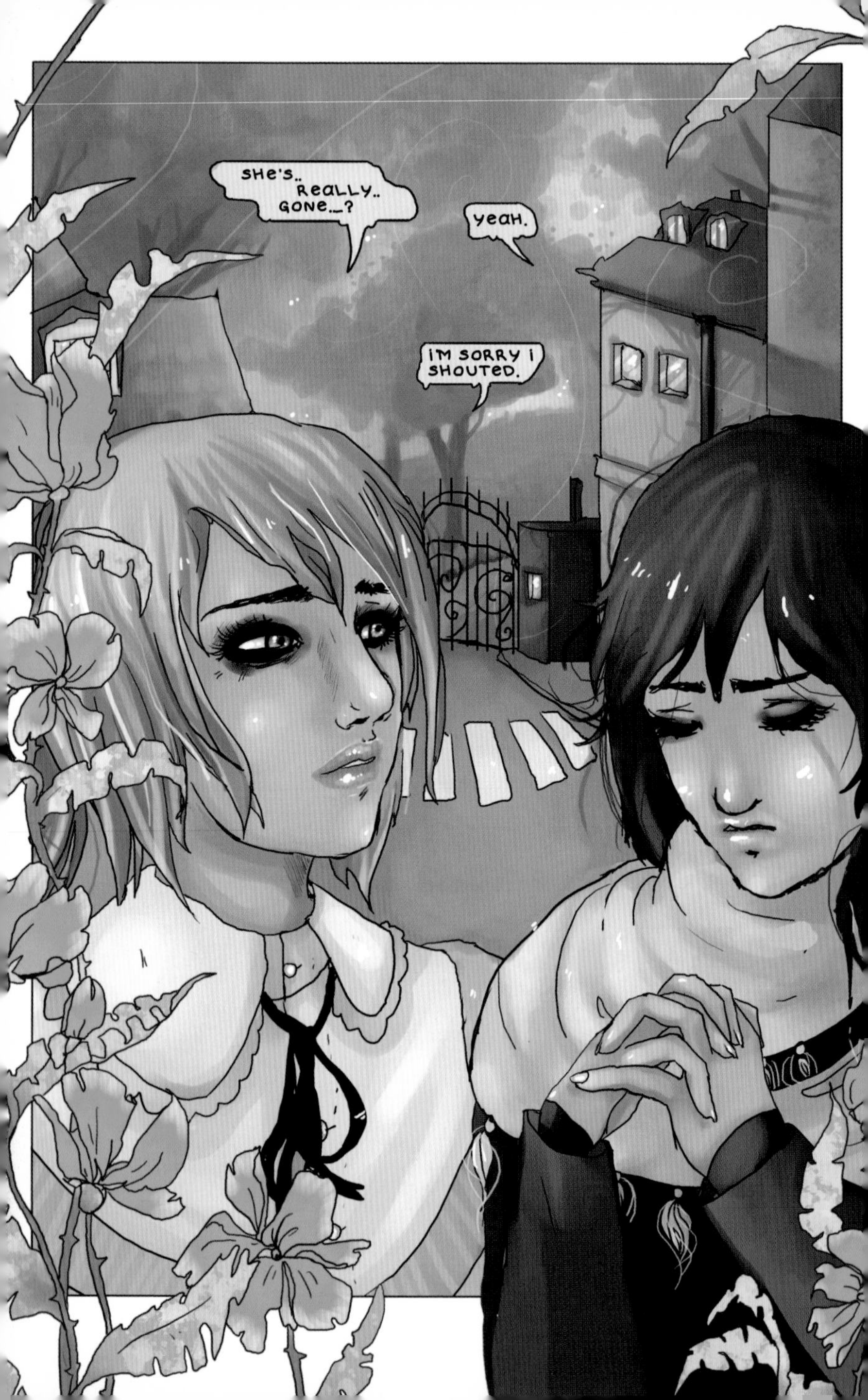
SHE'S.. REALLY.. GONE...?
YeaH.
I'M SORRY I SHOUTED.

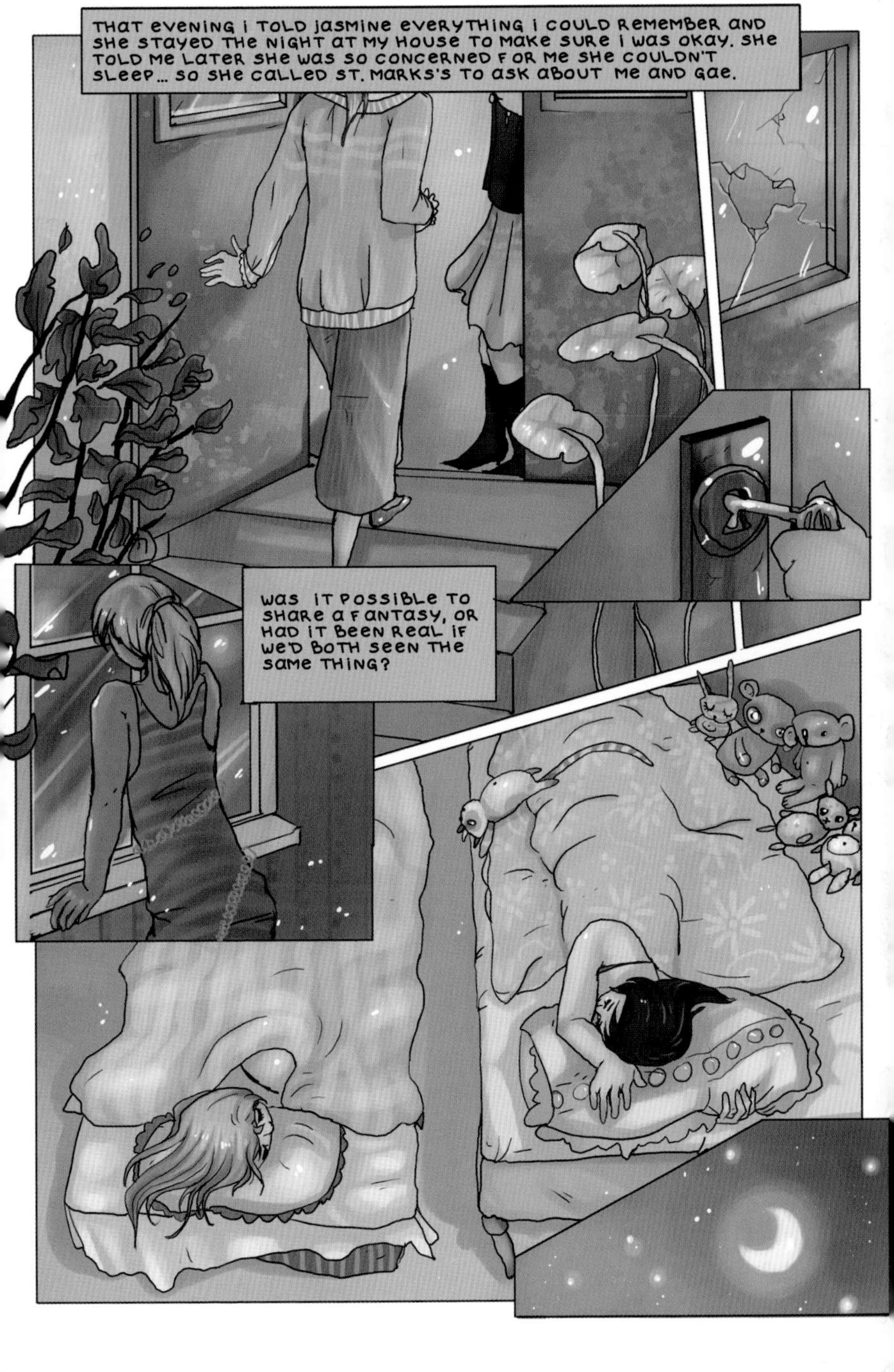
THAT EVENING I TOLD JASMINE EVERYTHING I COULD REMEMBER AND SHE STAYED THE NIGHT AT MY HOUSE TO MAKE SURE I WAS OKAY. SHE TOLD ME LATER SHE WAS SO CONCERNED FOR ME SHE COULDN'T SLEEP... SO SHE CALLED ST. MARKS'S TO ASK ABOUT ME AND GAE.
WAS IT POSSIBLE TO SHARE A FANTASY, OR HAD IT BEEN REAL IF WE'D BOTH SEEN THE SAME THING?

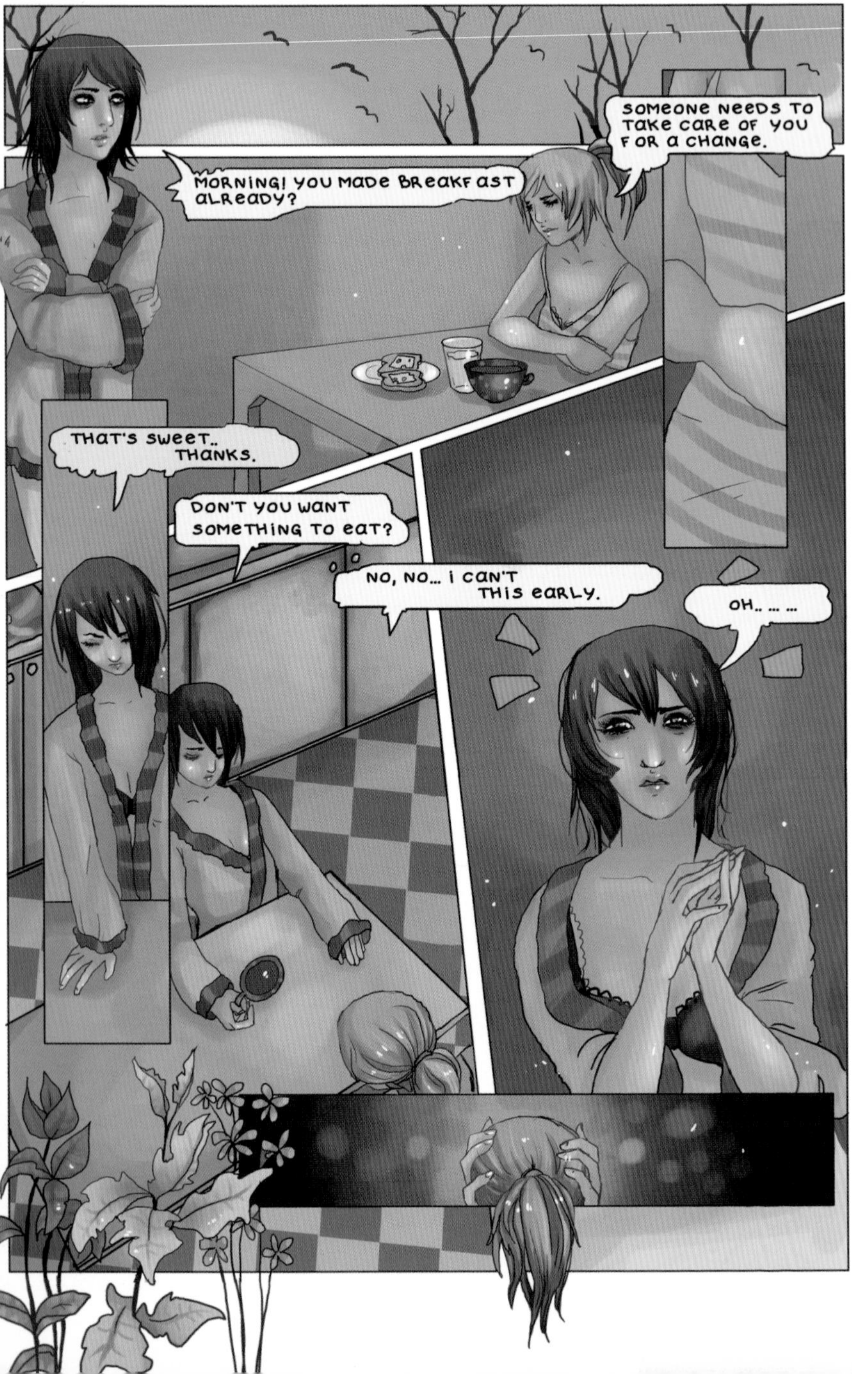
MORNING! YOU MADE BREAKFAST ALREADY?
SOMEONE NEEDS TO TAKE CARE OF YOU FOR A CHANGE.
THAT'S SWEET.. THANKS.
DON'T YOU WANT SOMETHING TO EAT?
NO, NO... I CAN'T THIS EARLY.
OH.. ... ...

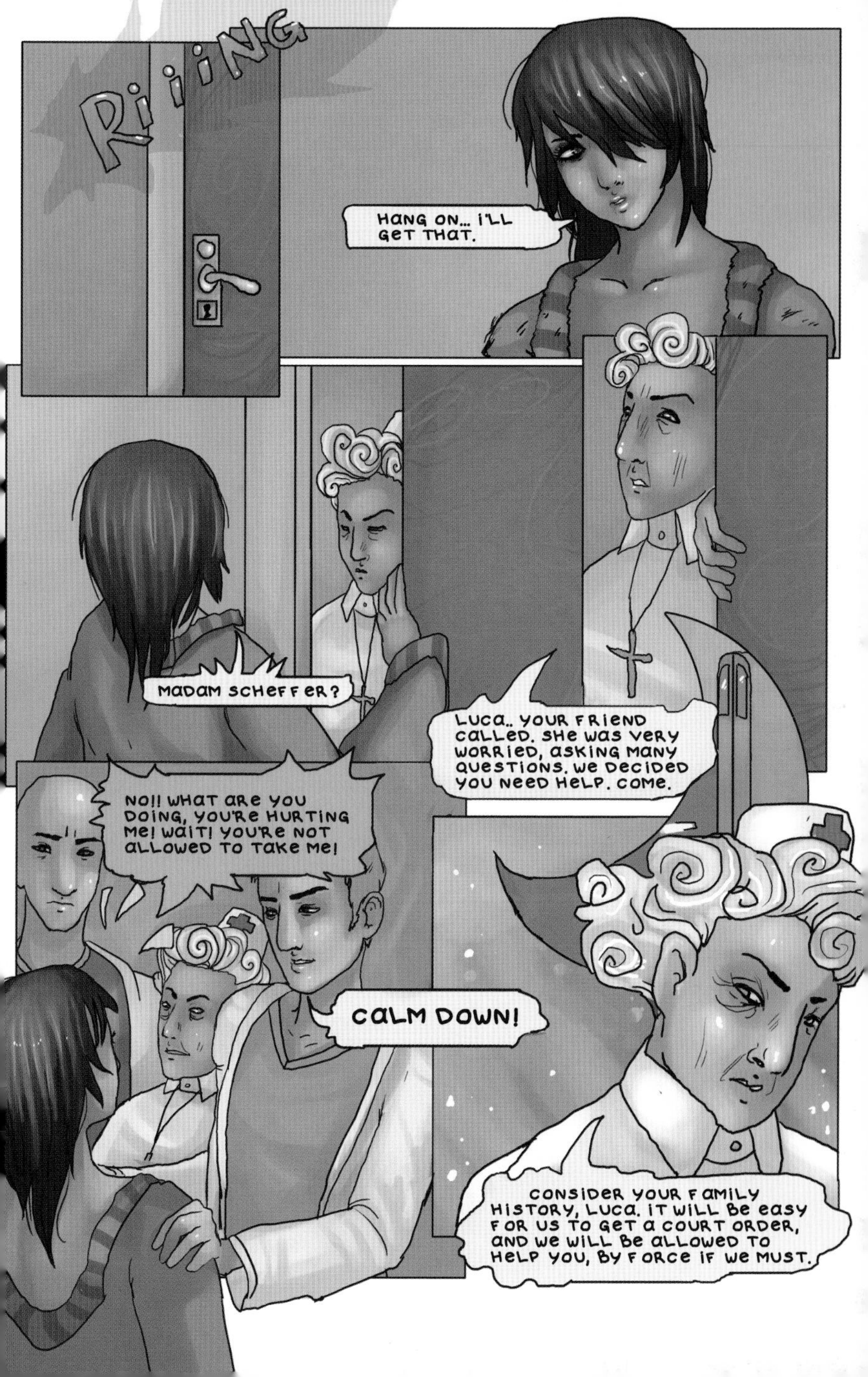
RiiiNG
HANG ON… I'LL GET THAT.
MADAM SCHEFFER?
LUCA.. YOUR FRIEND CALLED. SHE WAS VERY WORRIED, ASKING MANY QUESTIONS. WE DECIDED YOU NEED HELP. COME.
NO!! WHAT ARE YOU DOING, YOU'RE HURTING ME! WAIT! YOU'RE NOT ALLOWED TO TAKE ME!
CALM DOWN!
CONSIDER YOUR FAMILY HISTORY, LUCA. IT WILL BE EASY FOR US TO GET A COURT ORDER, AND WE WILL BE ALLOWED TO HELP YOU, BY FORCE IF WE MUST.

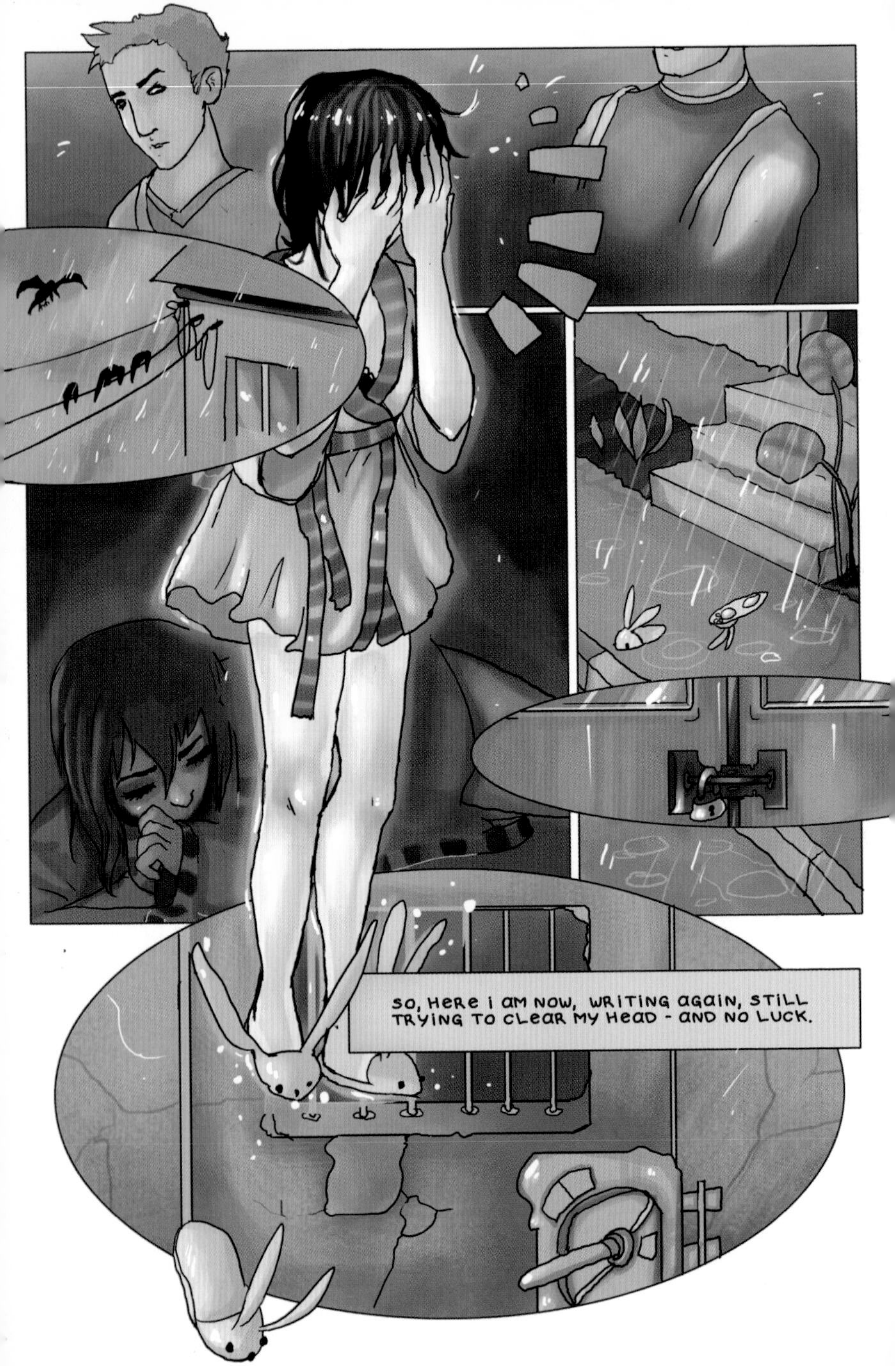
SO, HERE I AM NOW, WRITING AGAIN, STILL TRYING TO CLEAR MY HEAD - AND NO LUCK.

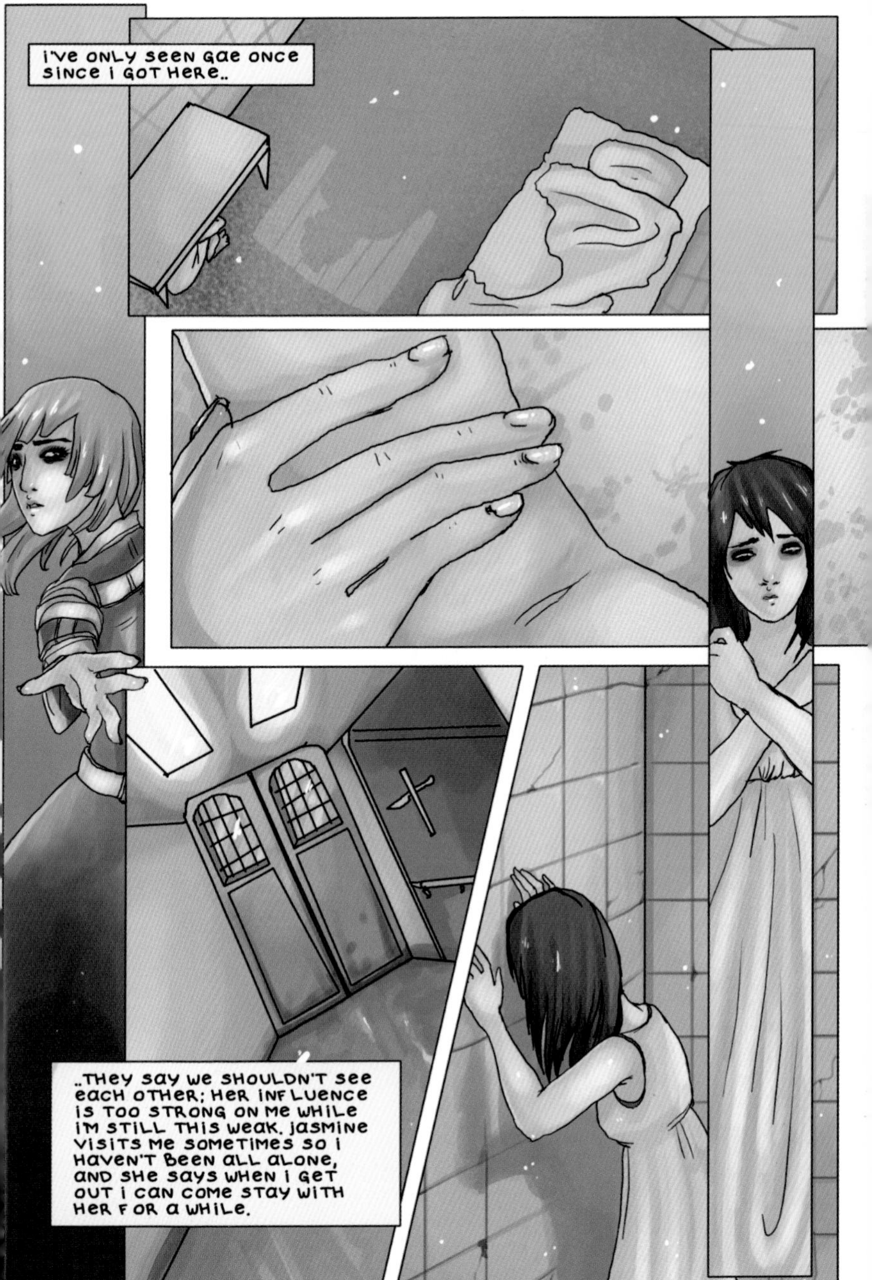
i've only seen gae once since i got here..
..they say we shouldn't see each other; her influence is too strong on me while im still this weak. jasmine visits me sometimes so i haven't been all alone, and she says when i get out i can come stay with her for a while.

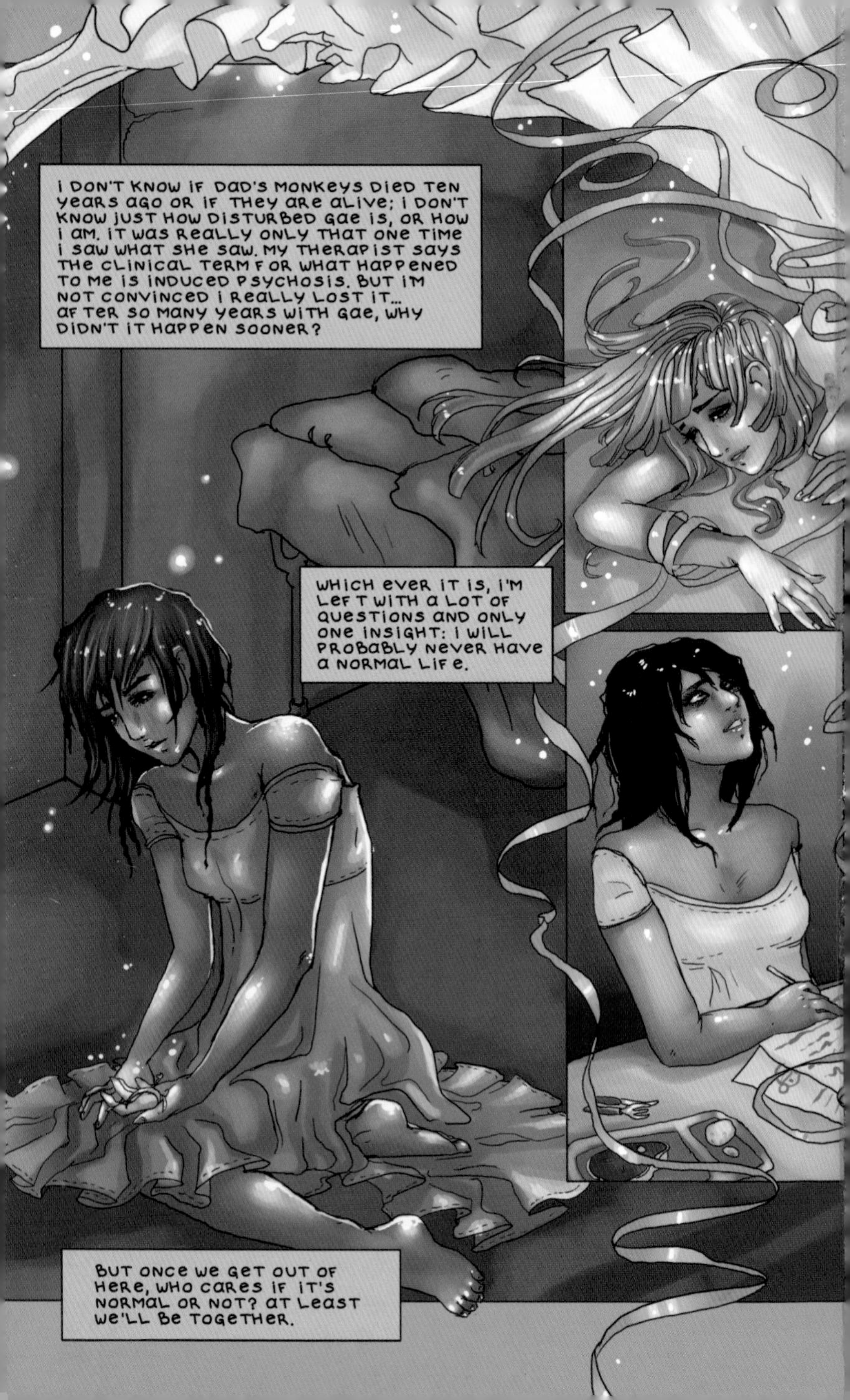
i DON'T KNOW iF DAD'S MONKEYS DIED TEN YEARS AGO OR IF THEY ARE ALIVE; i DON'T KNOW JUST HOW DISTURBED GAE IS, OR HOW i AM. iT WAS REALLY ONLY THAT ONE TIME i SAW WHAT SHE SAW. MY THERAPIST SAYS THE CLINICAL TERM FOR WHAT HAPPENED TO ME IS INDUCED PSYCHOSIS. BUT IM NOT CONVINCED i REALLY LOST IT... AFTER SO MANY YEARS WITH GAE, WHY DIDN'T IT HAPPEN SOONER?
WHICH EVER IT IS, I'M LEFT WITH A LOT OF QUESTIONS AND ONLY ONE INSIGHT: I WILL PROBABLY NEVER HAVE A NORMAL LIFE.
BUT ONCE WE GET OUT OF HERE, WHO CARES IF IT'S NORMAL OR NOT? AT LEAST WE'LL BE TOGETHER.